CLOSER

WRITTEN BY
Antony Johnston

ILLUSTRATED BY
Mike Norton
AND
Leanne Buckley

LETTERED BY
Christopher Butcher

COVER ILLUSTRATION BY
Mike Norton

BOOK DESIGN BY
Antony Johnston

EDITOR
James Lucas Jones

oni PRESS

PUBLISHED BY ONI PRESS, INC.

PUBLISHER JOE NOZEMACK
EDITOR IN CHIEF JAMIE S. RICH
SENIOR EDITOR JAMES LUCAS JONES
MANAGING EDITOR RANDAL C. JARRELL

6336 SE MILWAUKIE AVENUE, PMB 30
PORTLAND, OR 97202
USA

www.onipress.com
www.mostlyblack.com
www.ihatemike.com

FIRST EDITION MAY 2004
ISBN 1-929998-81-3

1 3 5 7 9 10 8 6 4 2
PRINTED IN CANADA

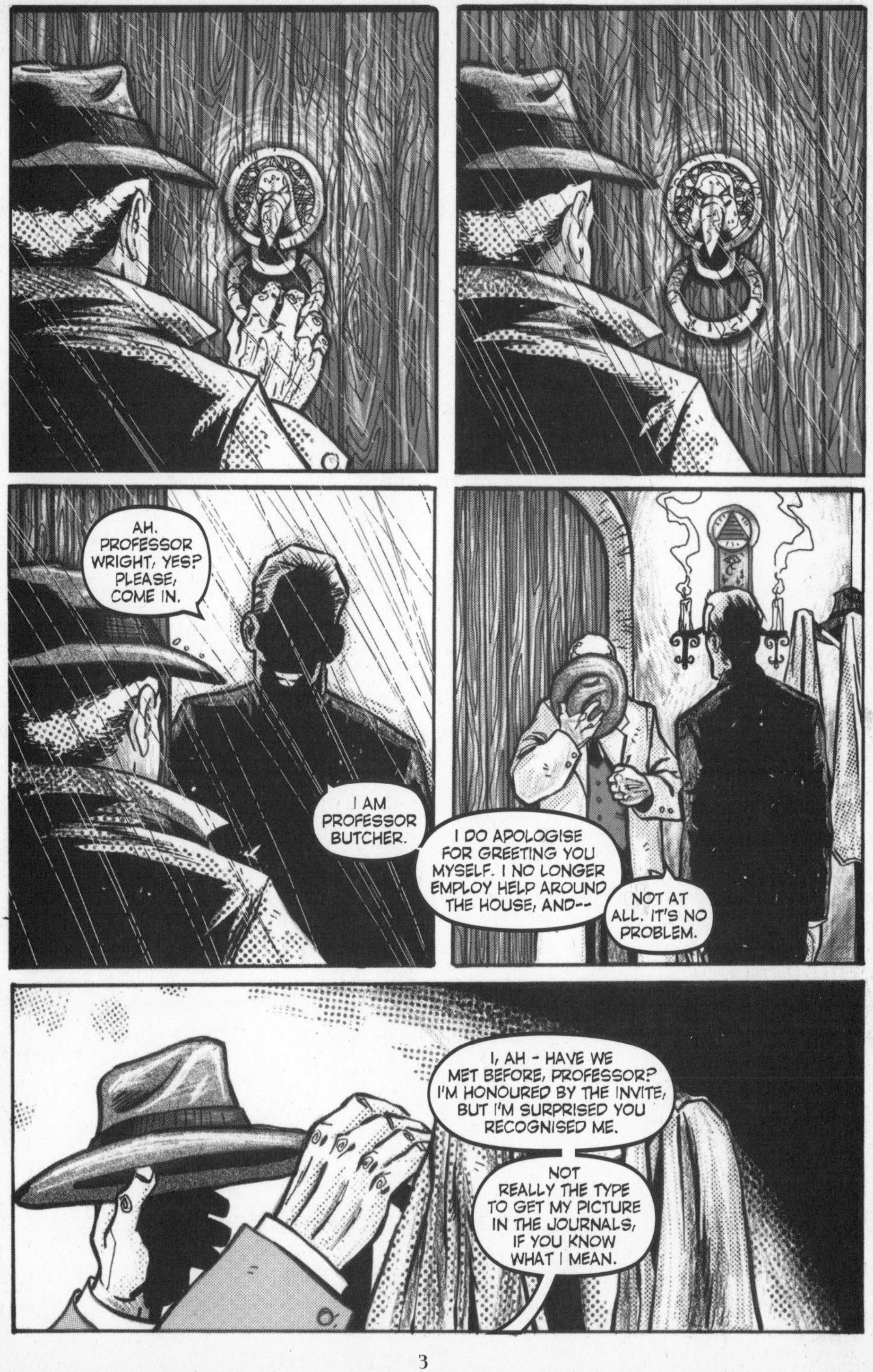
AH. PROFESSOR WRIGHT, YES? PLEASE, COME IN.
I AM PROFESSOR BUTCHER.
I DO APOLOGISE FOR GREETING YOU MYSELF. I NO LONGER EMPLOY HELP AROUND THE HOUSE, AND--
NOT AT ALL. IT'S NO PROBLEM.
I, AH - HAVE WE MET BEFORE, PROFESSOR? I'M HONOURED BY THE INVITE, BUT I'M SURPRISED YOU RECOGNISED ME.
NOT REALLY THE TYPE TO GET MY PICTURE IN THE JOURNALS, IF YOU KNOW WHAT I MEAN.

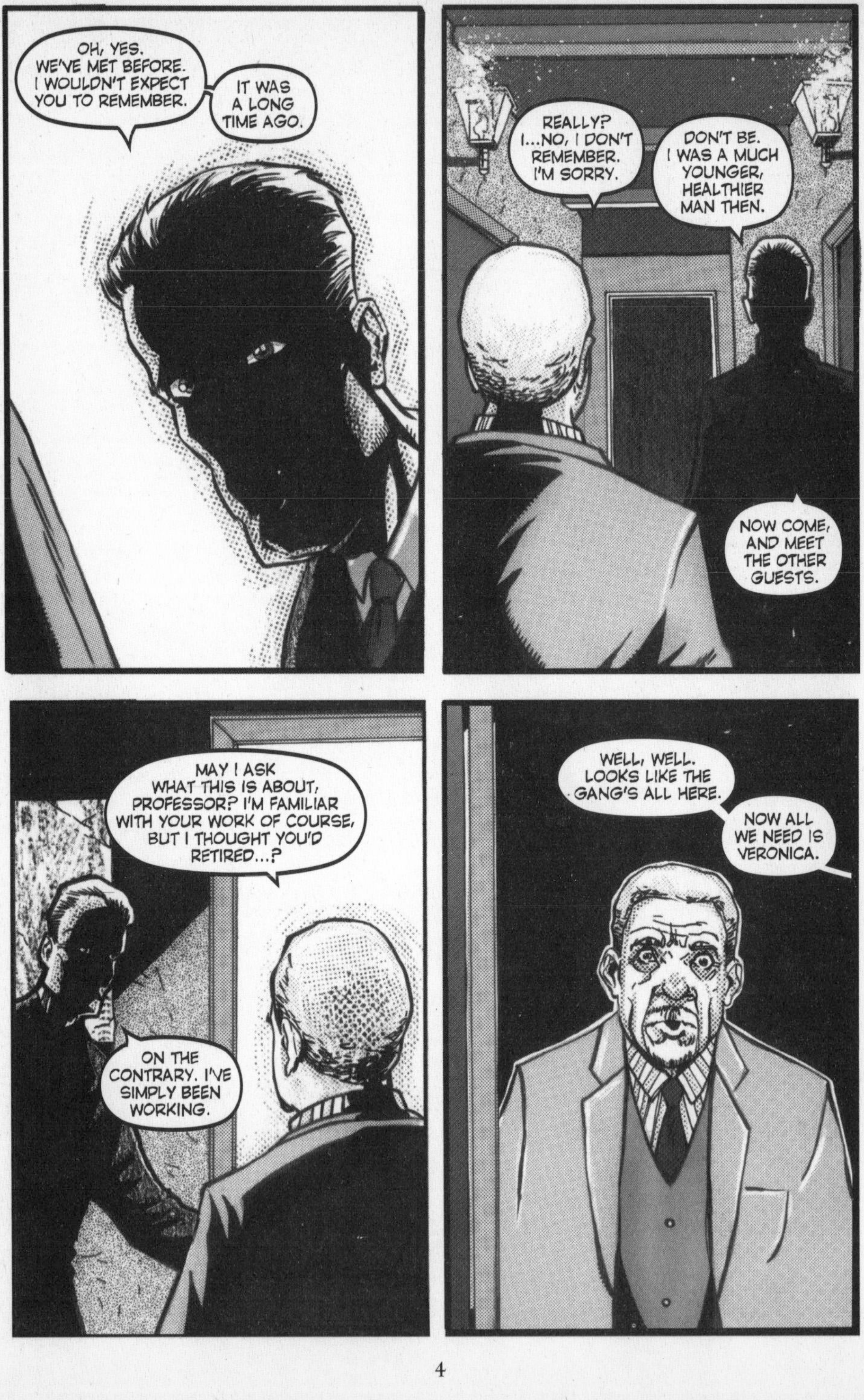
OH, YES. WE'VE MET BEFORE. I WOULDN'T EXPECT YOU TO REMEMBER.
IT WAS A LONG TIME AGO.
REALLY? I...NO, I DON'T REMEMBER. I'M SORRY.
DON'T BE. I WAS A MUCH YOUNGER, HEALTHIER MAN THEN.
NOW COME, AND MEET THE OTHER GUESTS.
MAY I ASK WHAT THIS IS ABOUT, PROFESSOR? I'M FAMILIAR WITH YOUR WORK OF COURSE, BUT I THOUGHT YOU'D RETIRED...?
ON THE CONTRARY. I'VE SIMPLY BEEN WORKING.
WELL, WELL. LOOKS LIKE THE GANG'S ALL HERE.
NOW ALL WE NEED IS VERONICA.

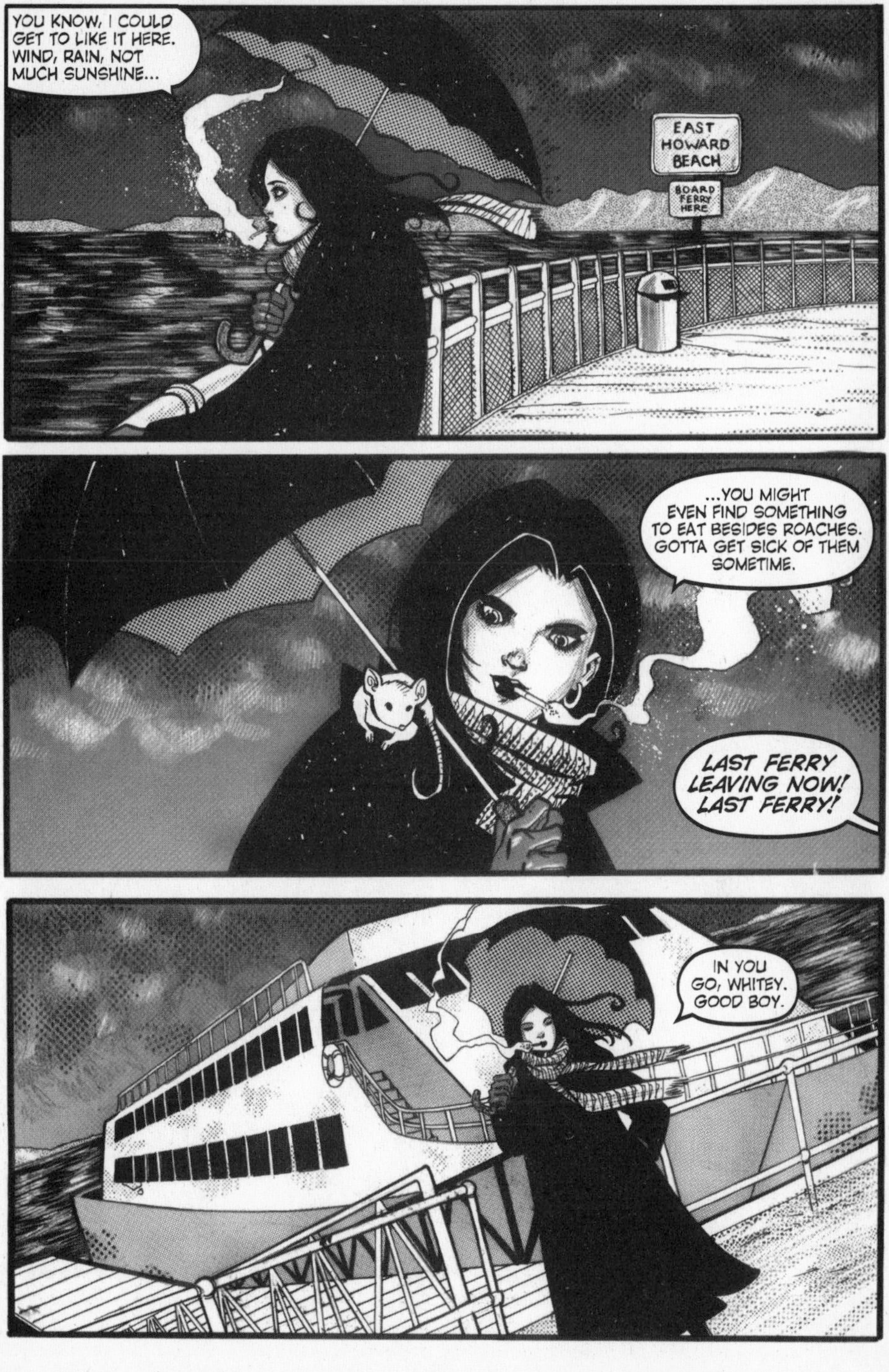
YOU KNOW, I COULD GET TO LIKE IT HERE. WIND, RAIN, NOT MUCH SUNSHINE...
EAST HOWARD BEACH
BOARD FERRY HERE
...YOU MIGHT EVEN FIND SOMETHING TO EAT BESIDES ROACHES. GOTTA GET SICK OF THEM SOMETIME.
LAST FERRY LEAVING NOW! LAST FERRY!
IN YOU GO, WHITEY. GOOD BOY.

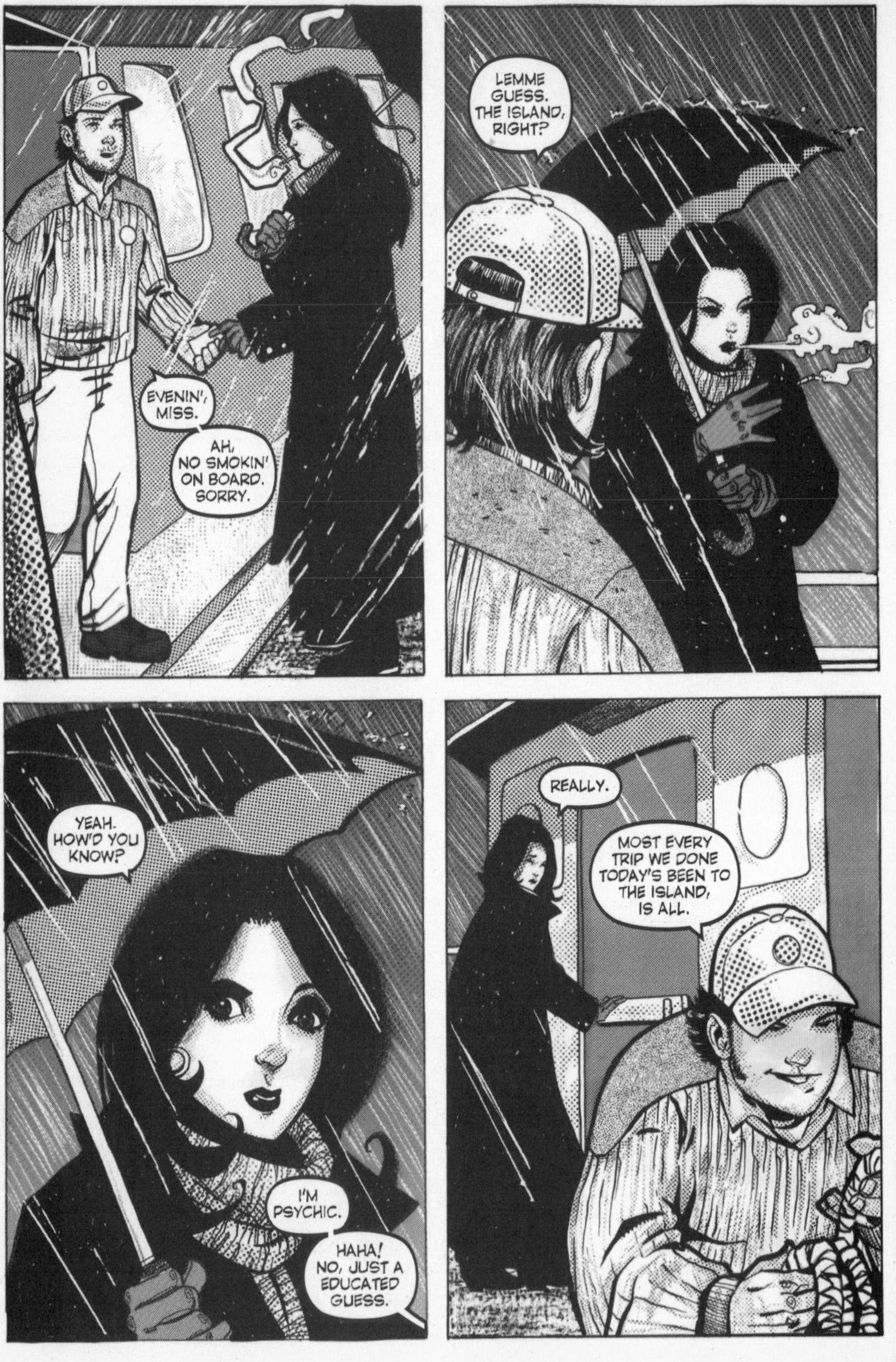
EVENIN', MISS.
AH, NO SMOKIN' ON BOARD. SORRY.
LEMME GUESS. THE ISLAND, RIGHT?
YEAH. HOW'D YOU KNOW?
I'M PSYCHIC.
HAHA! NO, JUST A EDUCATED GUESS.
REALLY.
MOST EVERY TRIP WE DONE TODAY'S BEEN TO THE ISLAND, IS ALL.

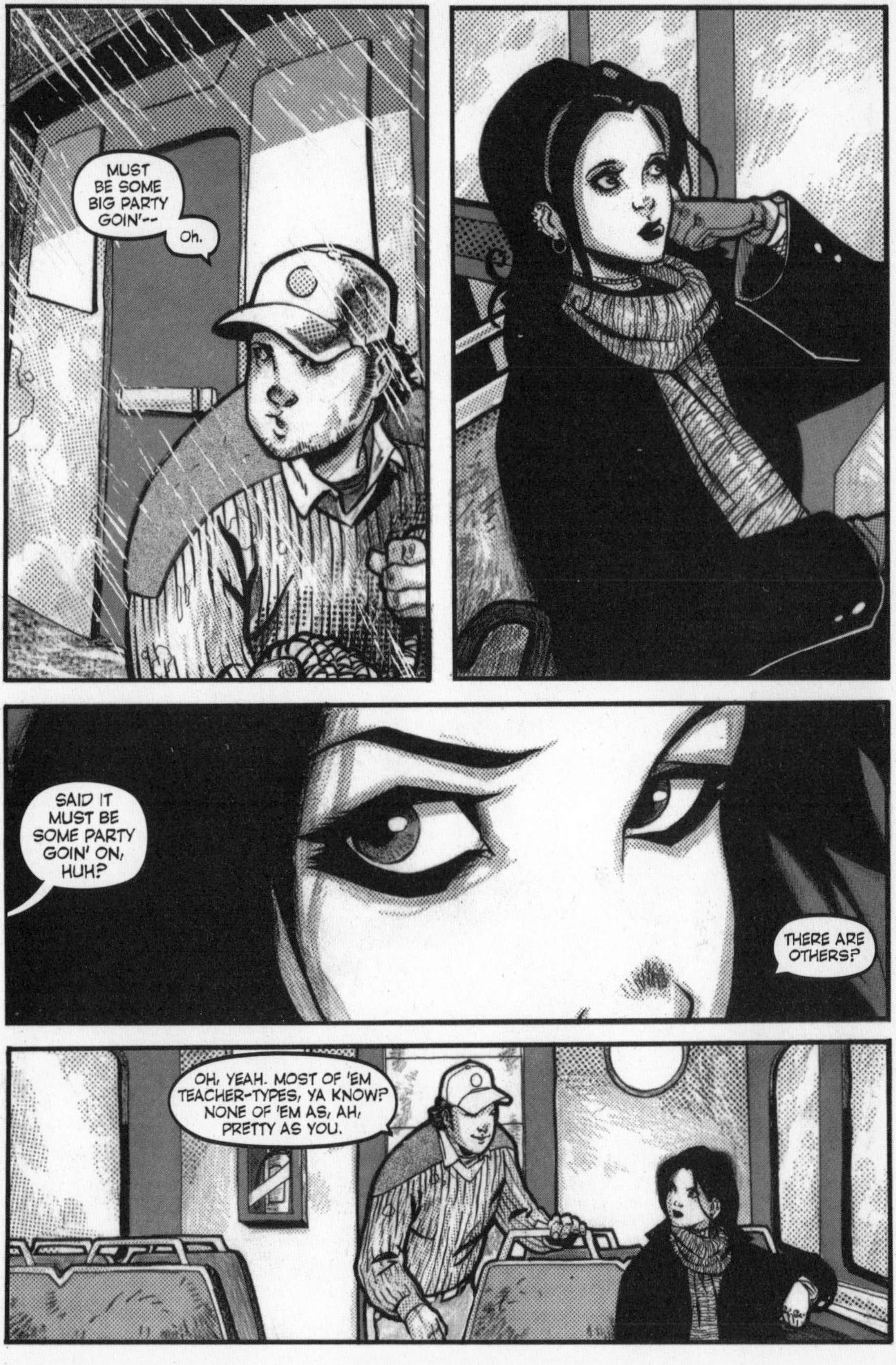
MUST BE SOME BIG PARTY GOIN'--
Oh.
SAID IT MUST BE SOME PARTY GOIN' ON, HUH?
THERE ARE OTHERS?
OH, YEAH. MOST OF 'EM TEACHER-TYPES, YA KNOW? NONE OF 'EM AS, AH, PRETTY AS YOU.

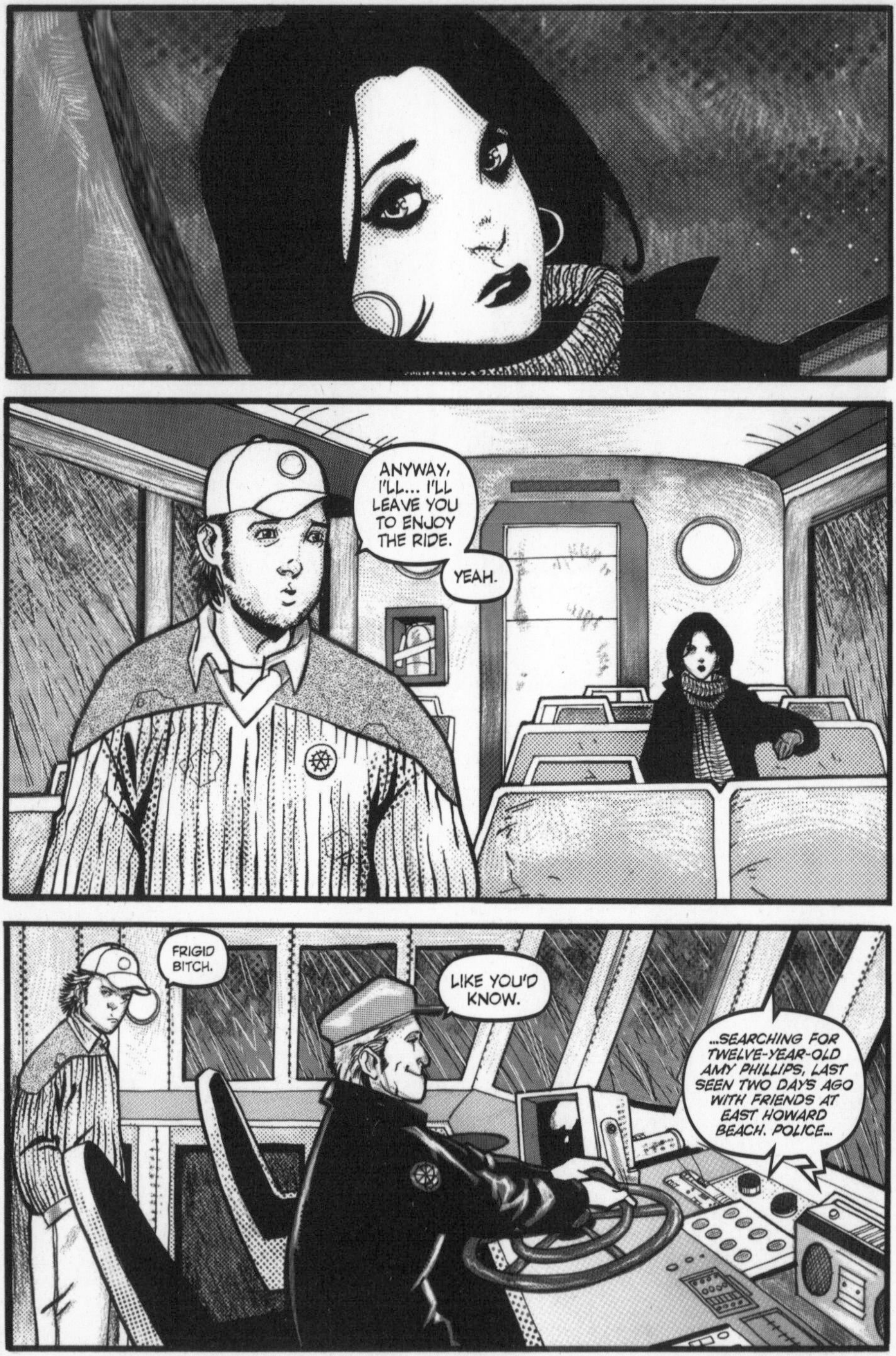
ANYWAY, I'LL... I'LL LEAVE YOU TO ENJOY THE RIDE.
YEAH.
FRIGID BITCH.
LIKE YOU'D KNOW.
...SEARCHING FOR TWELVE-YEAR-OLD AMY PHILLIPS, LAST SEEN TWO DAYS AGO WITH FRIENDS AT EAST HOWARD BEACH. POLICE...

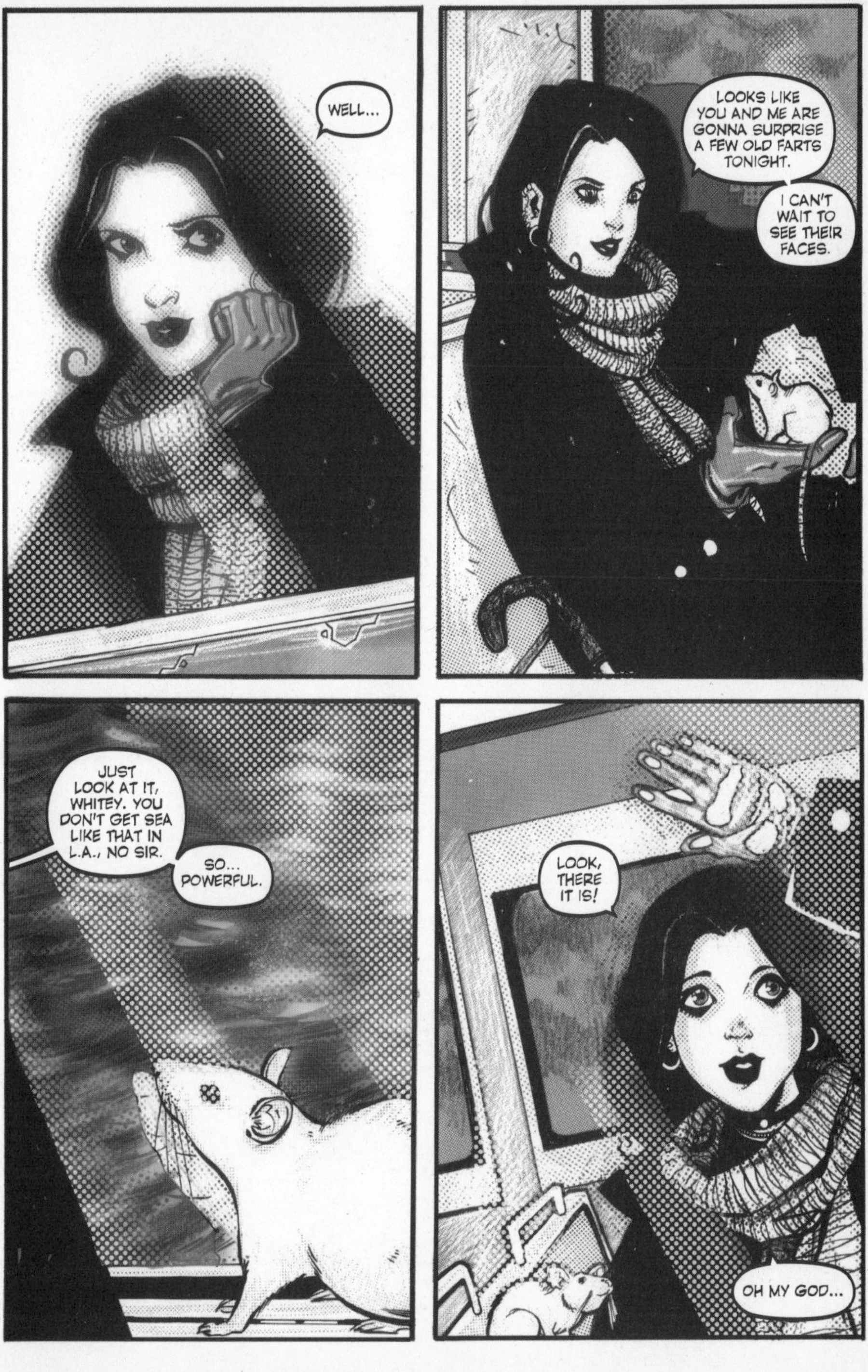
WELL...
LOOKS LIKE YOU AND ME ARE GONNA SURPRISE A FEW OLD FARTS TONIGHT.
I CAN'T WAIT TO SEE THEIR FACES.
JUST LOOK AT IT, WHITEY. YOU DON'T GET SEA LIKE THAT IN L.A., NO SIR.
SO... POWERFUL.
LOOK, THERE IT IS!
OH MY GOD...

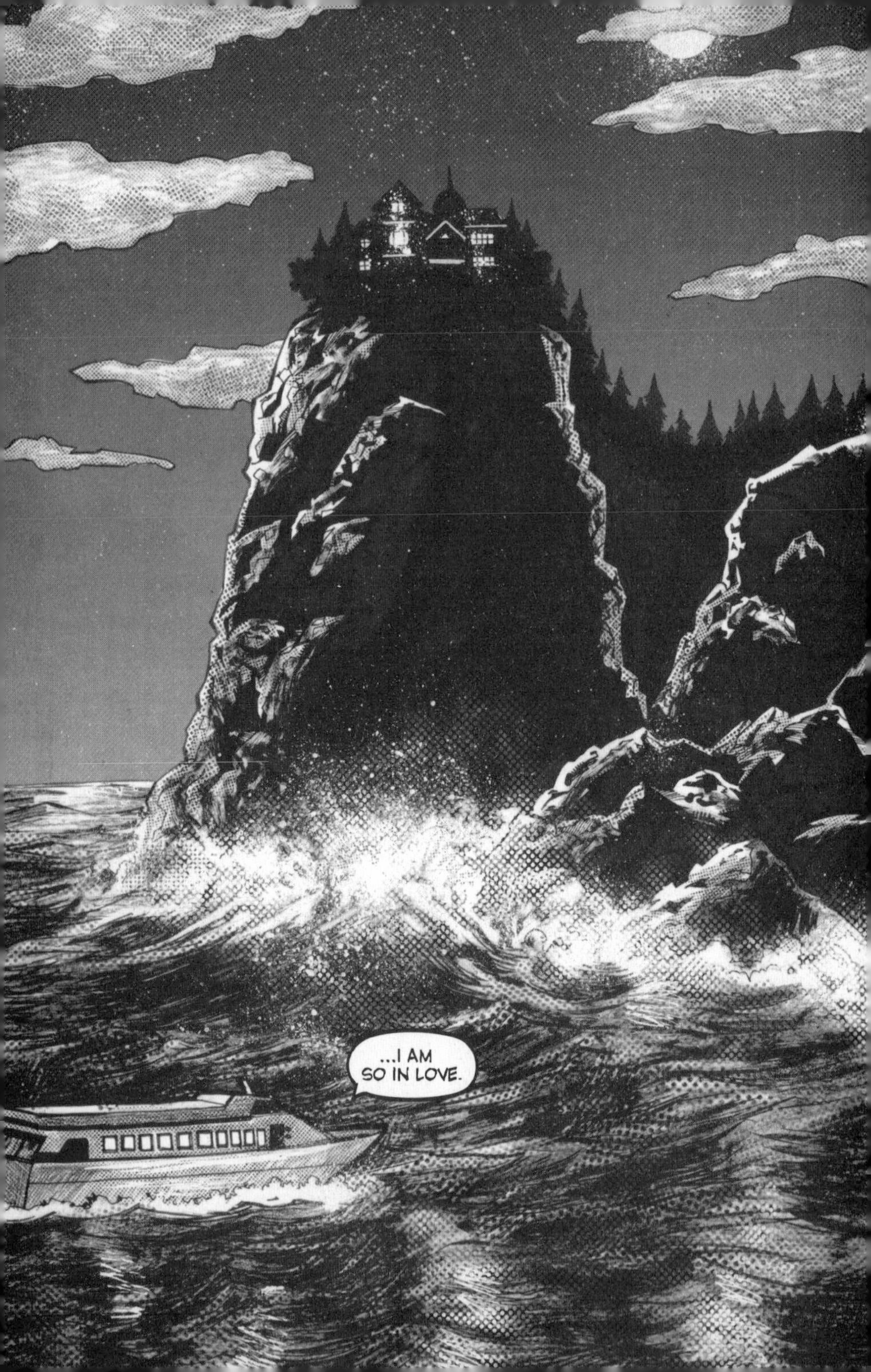
...I AM SO IN LOVE.

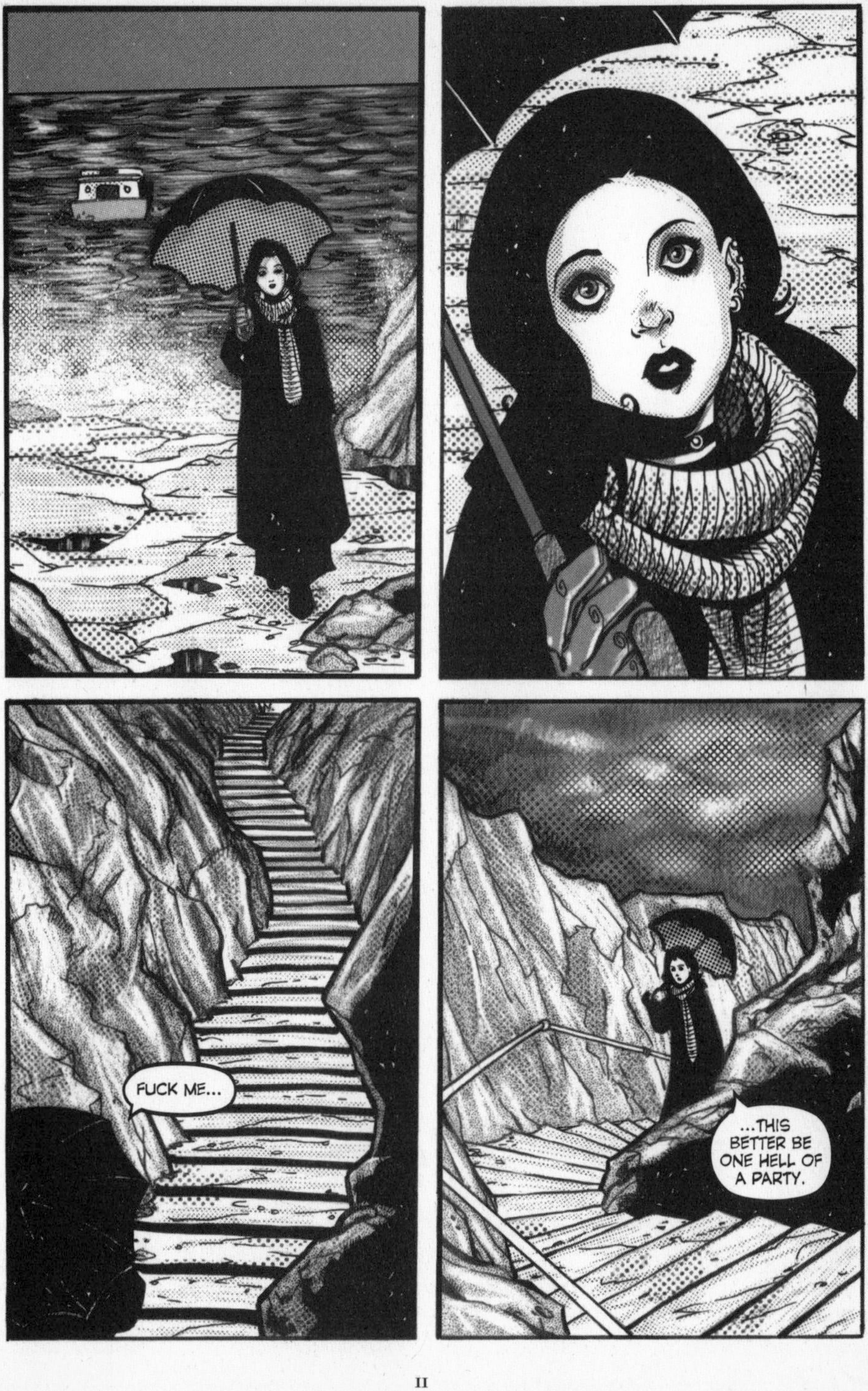
FUCK ME...
...THIS BETTER BE ONE HELL OF A PARTY.

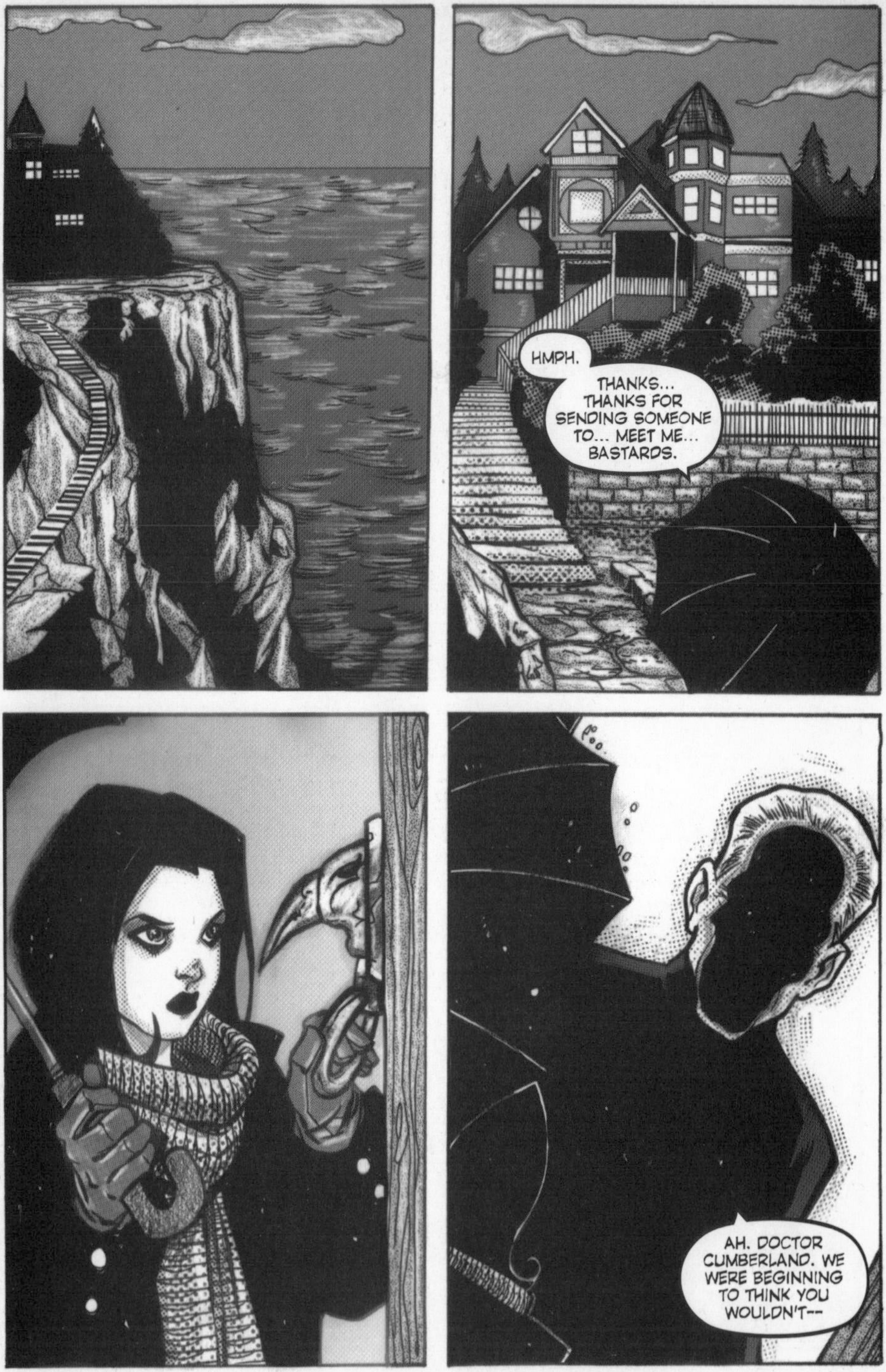
HMPH.
THANKS... THANKS FOR SENDING SOMEONE TO... MEET ME... BASTARDS.
AH. DOCTOR CUMBERLAND. WE WERE BEGINNING TO THINK YOU WOULDN'T--

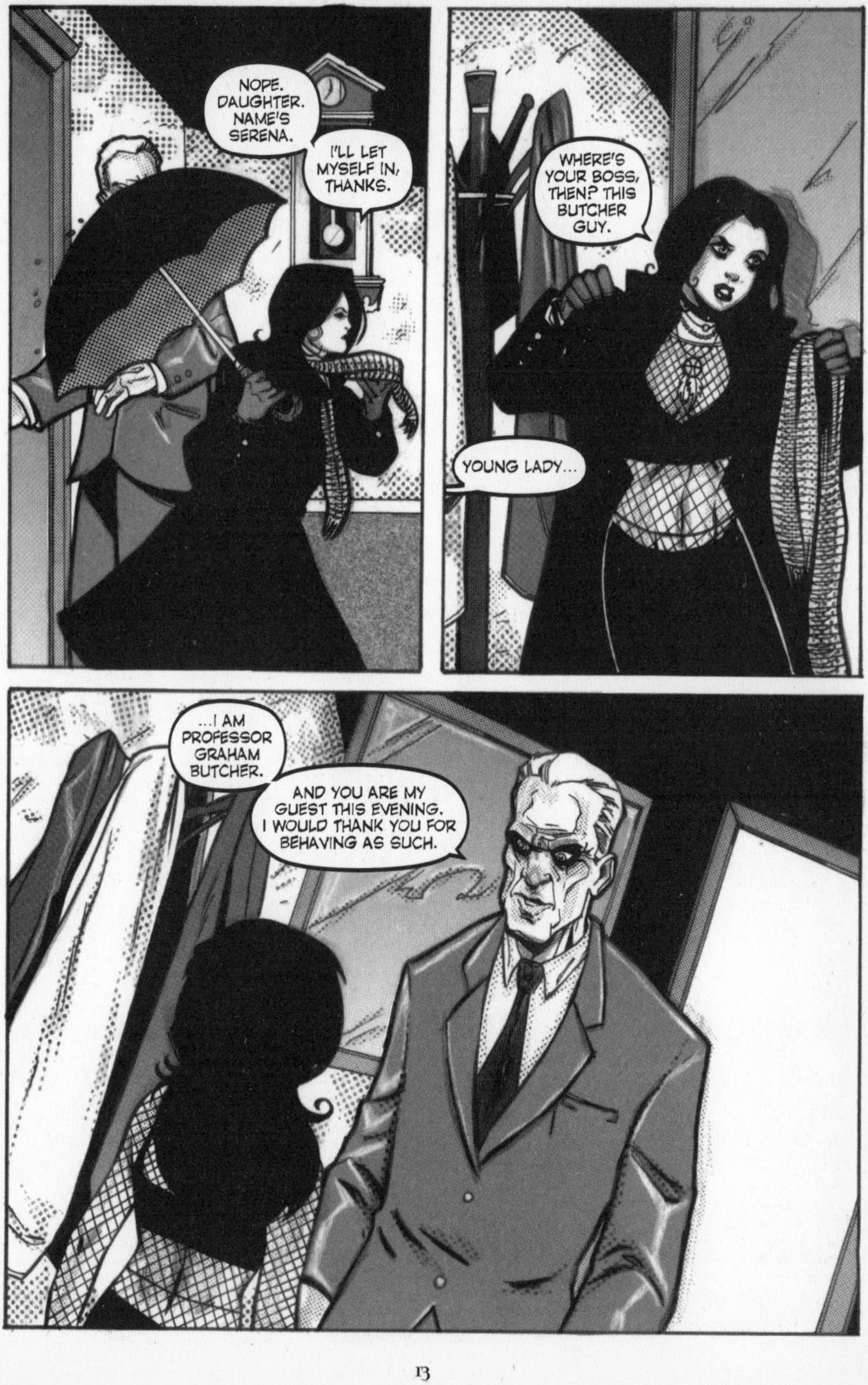
NOPE. DAUGHTER. NAME'S SERENA.
I'LL LET MYSELF IN, THANKS.
WHERE'S YOUR BOSS, THEN? THIS BUTCHER GUY.
YOUNG LADY...
...I AM PROFESSOR GRAHAM BUTCHER.
AND YOU ARE MY GUEST THIS EVENING. I WOULD THANK YOU FOR BEHAVING AS SUCH.

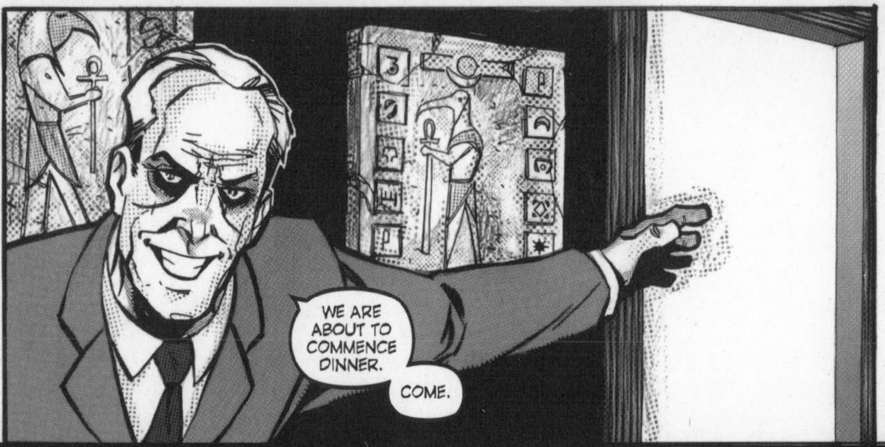
WE ARE ABOUT TO COMMENCE DINNER.
COME.

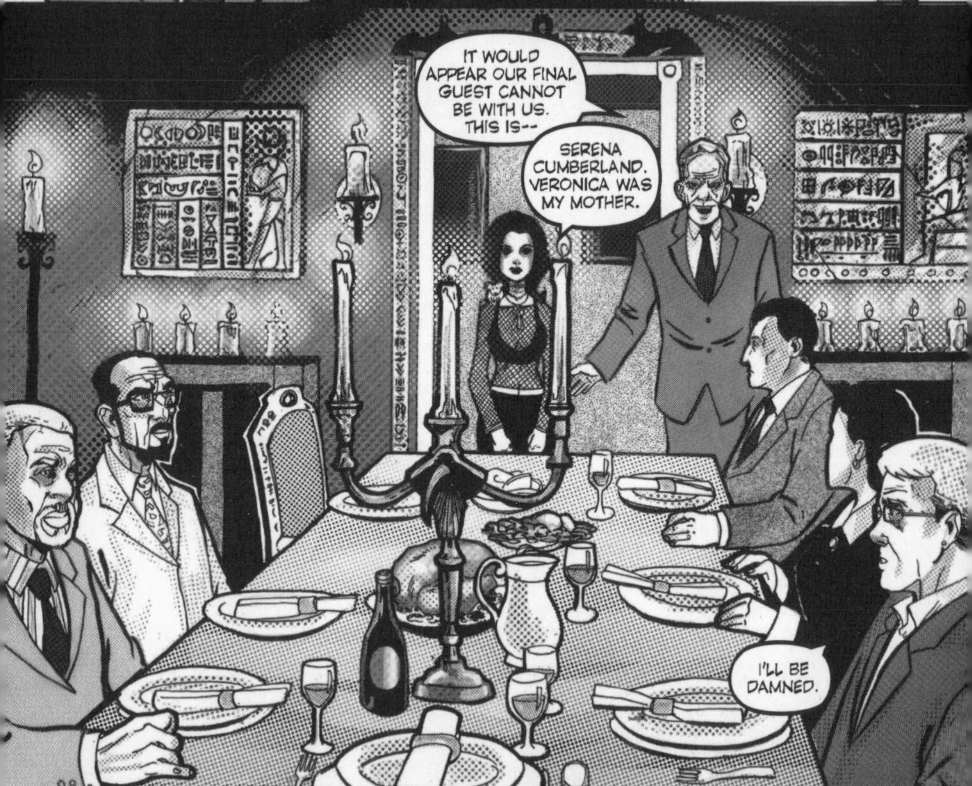
IT WOULD APPEAR OUR FINAL GUEST CANNOT BE WITH US. THIS IS--
SERENA CUMBERLAND. VERONICA WAS MY MOTHER.
I'LL BE DAMNED.

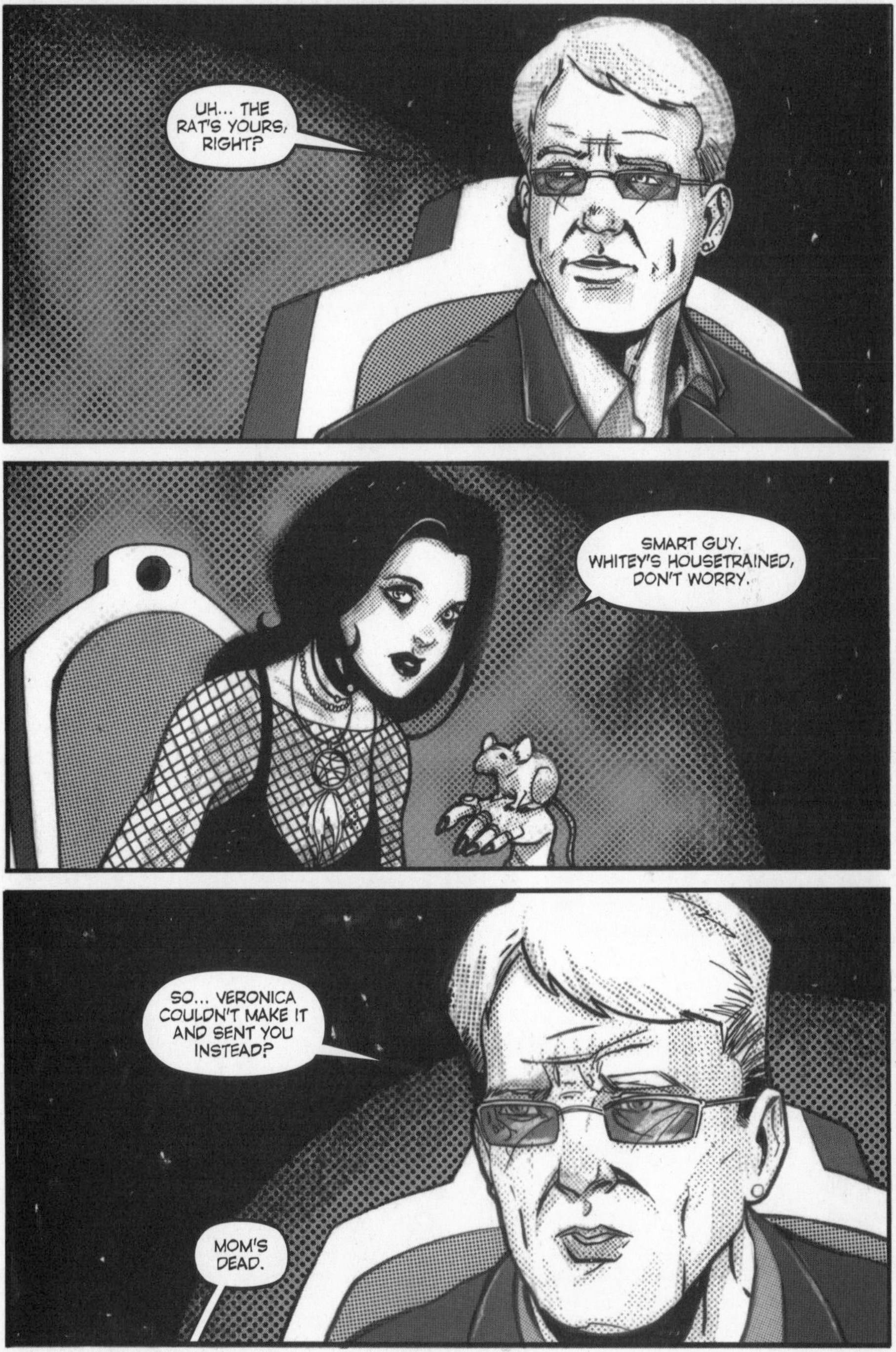
UH... THE RAT'S YOURS, RIGHT?
SMART GUY. WHITEY'S HOUSETRAINED, DON'T WORRY.
SO... VERONICA COULDN'T MAKE IT AND SENT YOU INSTEAD?
MOM'S DEAD.

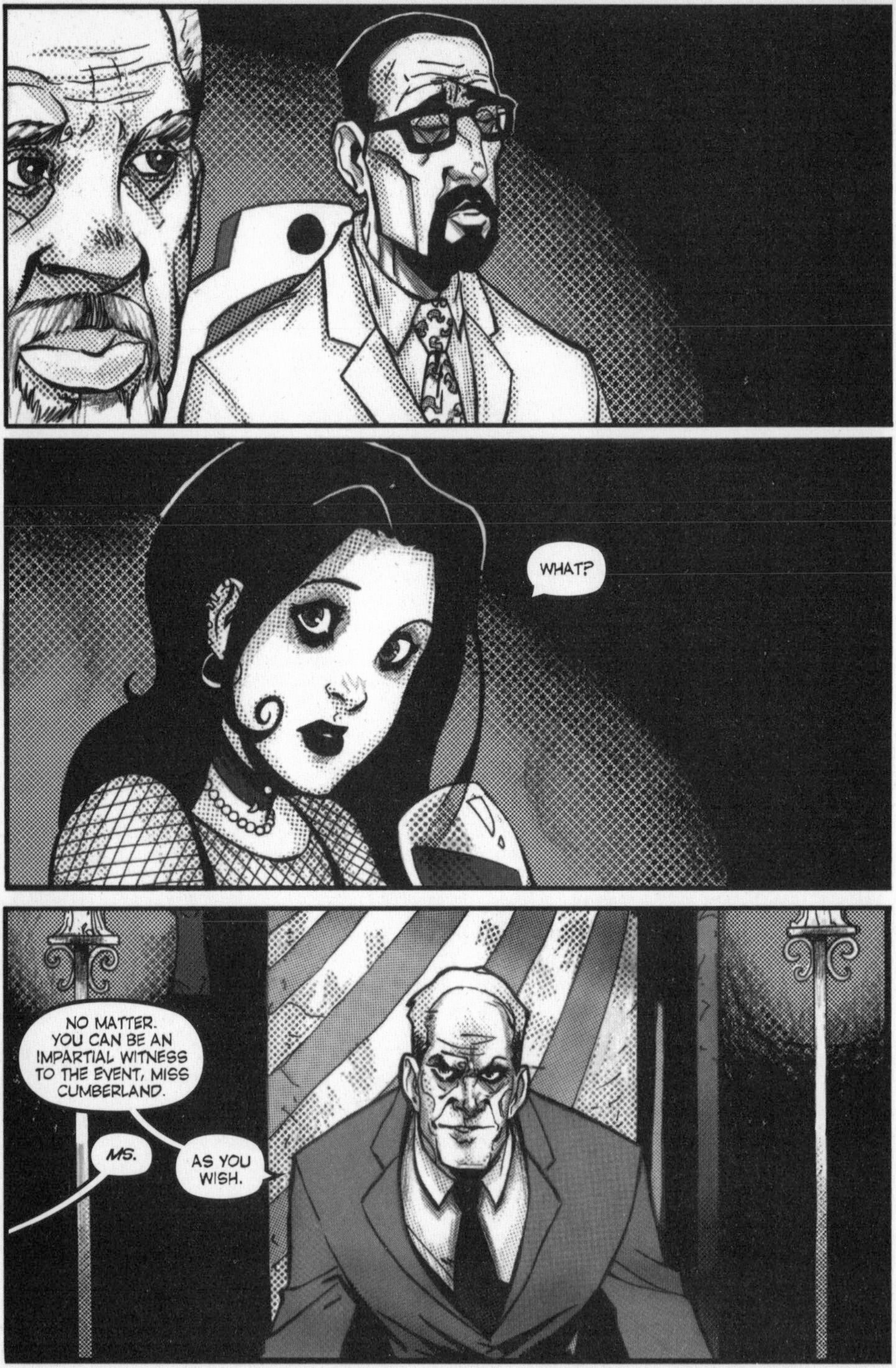
WHAT?
NO MATTER. YOU CAN BE AN IMPARTIAL WITNESS TO THE EVENT, MISS CUMBERLAND.
MS.
AS YOU WISH.

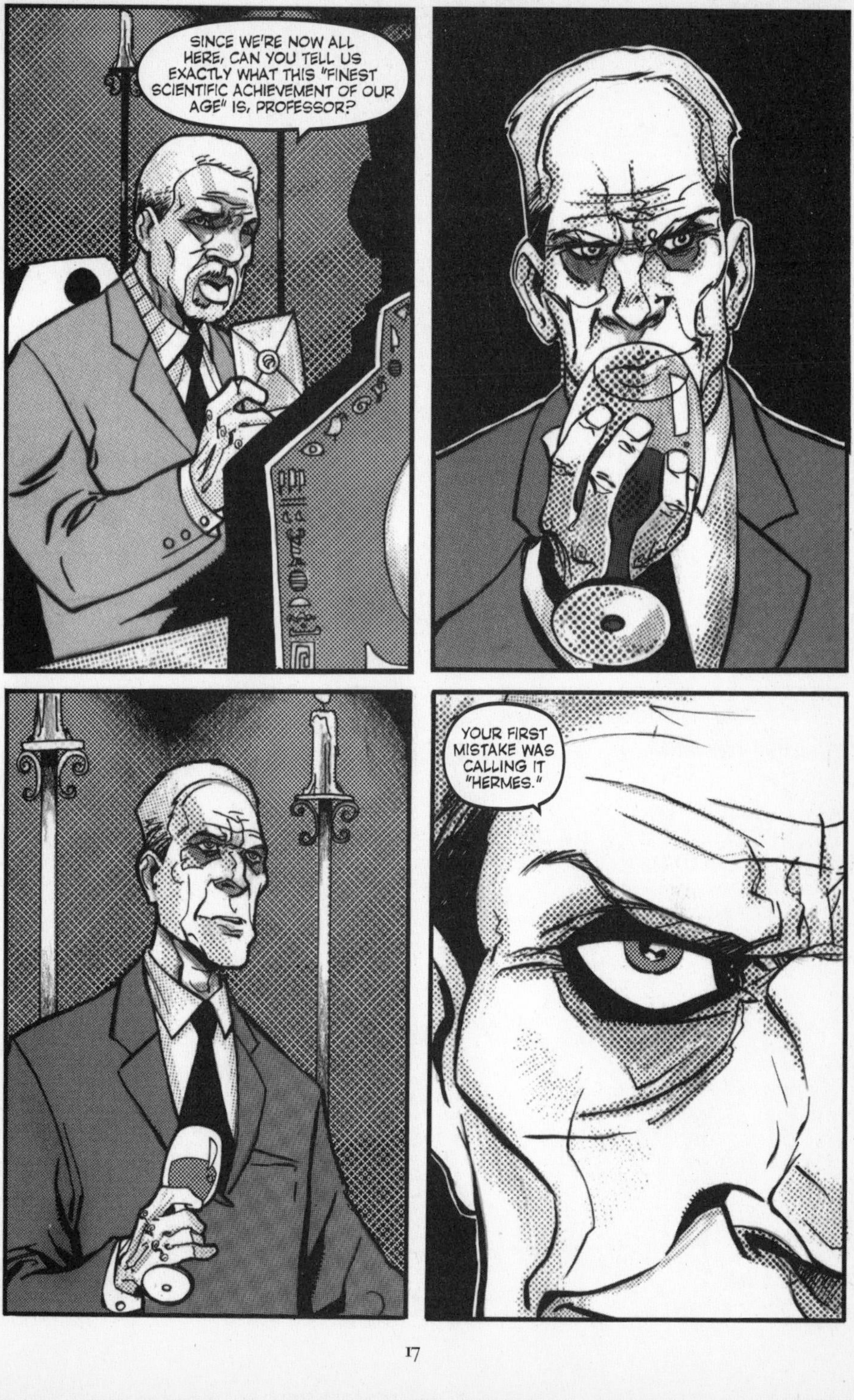
SINCE WE'RE NOW ALL HERE, CAN YOU TELL US EXACTLY WHAT THIS "FINEST SCIENTIFIC ACHIEVEMENT OF OUR AGE" IS, PROFESSOR?
YOUR FIRST MISTAKE WAS CALLING IT "HERMES."

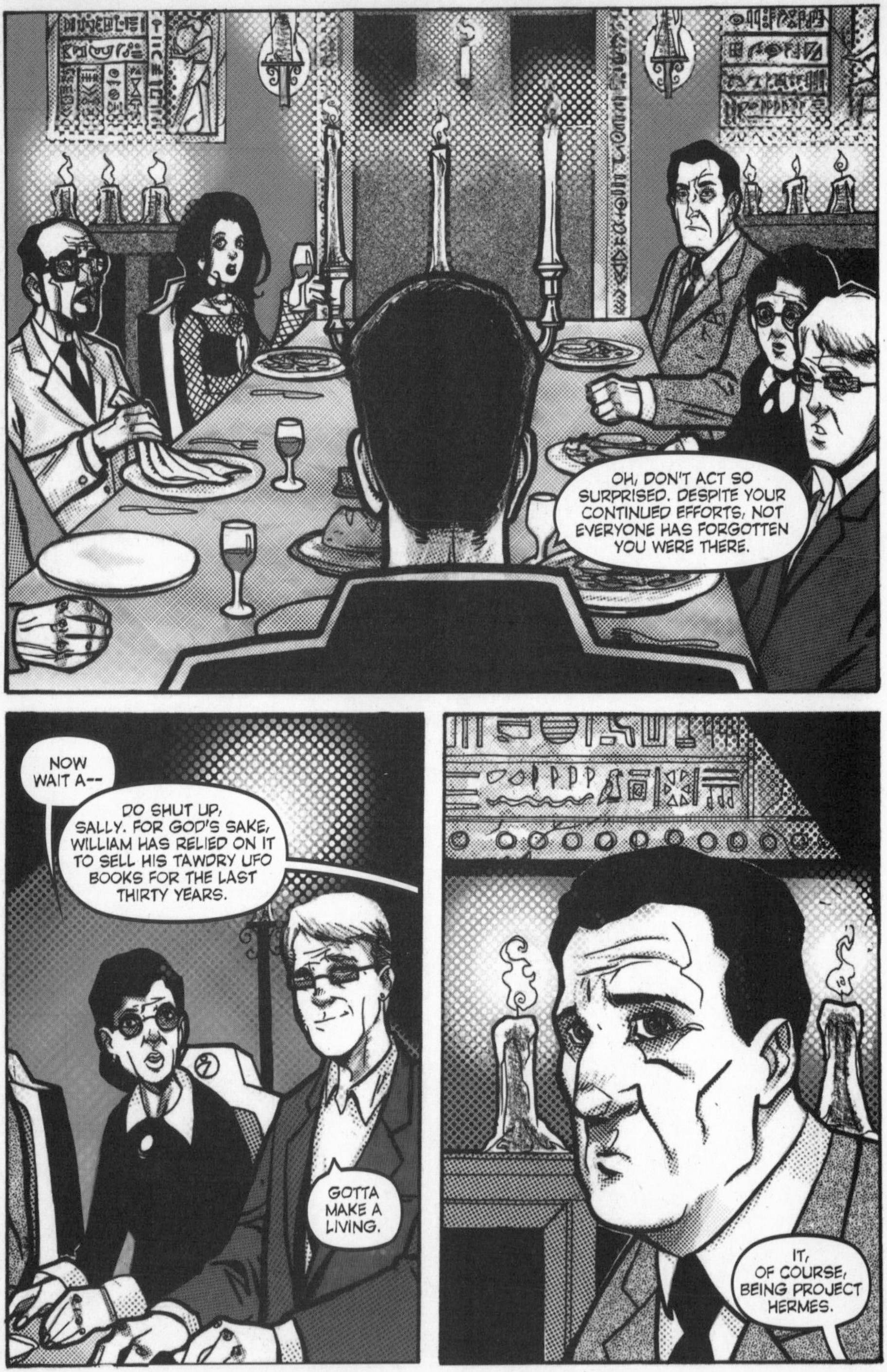
OH, DON'T ACT SO SURPRISED. DESPITE YOUR CONTINUED EFFORTS, NOT EVERYONE HAS FORGOTTEN YOU WERE THERE.
NOW WAIT A--
DO SHUT UP, SALLY. FOR GOD'S SAKE, WILLIAM HAS RELIED ON IT TO SELL HIS TAWDRY UFO BOOKS FOR THE LAST THIRTY YEARS.
GOTTA MAKE A LIVING.
IT, OF COURSE, BEING PROJECT HERMES.

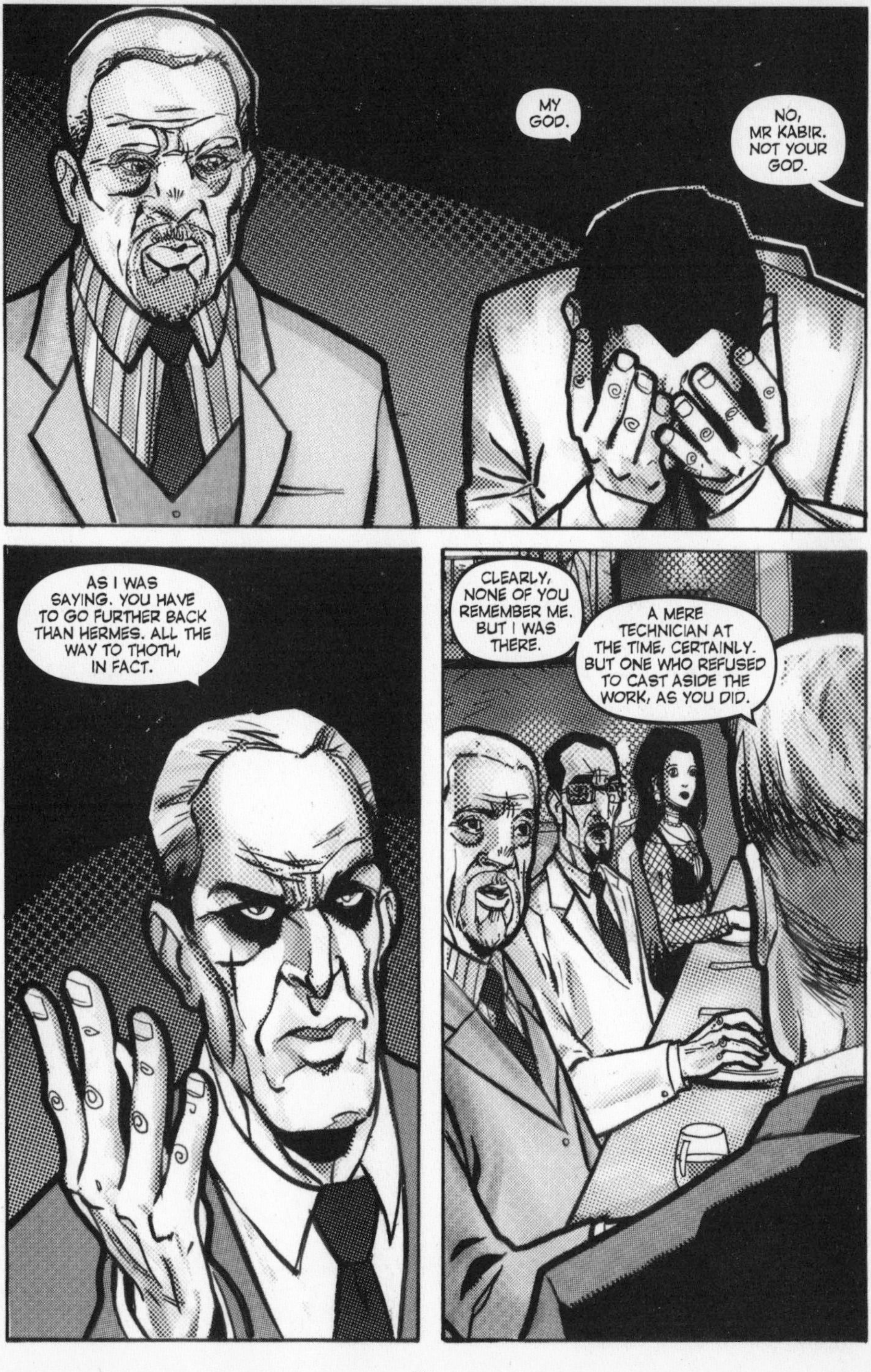
MY GOD.
NO, MR KABIR. NOT YOUR GOD.
AS I WAS SAYING. YOU HAVE TO GO FURTHER BACK THAN HERMES. ALL THE WAY TO THOTH, IN FACT.
CLEARLY, NONE OF YOU REMEMBER ME. BUT I WAS THERE.
A MERE TECHNICIAN AT THE TIME, CERTAINLY. BUT ONE WHO REFUSED TO CAST ASIDE THE WORK, AS YOU DID.

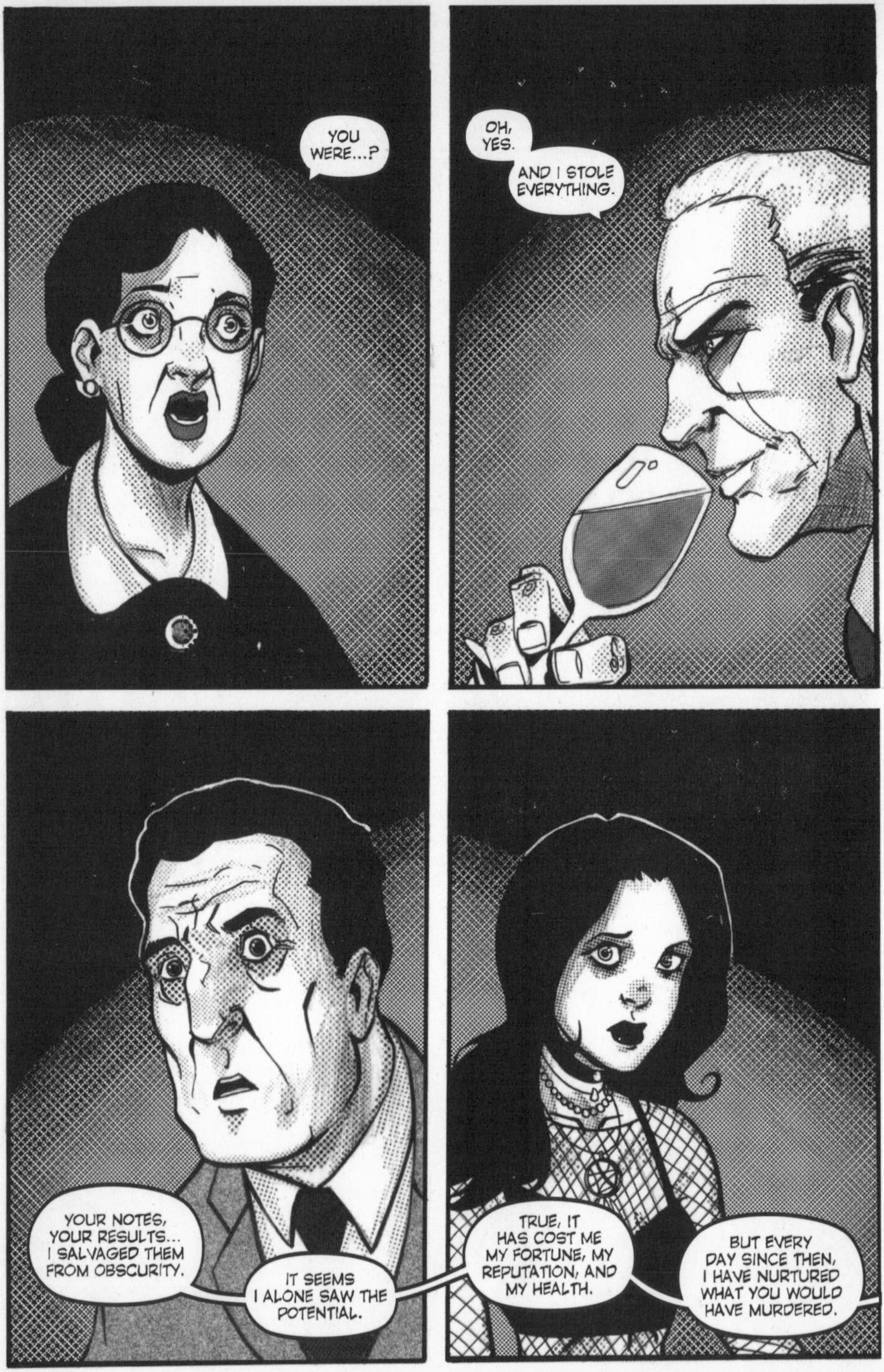
YOU WERE...?
OH, YES.
AND I STOLE EVERYTHING.
YOUR NOTES, YOUR RESULTS... I SALVAGED THEM FROM OBSCURITY.
IT SEEMS I ALONE SAW THE POTENTIAL.
TRUE, IT HAS COST ME MY FORTUNE, MY REPUTATION, AND MY HEALTH.
BUT EVERY DAY SINCE THEN, I HAVE NURTURED WHAT YOU WOULD HAVE MURDERED.

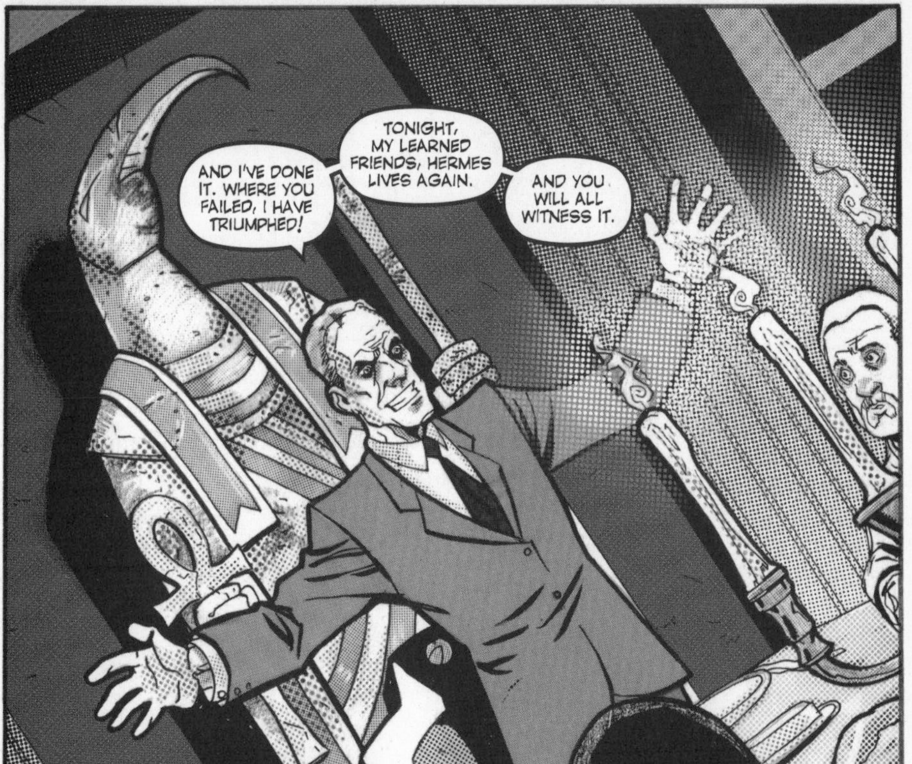
AND I'VE DONE IT. WHERE YOU FAILED, I HAVE TRIUMPHED!
TONIGHT, MY LEARNED FRIENDS, HERMES LIVES AGAIN.
AND YOU WILL ALL WITNESS IT.

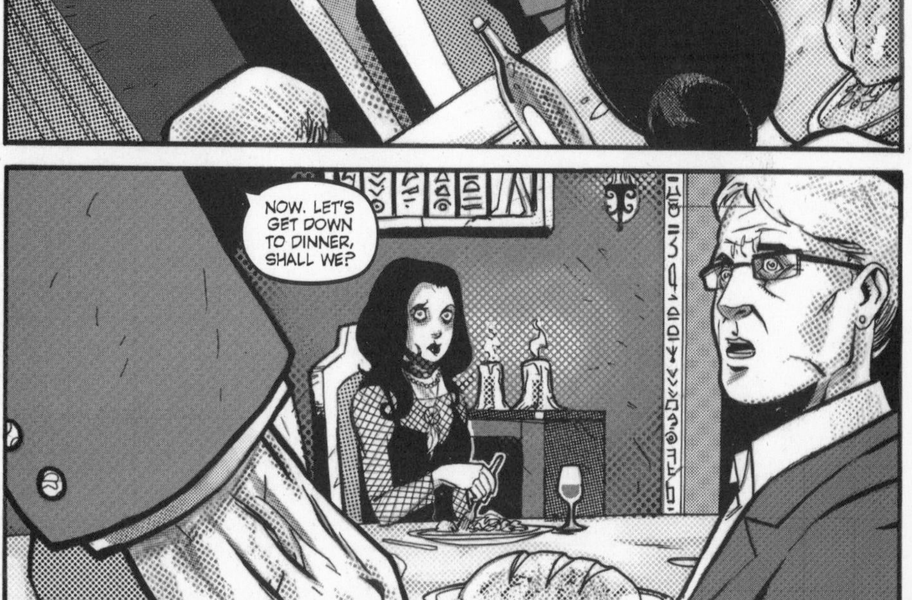
NOW. LET'S GET DOWN TO DINNER, SHALL WE?

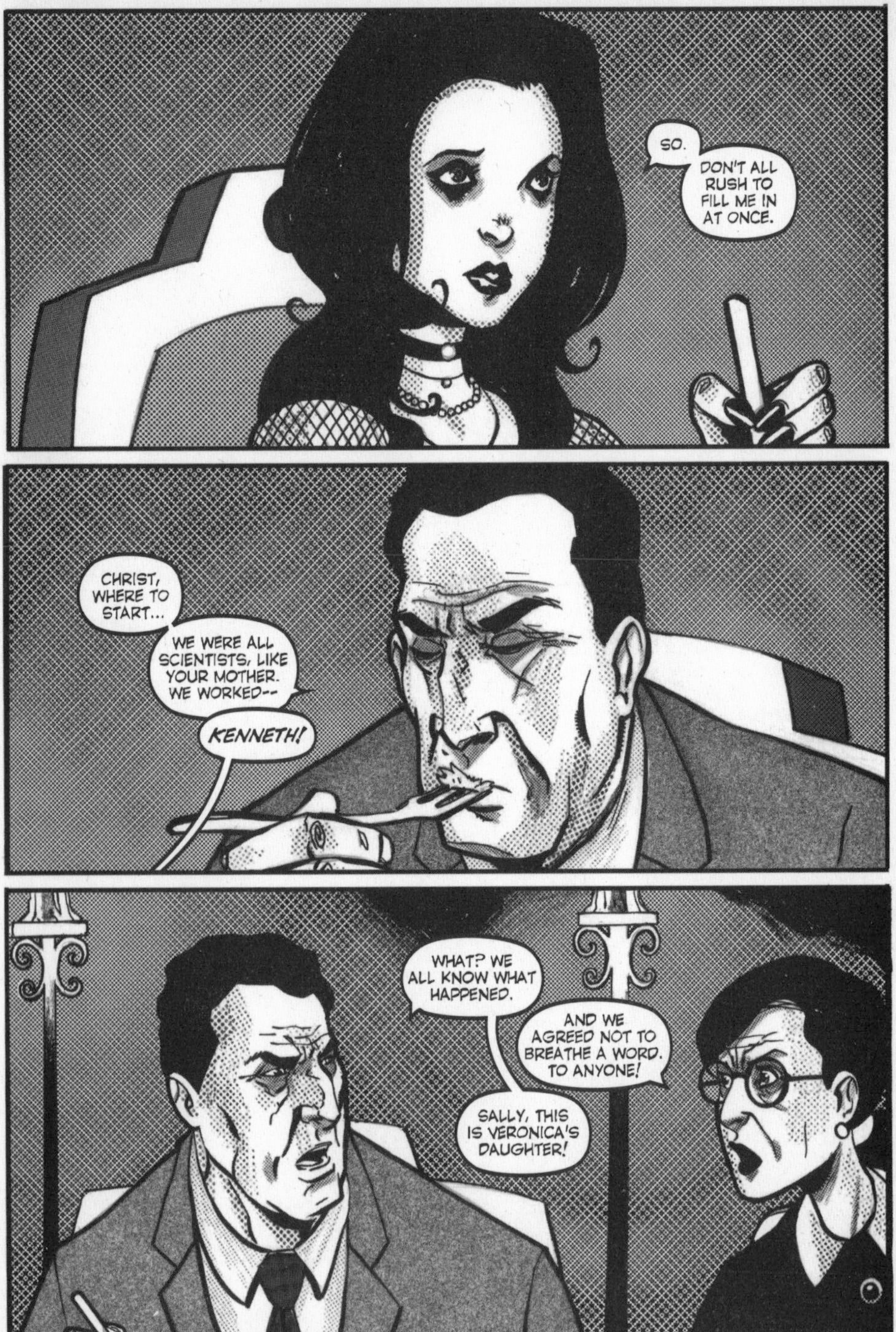
SO.
DON'T ALL RUSH TO FILL ME IN AT ONCE.
CHRIST, WHERE TO START...
WE WERE ALL SCIENTISTS, LIKE YOUR MOTHER. WE WORKED--
KENNETH!
WHAT? WE ALL KNOW WHAT HAPPENED.
AND WE AGREED NOT TO BREATHE A WORD. TO ANYONE!
SALLY, THIS IS VERONICA'S DAUGHTER!

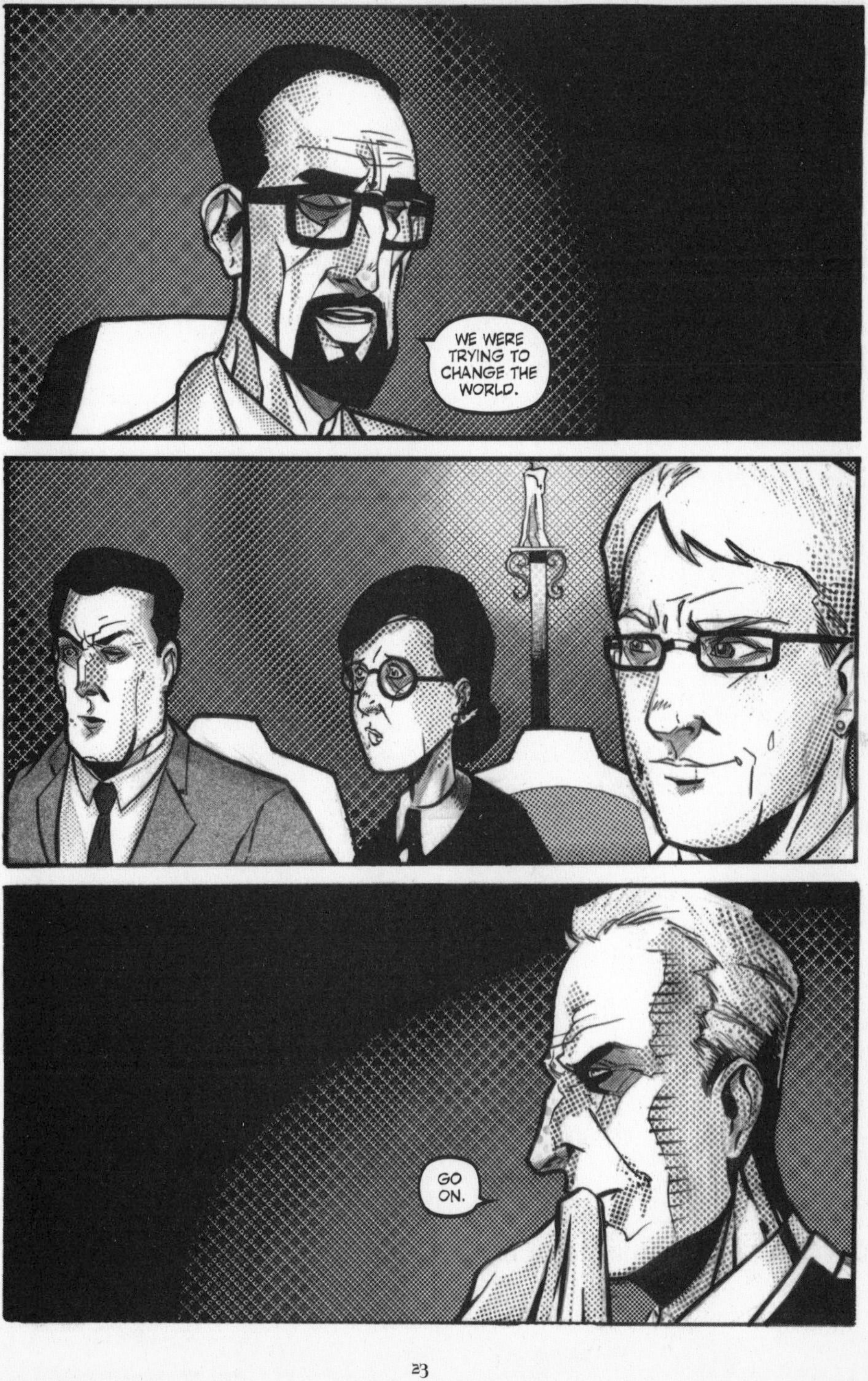
WE WERE TRYING TO CHANGE THE WORLD.
GO ON.

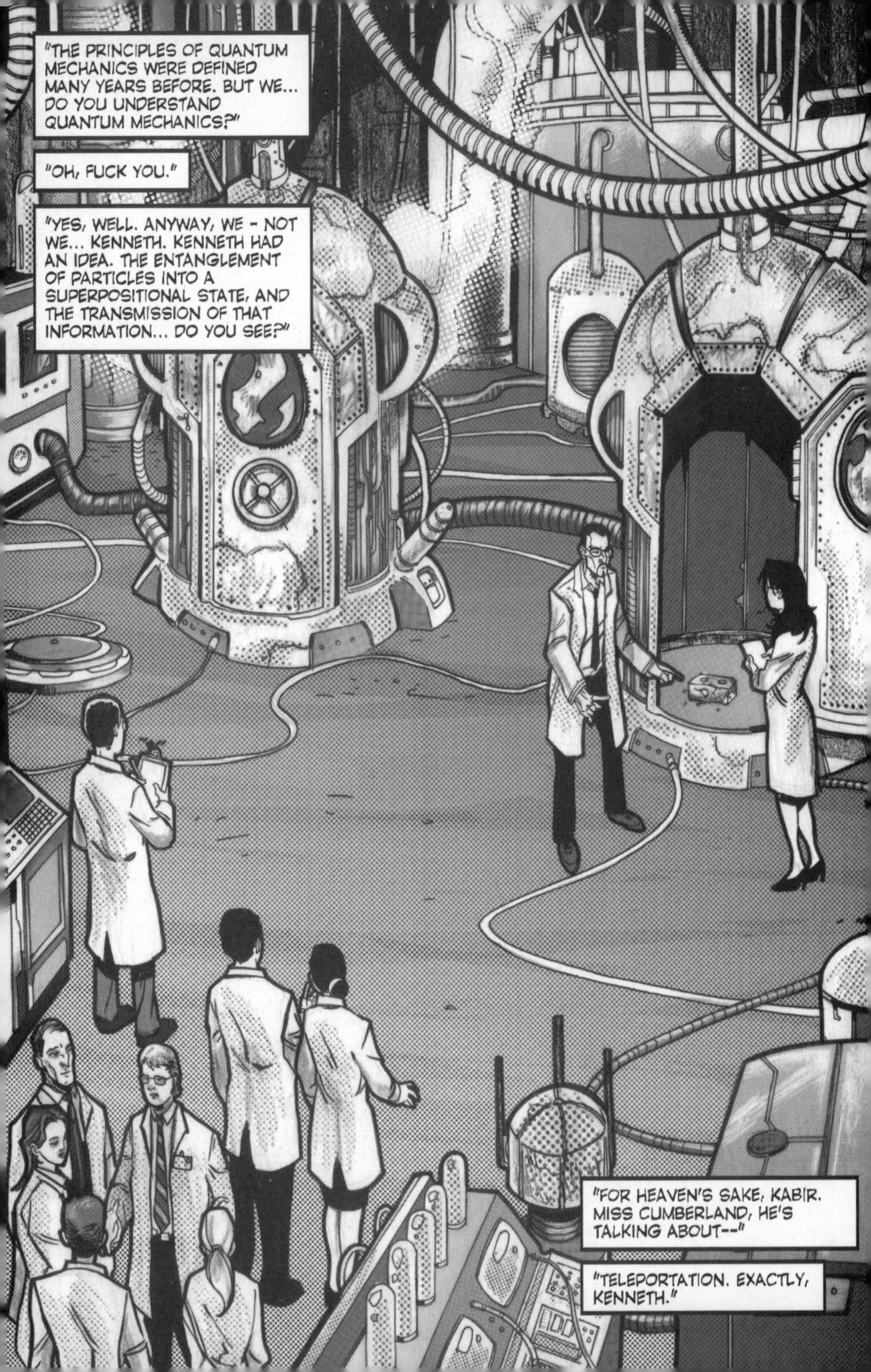
"THE PRINCIPLES OF QUANTUM MECHANICS WERE DEFINED MANY YEARS BEFORE. BUT WE... DO YOU UNDERSTAND QUANTUM MECHANICS?"
"OH, FUCK YOU."
"YES, WELL. ANYWAY, WE - NOT WE... KENNETH. KENNETH HAD AN IDEA. THE ENTANGLEMENT OF PARTICLES INTO A SUPERPOSITIONAL STATE, AND THE TRANSMISSION OF THAT INFORMATION... DO YOU SEE?"
"FOR HEAVEN'S SAKE, KABIR. MISS CUMBERLAND, HE'S TALKING ABOUT--"
"TELEPORTATION. EXACTLY, KENNETH."

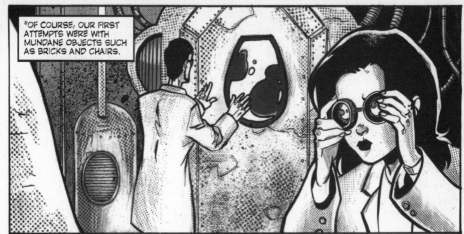

"OF COURSE, OUR FIRST ATTEMPTS WERE WITH MUNDANE OBJECTS SUCH AS BRICKS AND CHAIRS."

"IT WAS AN UNQUALIFIED SUCCESS. WE CALLED OUR DISCOVERY HERMES.

"AND WE BECAME AMBITIOUS."

"YOUR MOTHER, VERONICA, WAS MY ASSISTANT. A BRILLIANT WOMAN..."

"GET ON WITH IT, KABIR."

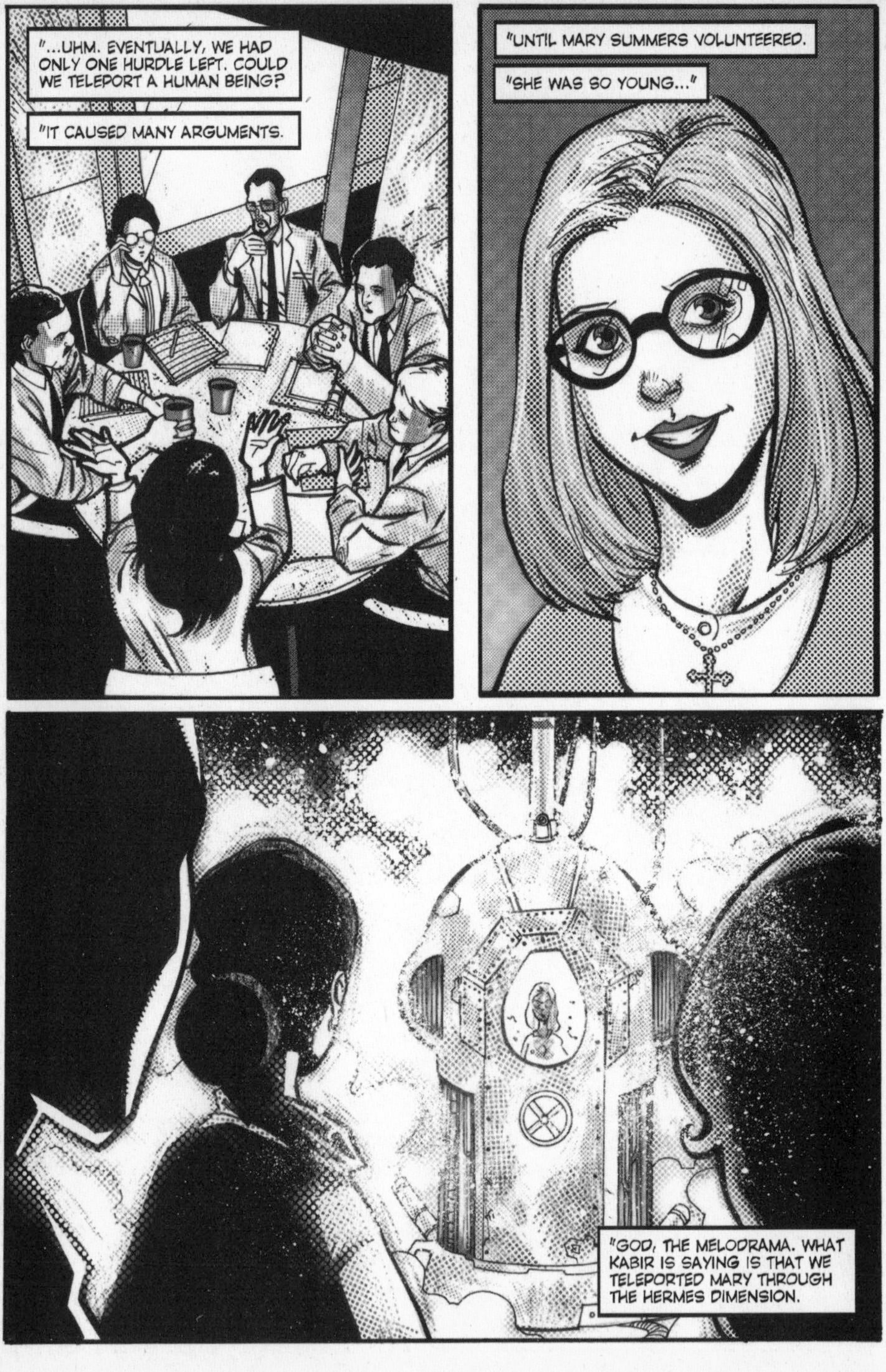
"...UHM. EVENTUALLY, WE HAD ONLY ONE HURDLE LEFT. COULD WE TELEPORT A HUMAN BEING?
"IT CAUSED MANY ARGUMENTS.
"UNTIL MARY SUMMERS VOLUNTEERED.
"SHE WAS SO YOUNG..."
"GOD, THE MELODRAMA. WHAT KABIR IS SAYING IS THAT WE TELEPORTED MARY THROUGH THE HERMES DIMENSION.

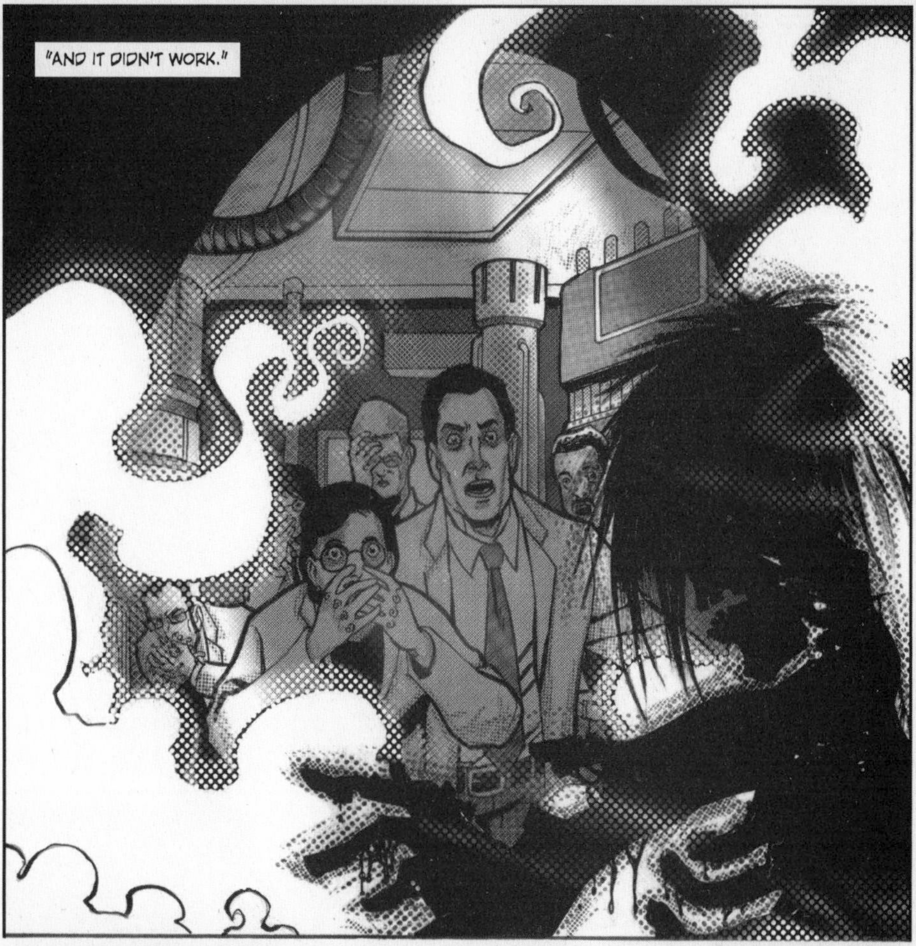
"AND IT DIDN'T WORK."

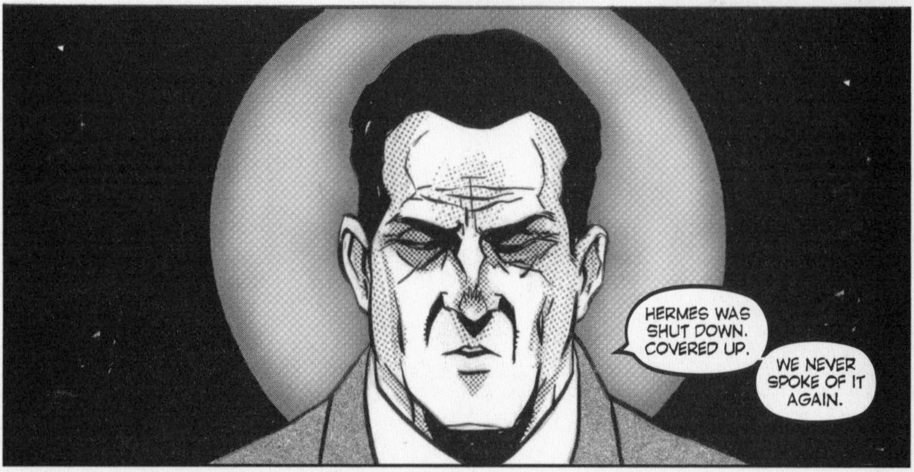
HERMES WAS SHUT DOWN. COVERED UP.
WE NEVER SPOKE OF IT AGAIN.

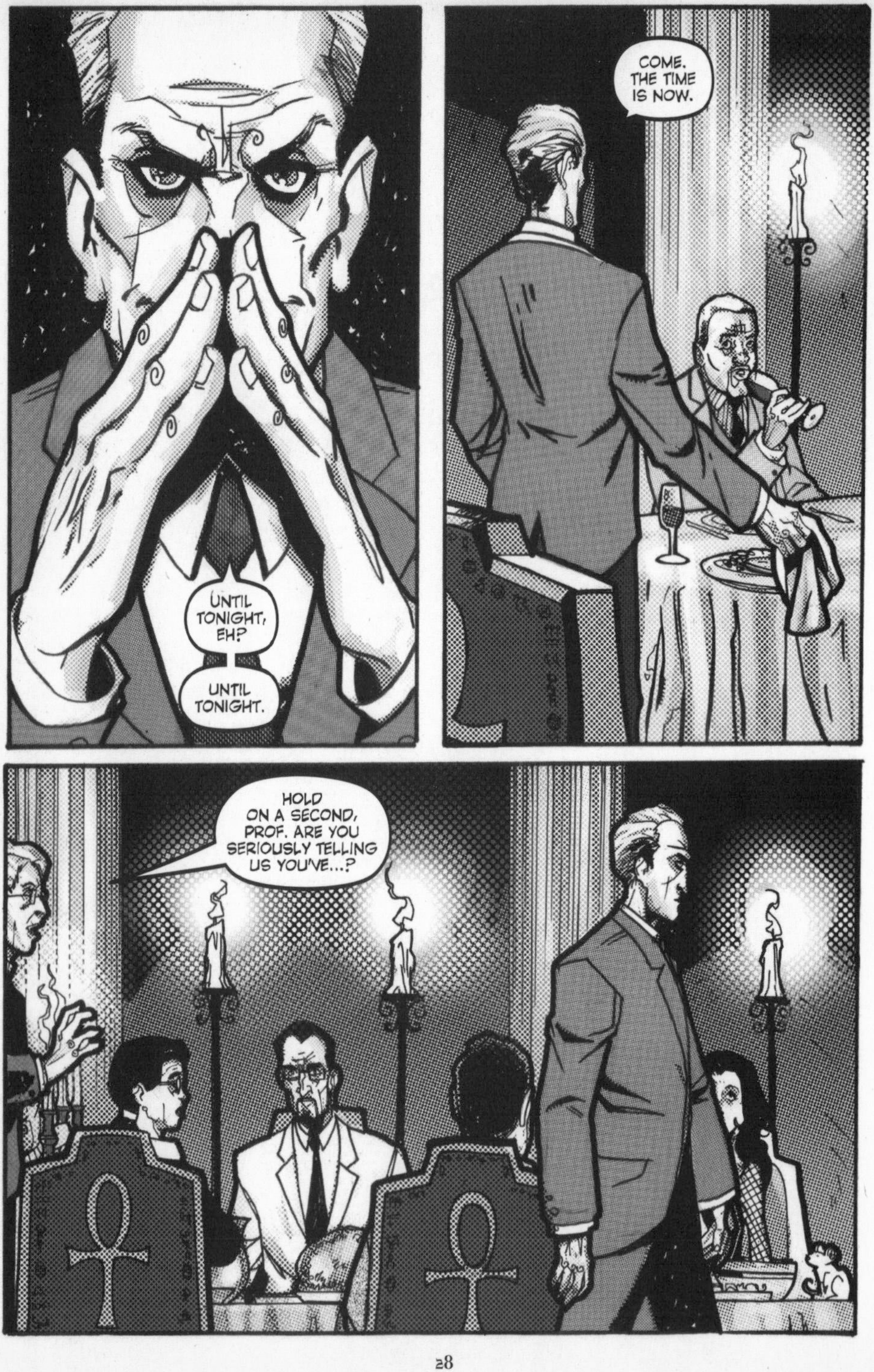
UNTIL TONIGHT, EH?
UNTIL TONIGHT.
COME. THE TIME IS NOW.
HOLD ON A SECOND, PROF. ARE YOU SERIOUSLY TELLING US YOU'VE...?

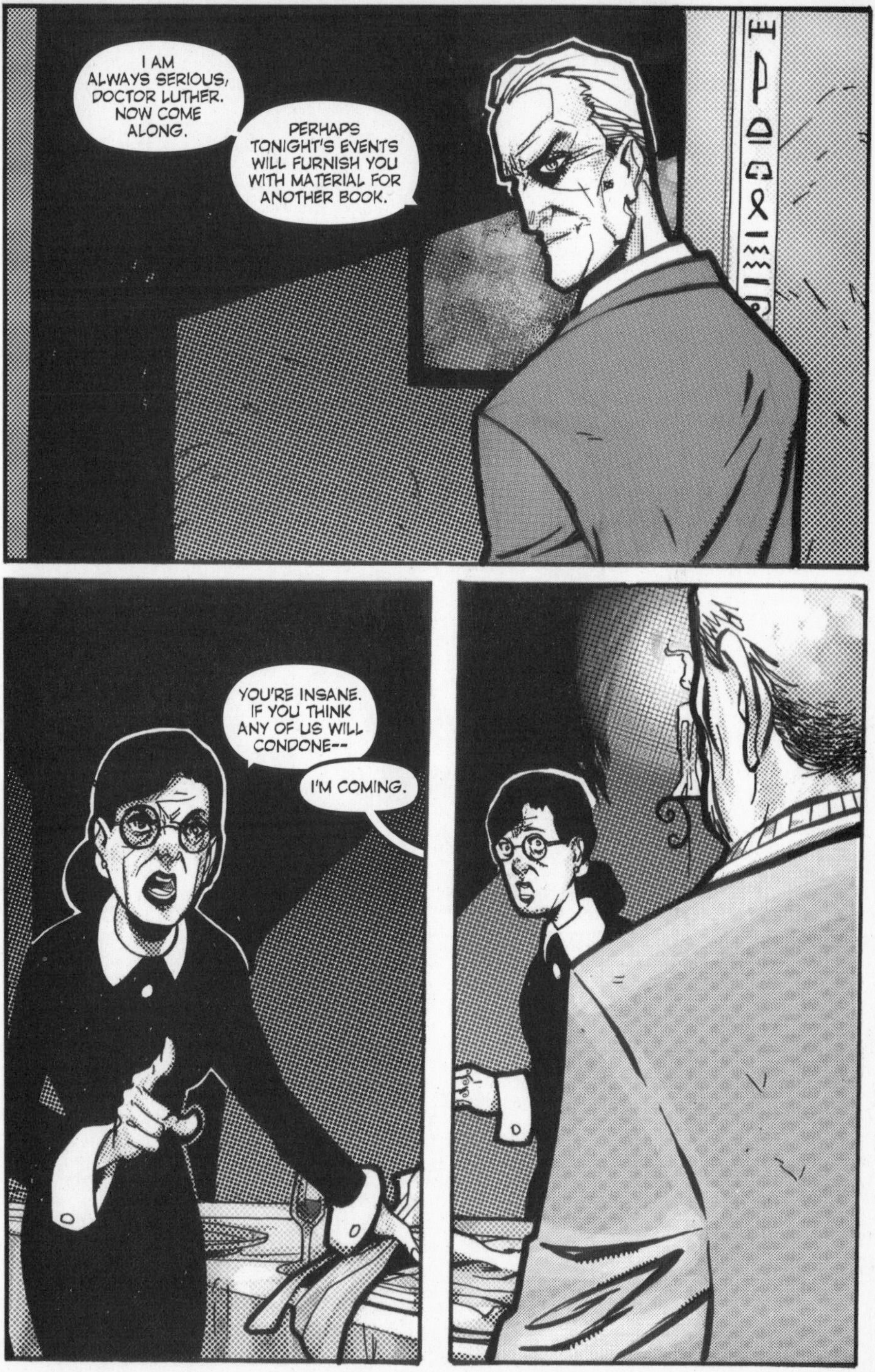
I AM ALWAYS SERIOUS, DOCTOR LUTHER. NOW COME ALONG.
PERHAPS TONIGHT'S EVENTS WILL FURNISH YOU WITH MATERIAL FOR ANOTHER BOOK.
YOU'RE INSANE. IF YOU THINK ANY OF US WILL CONDONE--
I'M COMING.

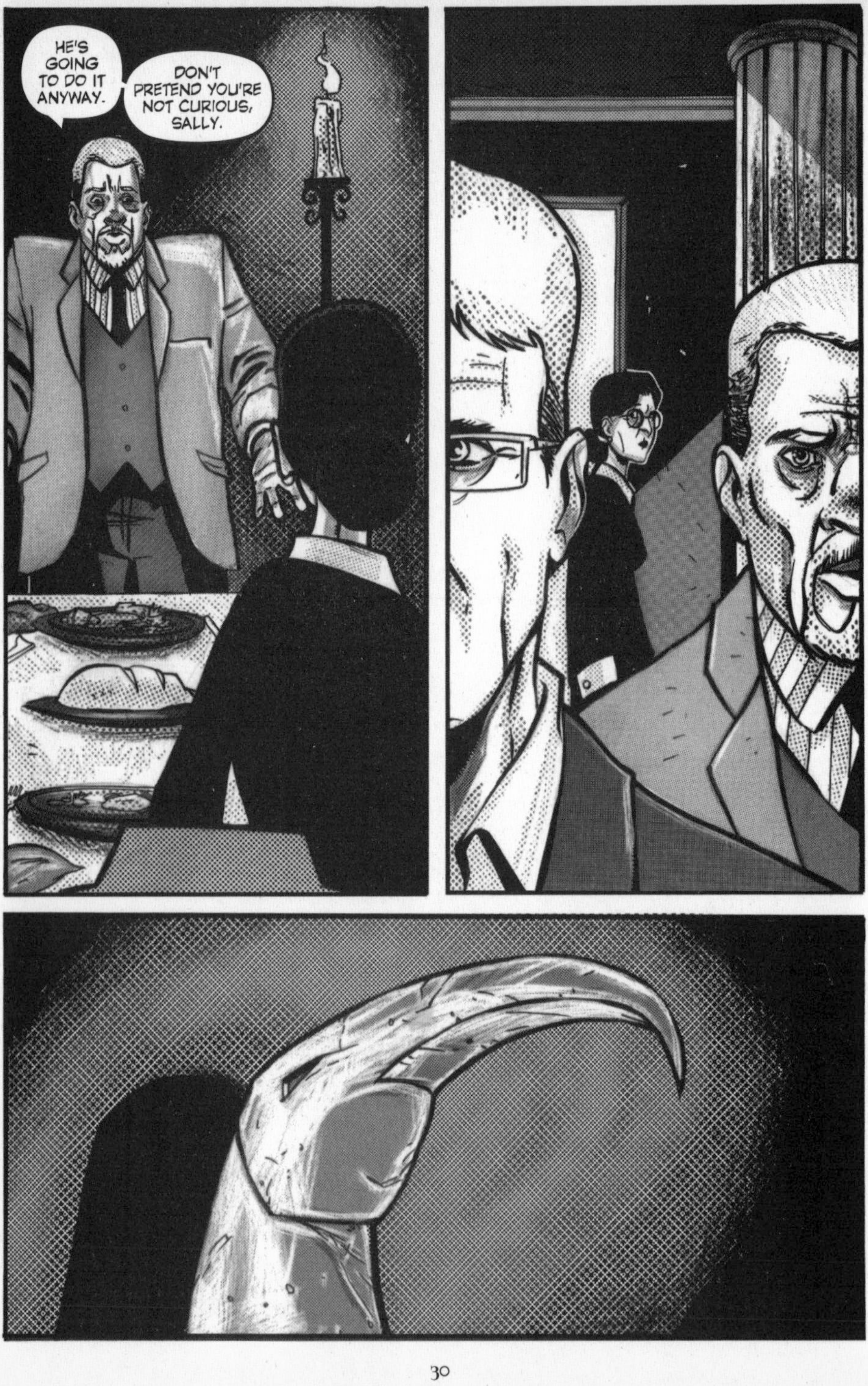
HE'S GOING TO DO IT ANYWAY.
DON'T PRETEND YOU'RE NOT CURIOUS, SALLY.

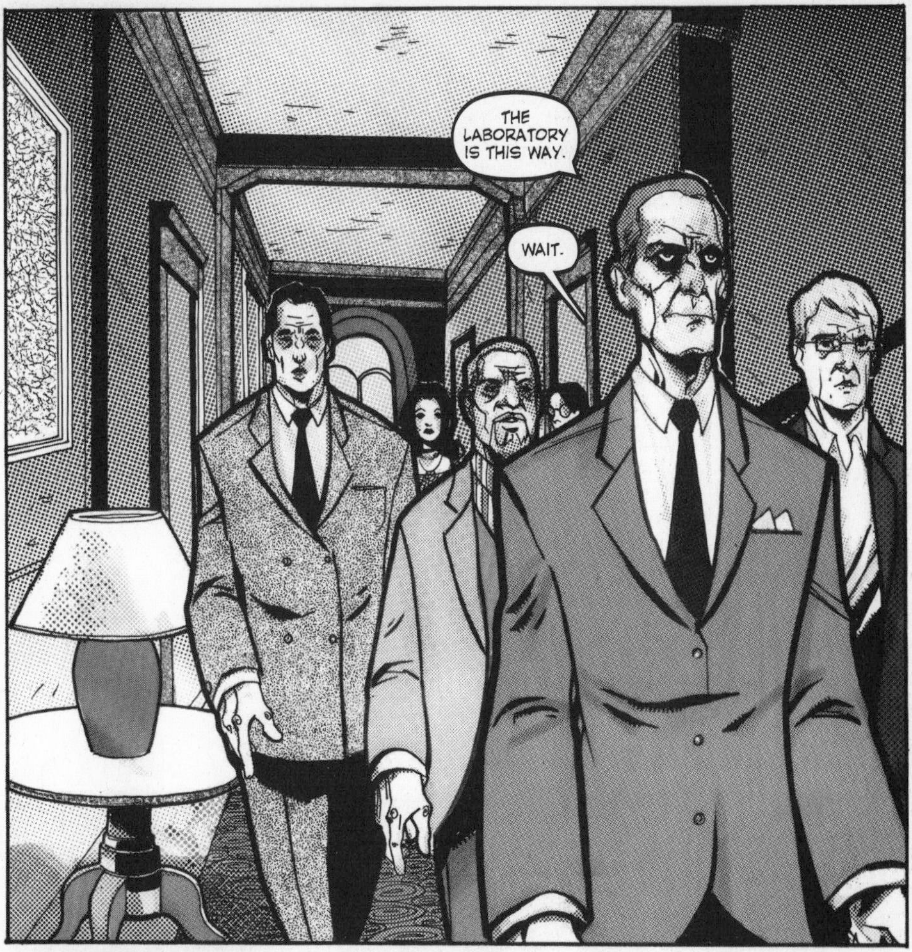
THE LABORATORY IS THIS WAY.
WAIT.

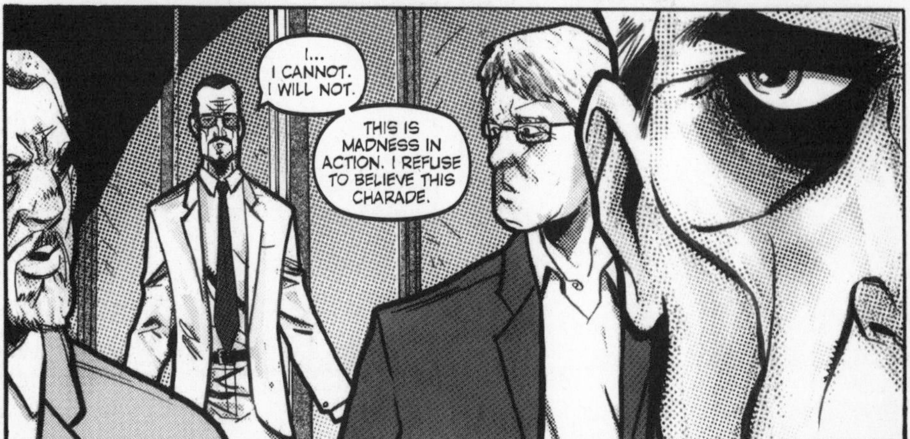
I... I CANNOT. I WILL NOT.
THIS IS MADNESS IN ACTION. I REFUSE TO BELIEVE THIS CHARADE.

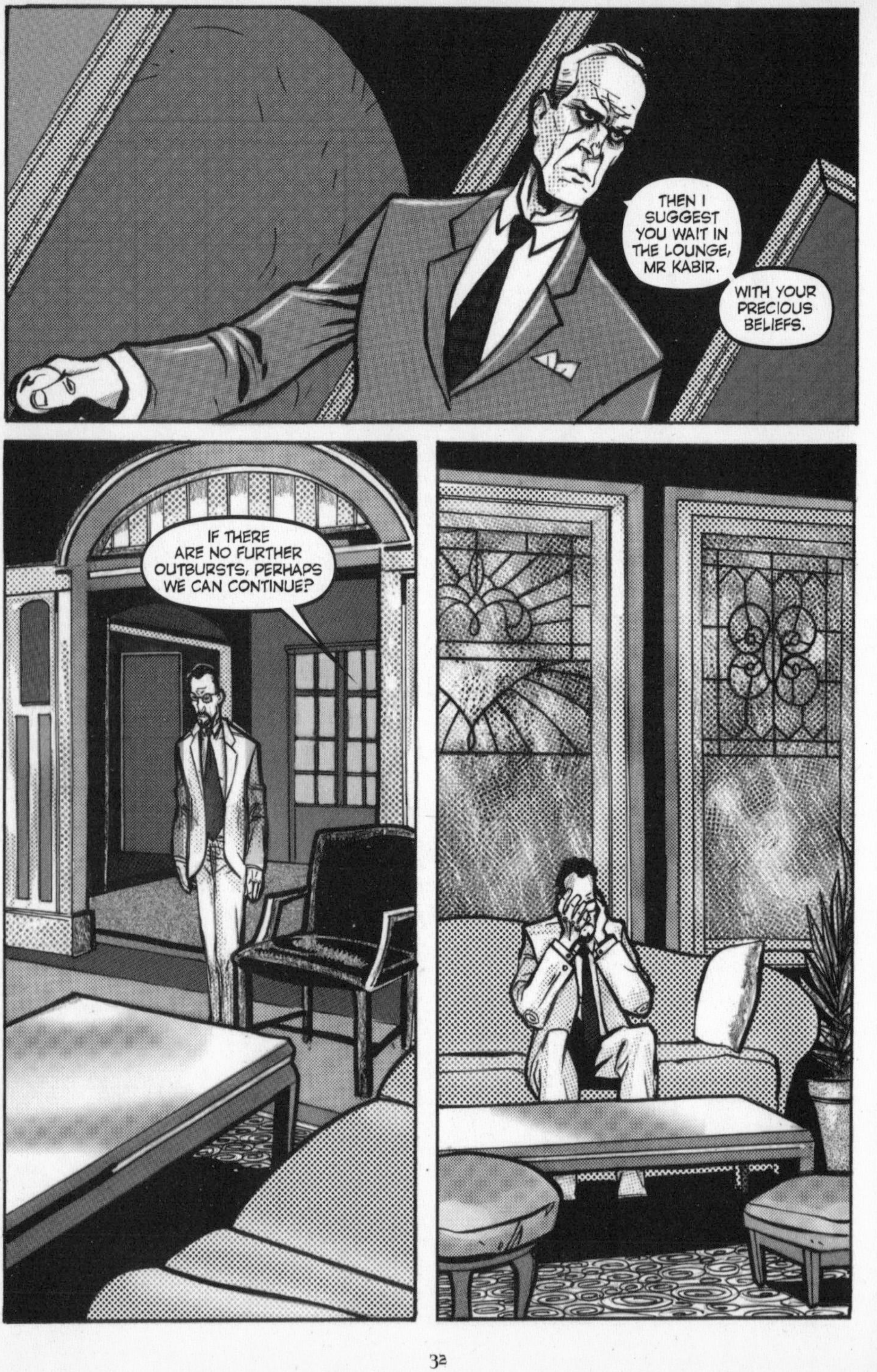
THEN I SUGGEST YOU WAIT IN THE LOUNGE, MR KABIR.
WITH YOUR PRECIOUS BELIEFS.
IF THERE ARE NO FURTHER OUTBURSTS, PERHAPS WE CAN CONTINUE?

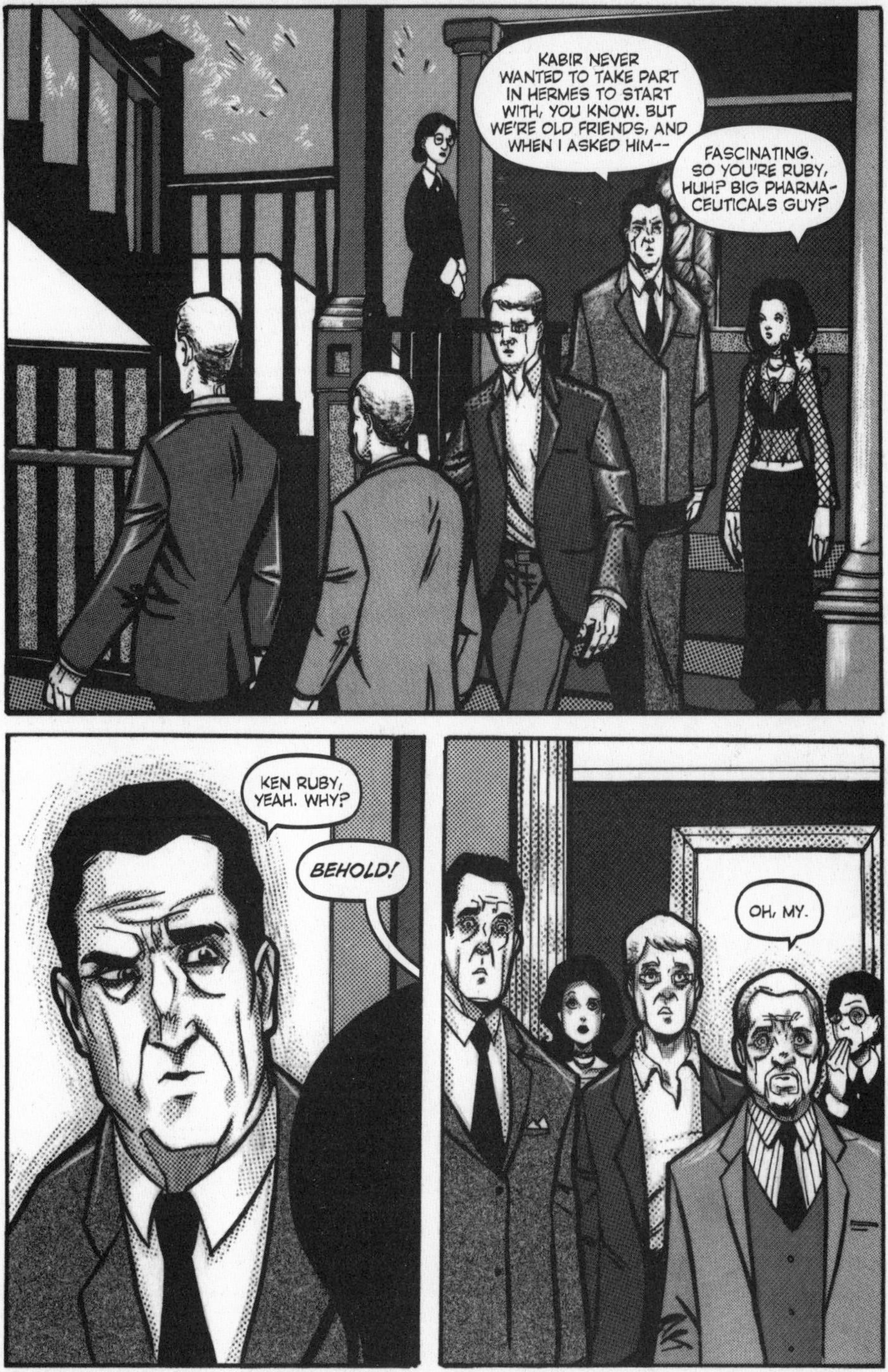
KABIR NEVER WANTED TO TAKE PART IN HERMES TO START WITH, YOU KNOW. BUT WE'RE OLD FRIENDS, AND WHEN I ASKED HIM--
FASCINATING. SO YOU'RE RUBY, HUH? BIG PHARMACEUTICALS GUY?
KEN RUBY, YEAH. WHY?
BEHOLD!
OH, MY.

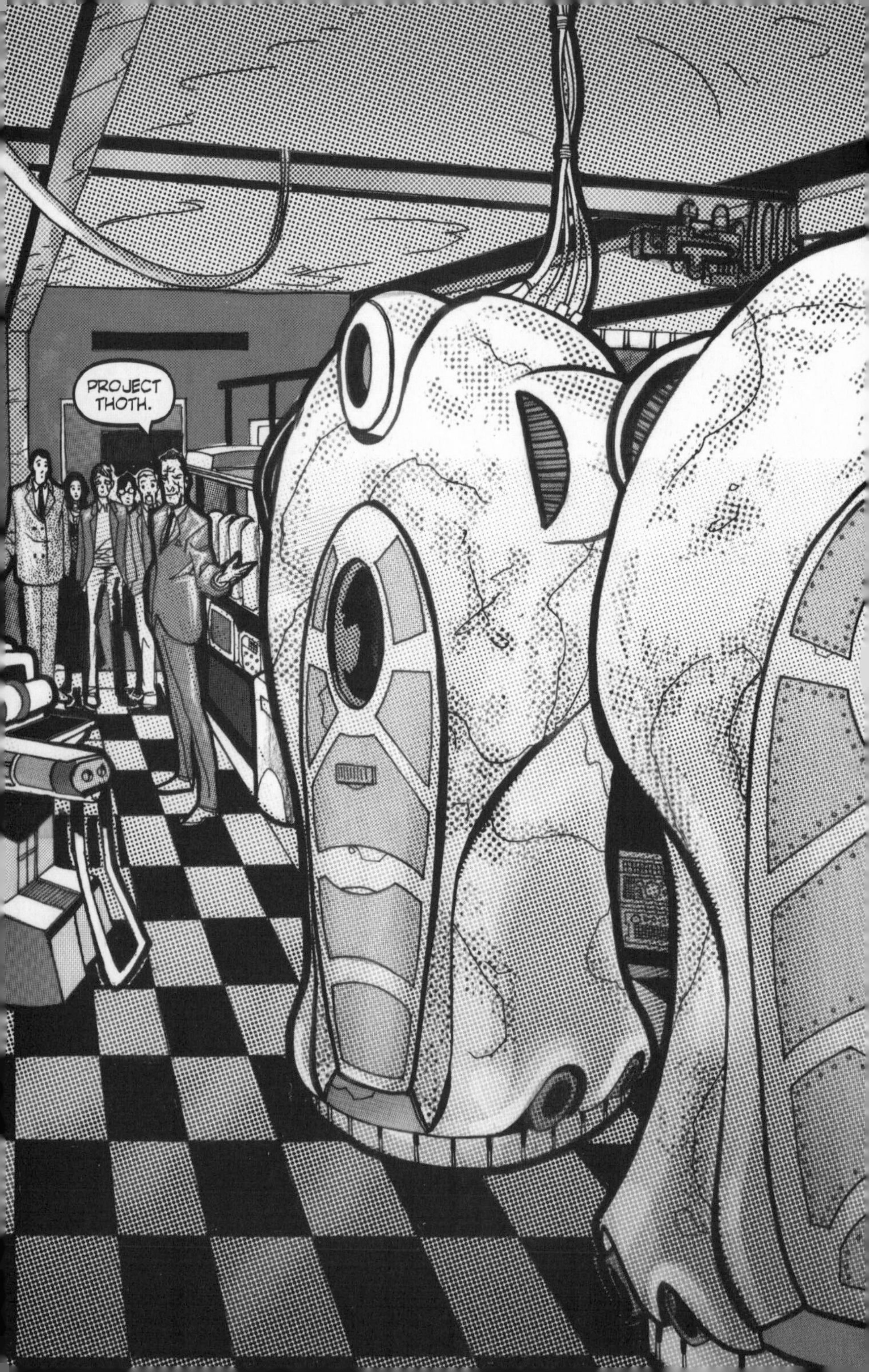
PROJECT THOTH.

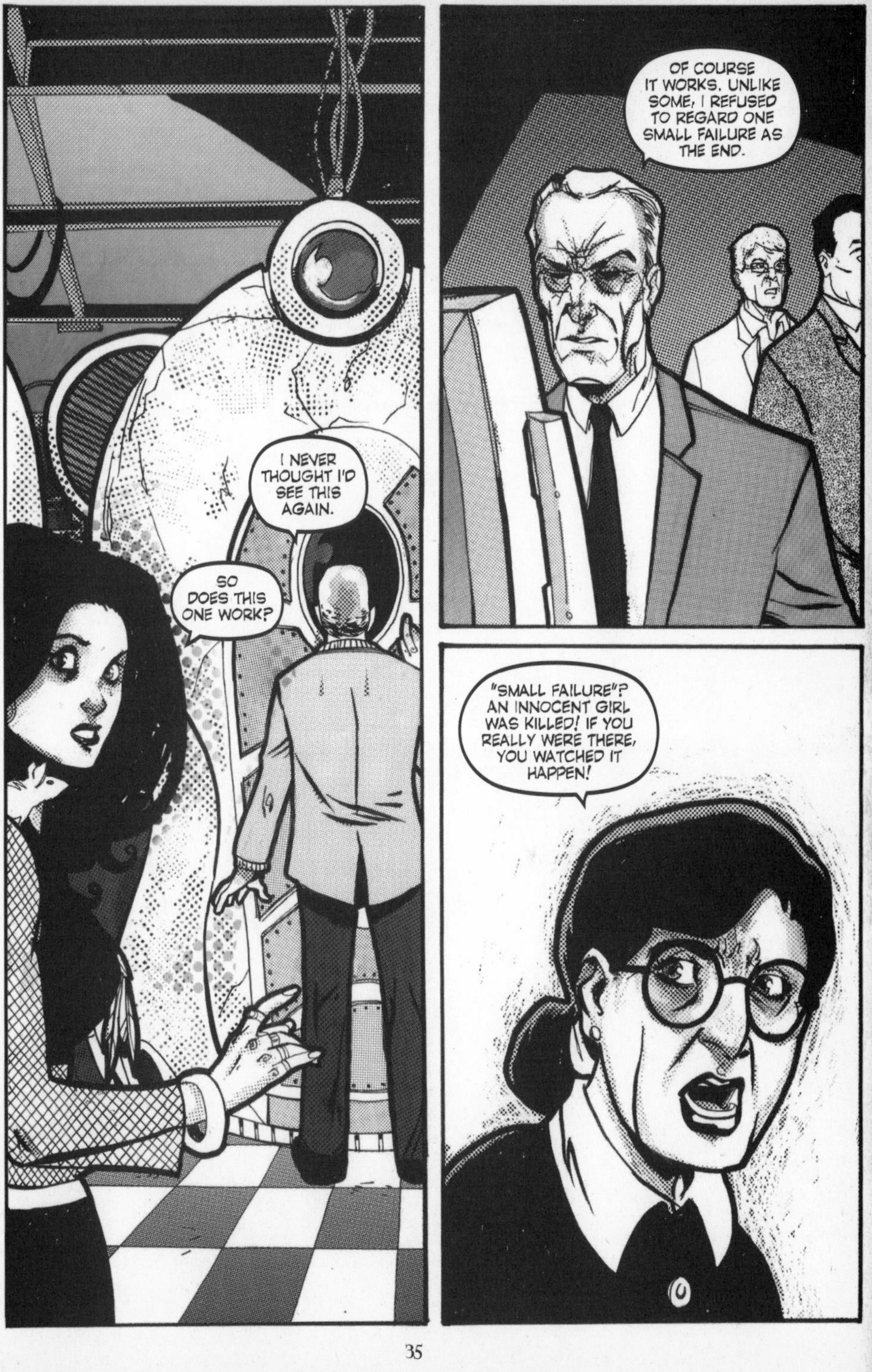
I NEVER THOUGHT I'D SEE THIS AGAIN.
SO DOES THIS ONE WORK?
OF COURSE IT WORKS. UNLIKE SOME, I REFUSED TO REGARD ONE SMALL FAILURE AS THE END.
"SMALL FAILURE"? AN INNOCENT GIRL WAS KILLED! IF YOU REALLY WERE THERE, YOU WATCHED IT HAPPEN!

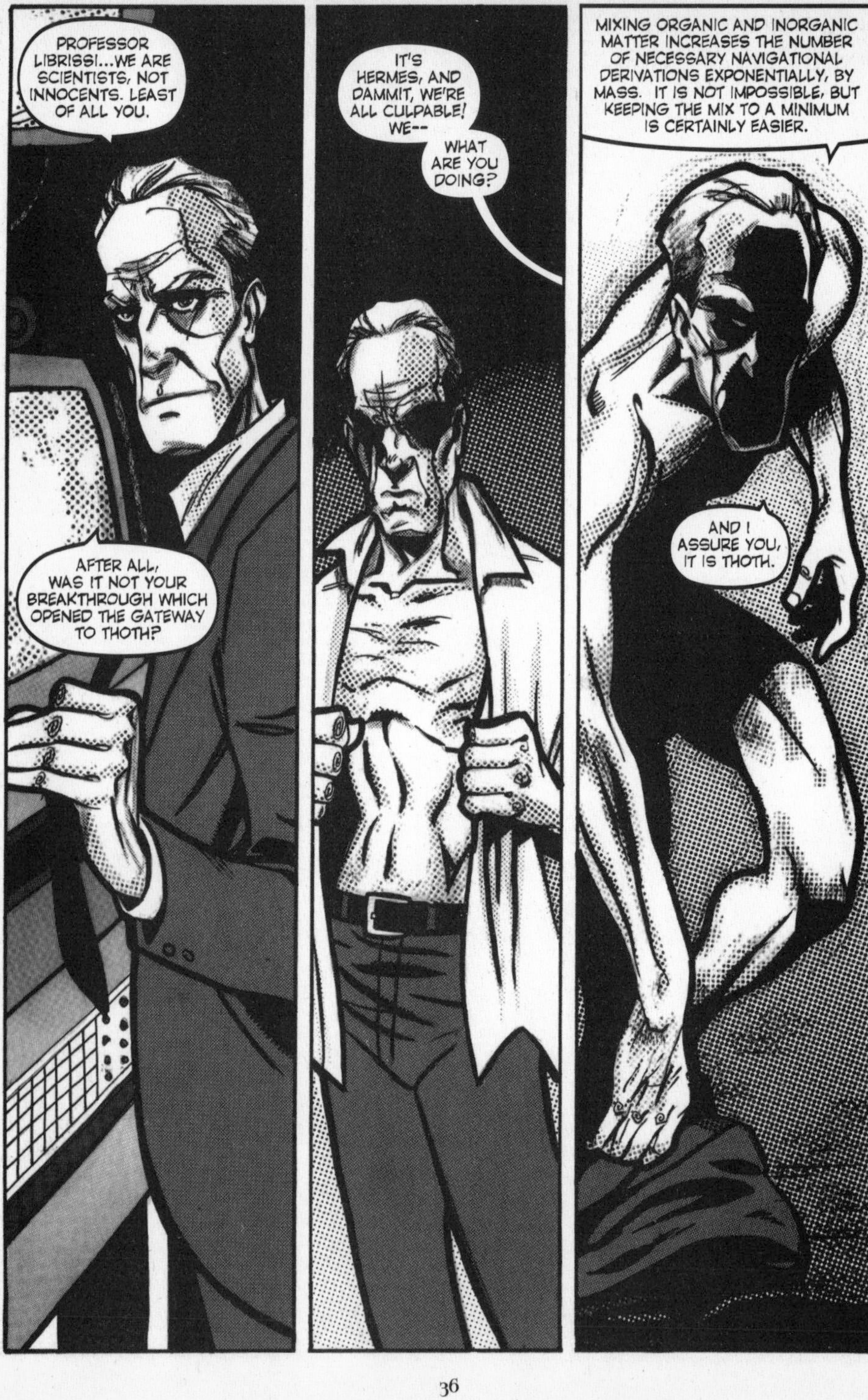
PROFESSOR LIBRISSI...WE ARE SCIENTISTS, NOT INNOCENTS. LEAST OF ALL YOU.
AFTER ALL, WAS IT NOT YOUR BREAKTHROUGH WHICH OPENED THE GATEWAY TO THOTH?
IT'S HERMES, AND DAMMIT, WE'RE ALL CULPABLE! WE--
WHAT ARE YOU DOING?
MIXING ORGANIC AND INORGANIC MATTER INCREASES THE NUMBER OF NECESSARY NAVIGATIONAL DERIVATIONS EXPONENTIALLY, BY MASS. IT IS NOT IMPOSSIBLE, BUT KEEPING THE MIX TO A MINIMUM IS CERTAINLY EASIER.
AND I ASSURE YOU, IT IS THOTH.

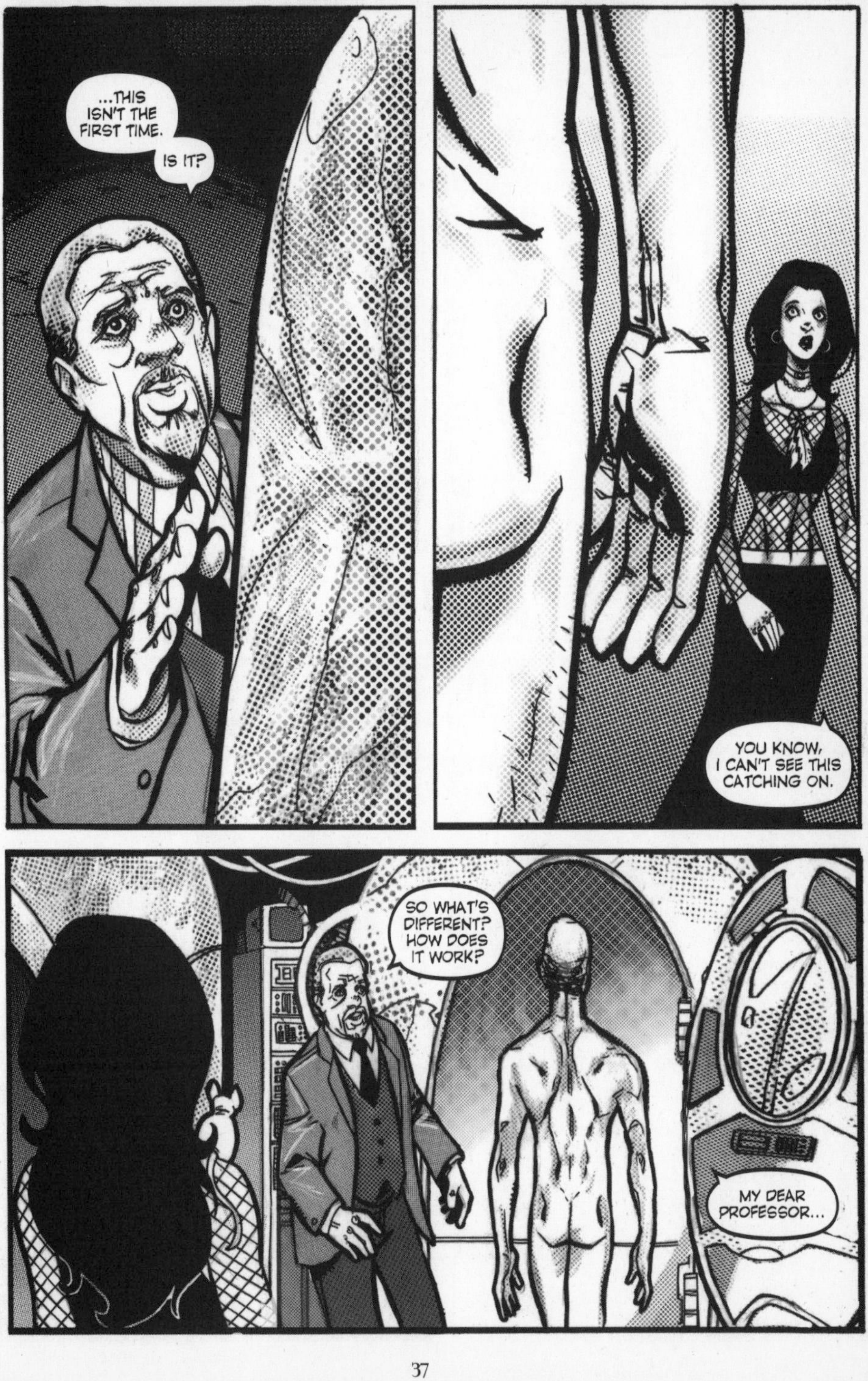
...THIS ISN'T THE FIRST TIME.
IS IT?
YOU KNOW, I CAN'T SEE THIS CATCHING ON.
SO WHAT'S DIFFERENT? HOW DOES IT WORK?
MY DEAR PROFESSOR...

...A MAGICIAN NEVER REVEALS HIS SECRETS.

PLEASE STAND BACK. THE PROGRAM WILL COMMENCE AUTOMATICALLY.

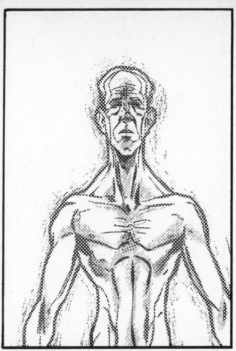

INCREDIBLE. WE WERE SO CLOSE!

OH, COME ON. IT'S A SCAM! WE KNOW WHAT HAPPENS IF HE REALLY TRIES TO TELEPORT. WE'VE ALREADY SEEN IT!

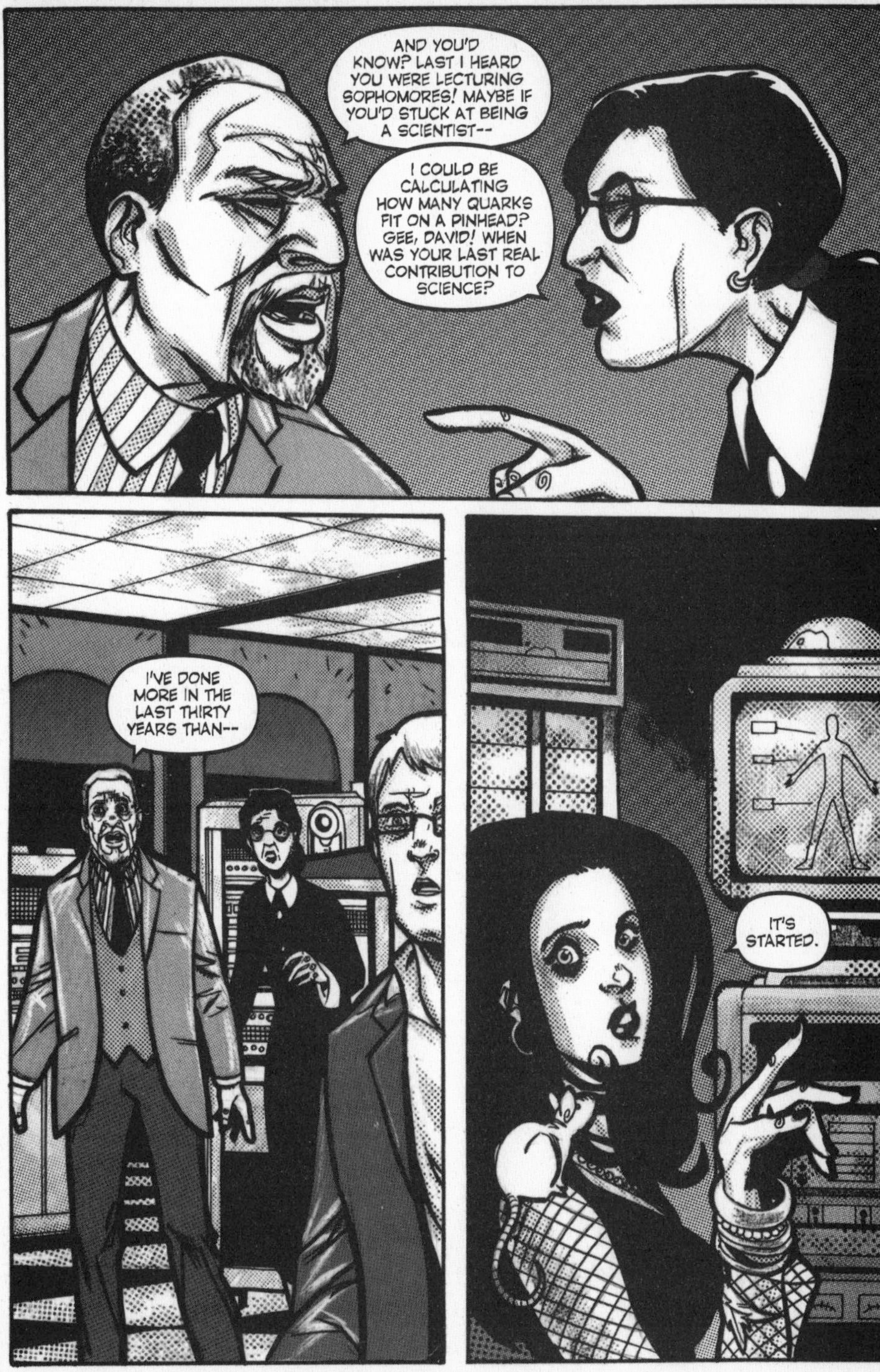
AND YOU'D KNOW? LAST I HEARD YOU WERE LECTURING SOPHOMORES! MAYBE IF YOU'D STUCK AT BEING A SCIENTIST--
I COULD BE CALCULATING HOW MANY QUARKS FIT ON A PINHEAD? GEE, DAVID! WHEN WAS YOUR LAST REAL CONTRIBUTION TO SCIENCE?
I'VE DONE MORE IN THE LAST THIRTY YEARS THAN--
IT'S STARTED.

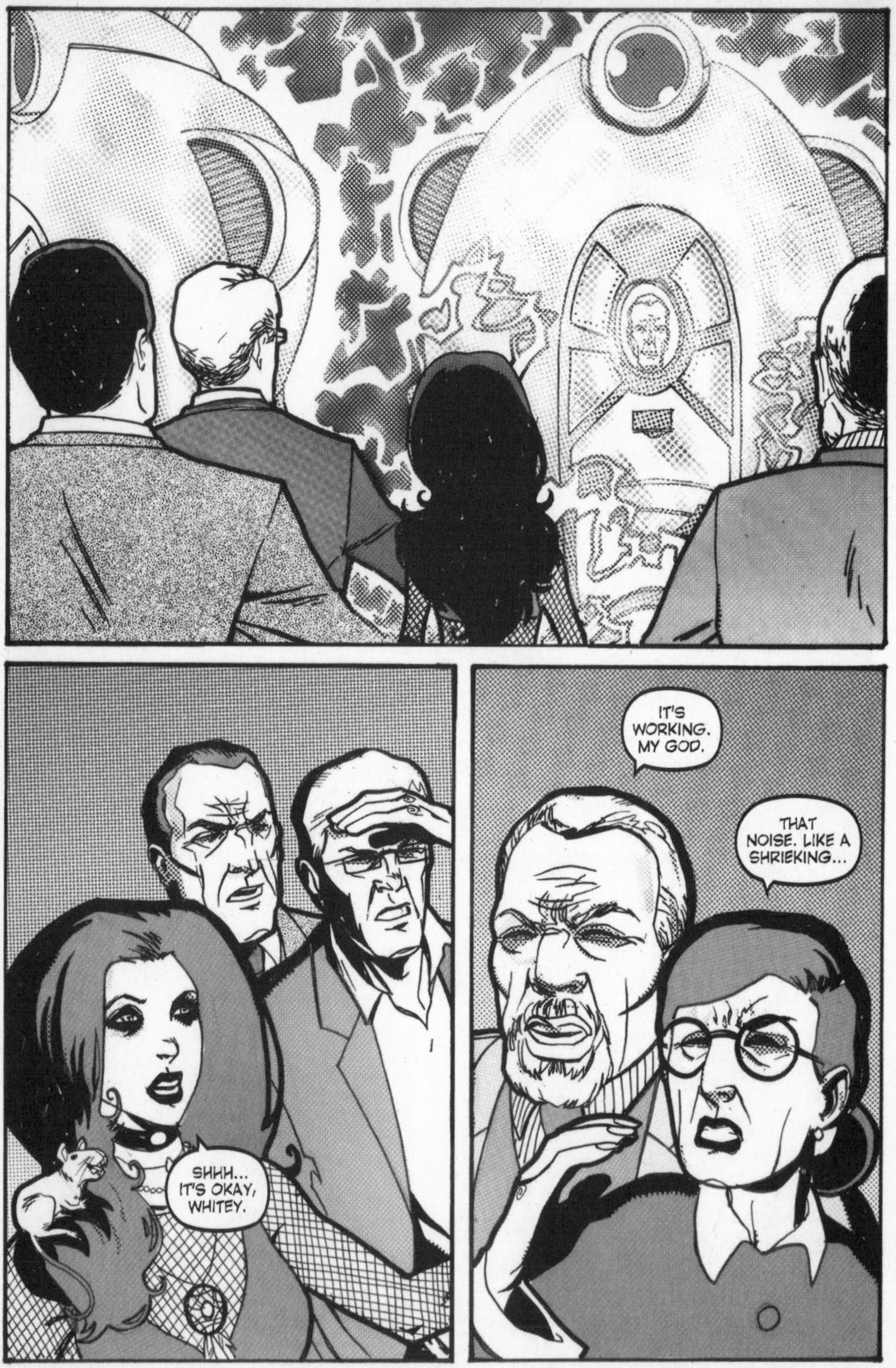
SHHH...
IT'S OKAY,
WHITEY.
IT'S
WORKING.
MY GOD.
THAT
NOISE. LIKE A
SHRIEKING...

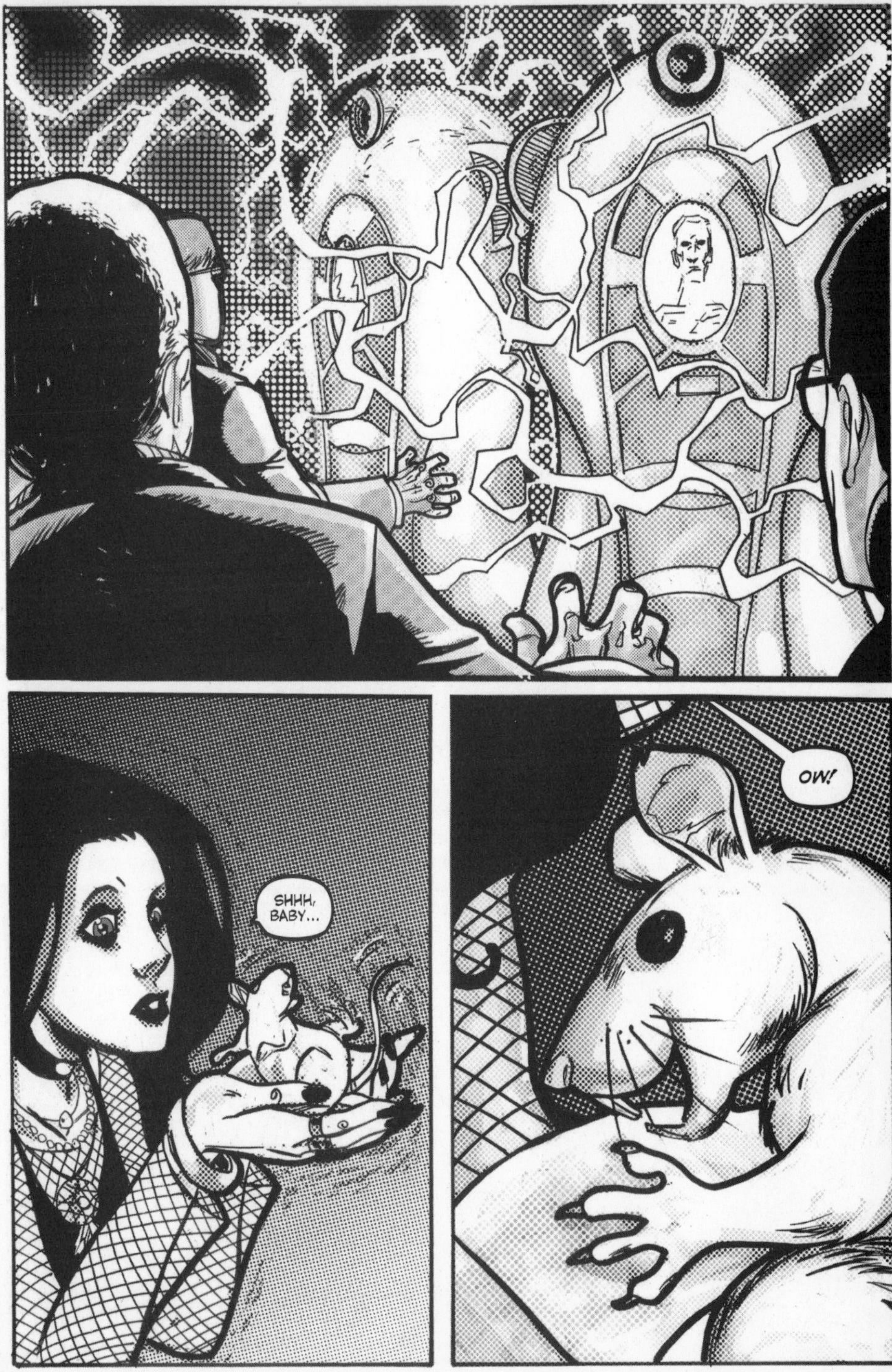
SHHH, BABY...
OW!

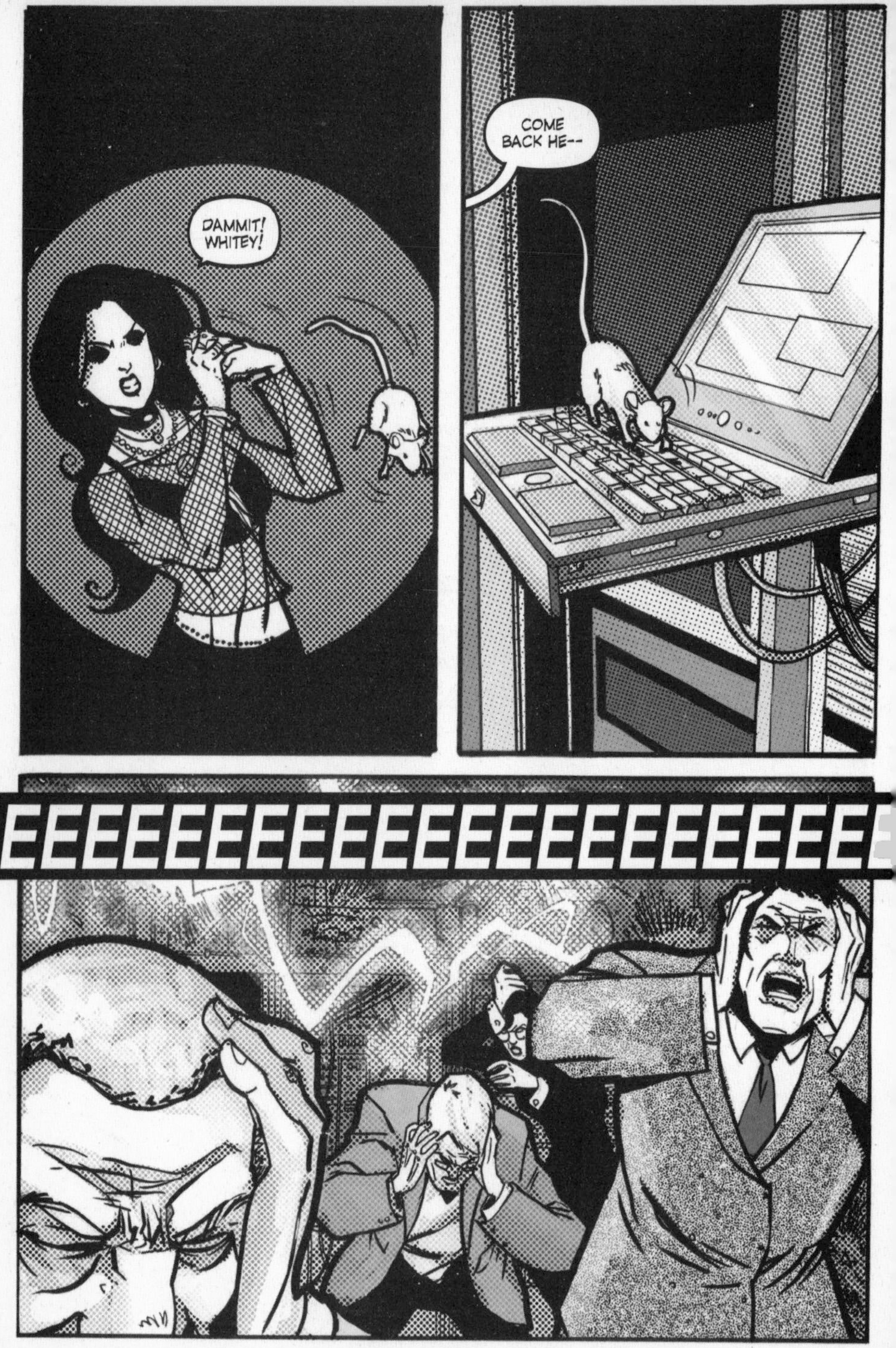
DAMMIT! WHITEY!
COME BACK HE--
EEEEEEEEEEEEEEEEEEEEEEEE

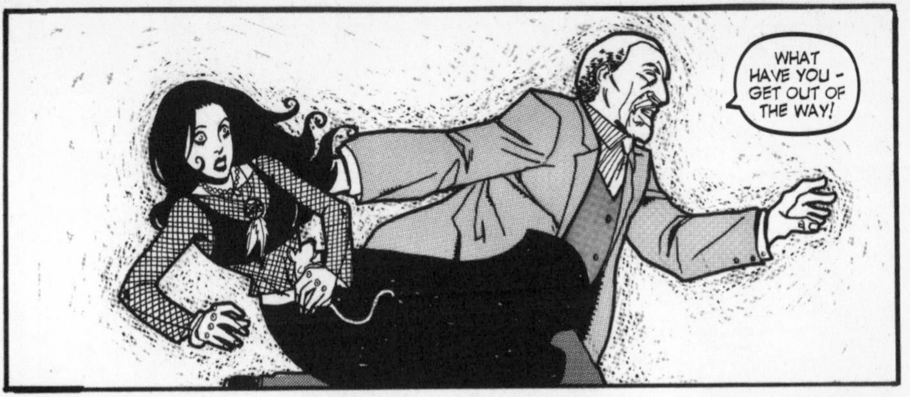
WHAT HAVE YOU - GET OUT OF THE WAY!

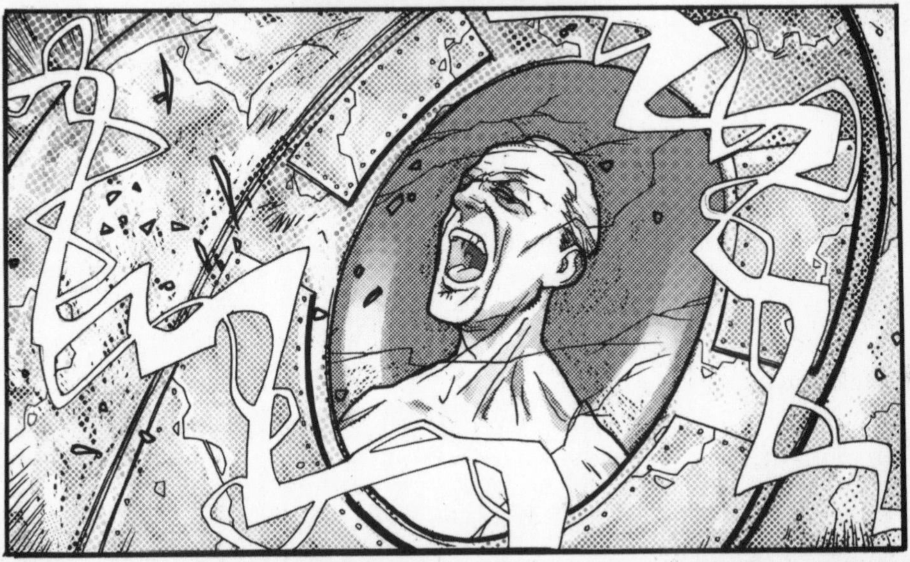

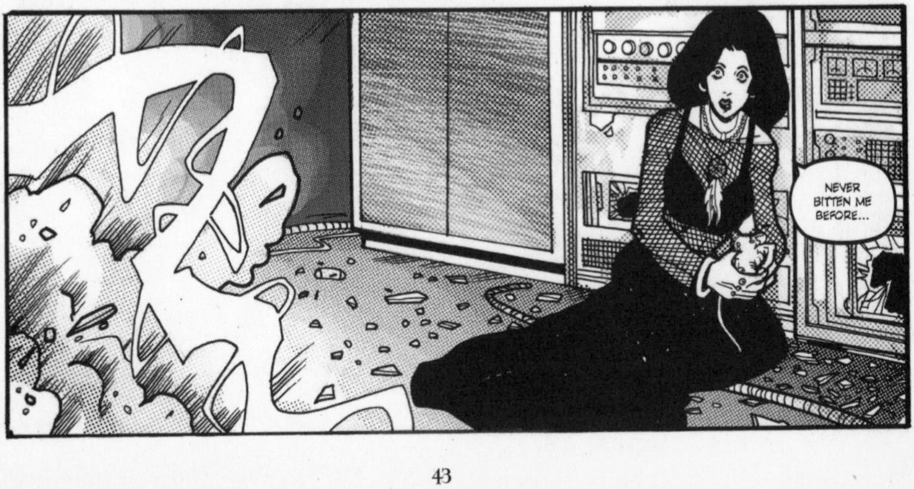
NEVER BITTEN ME BEFORE...

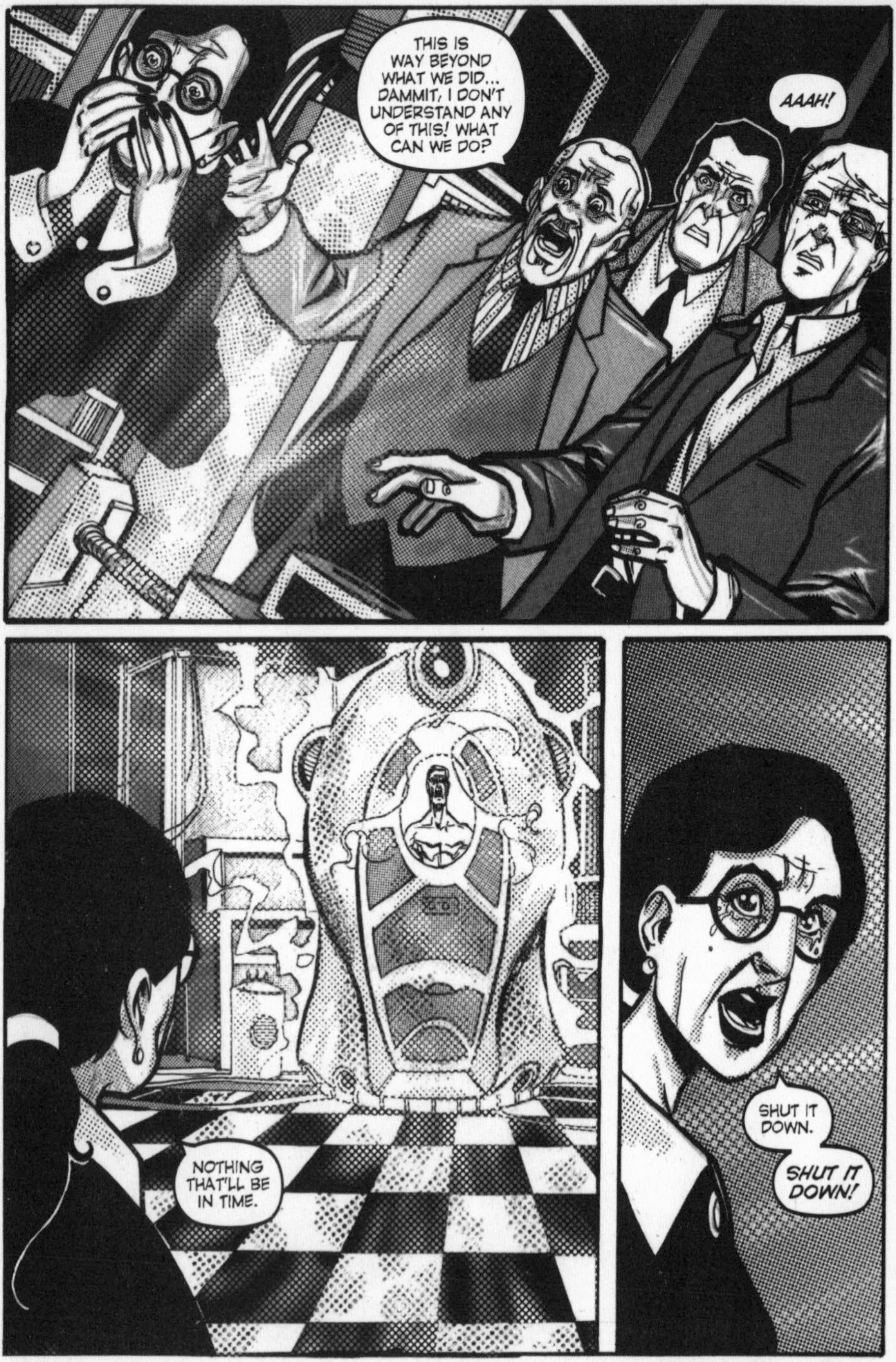
THIS IS WAY BEYOND WHAT WE DID... DAMMIT, I DON'T UNDERSTAND ANY OF THIS! WHAT CAN WE DO?
AAAH!
NOTHING THAT'LL BE IN TIME.
SHUT IT DOWN.
SHUT IT DOWN!

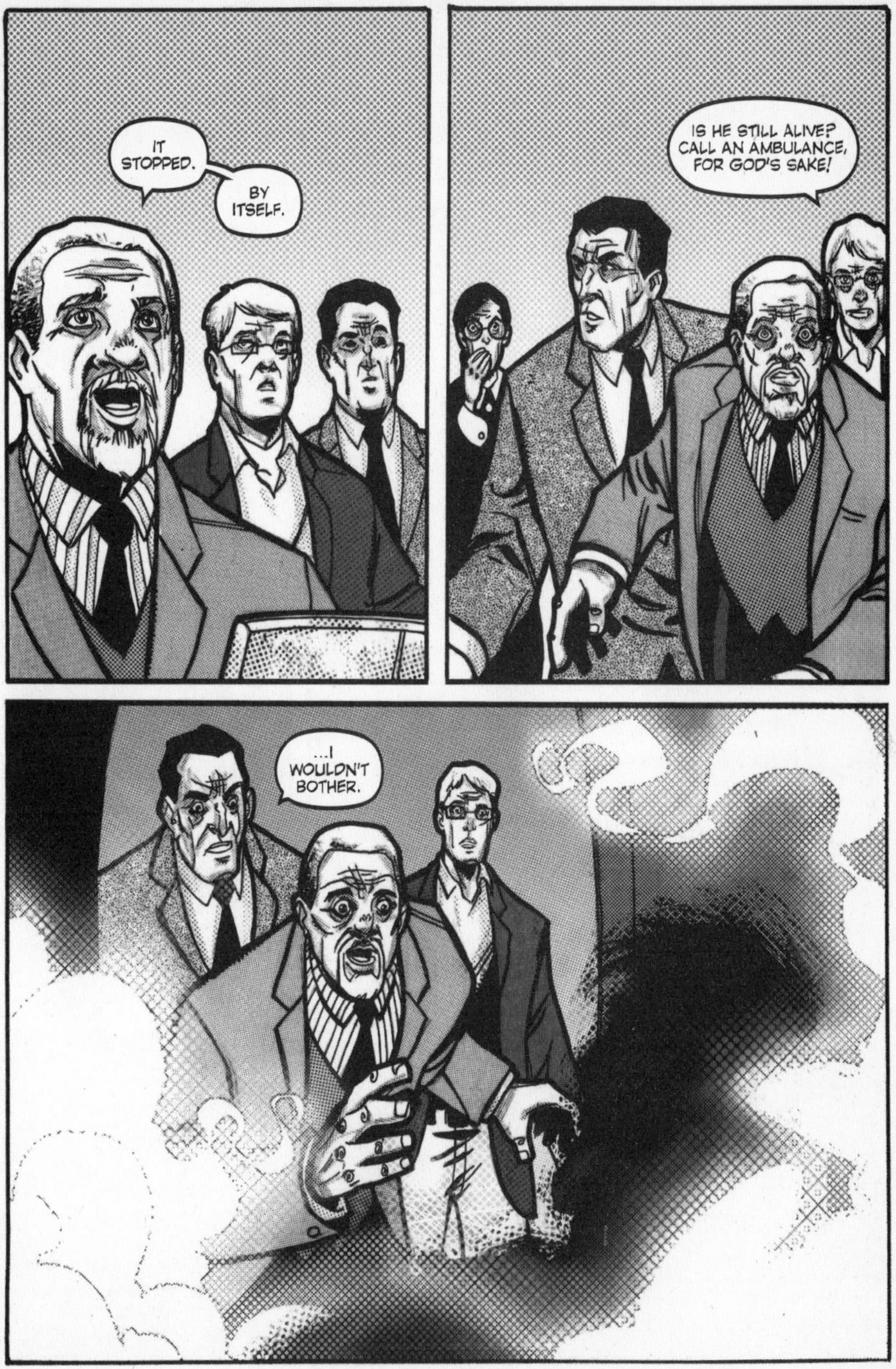
IT STOPPED.
BY ITSELF.
IS HE STILL ALIVE? CALL AN AMBULANCE, FOR GOD'S SAKE!
...I WOULDN'T BOTHER.

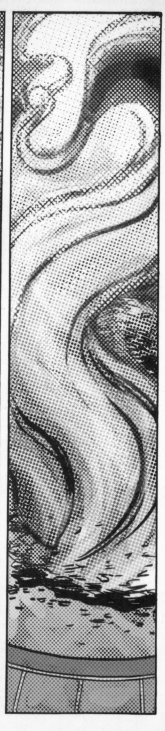

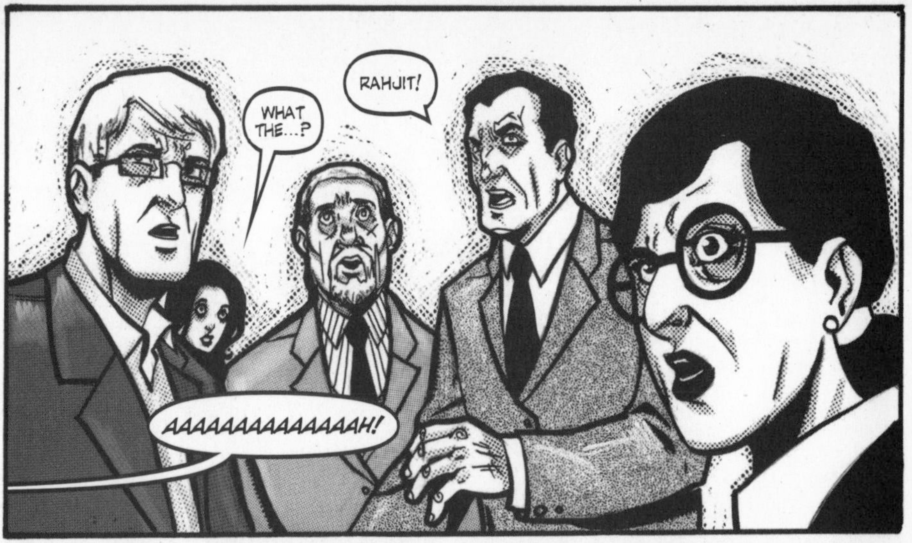
WHAT THE...?
RAHJIT!
AAAAAAAAAAAAAAH!

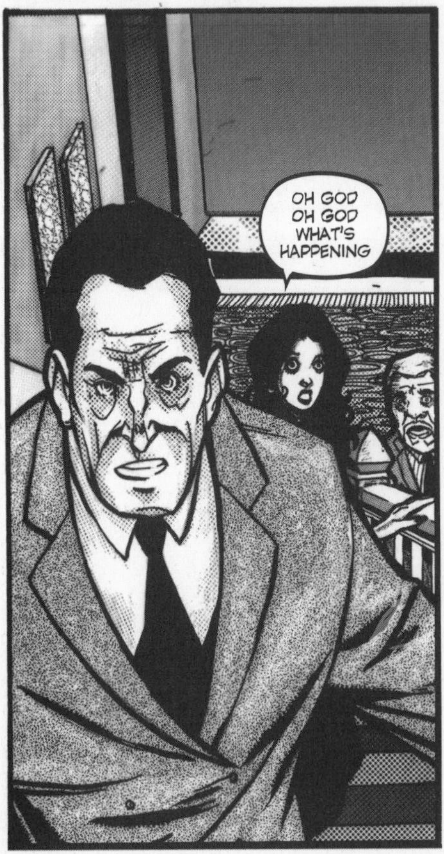
OH GOD OH GOD WHAT'S HAPPENING

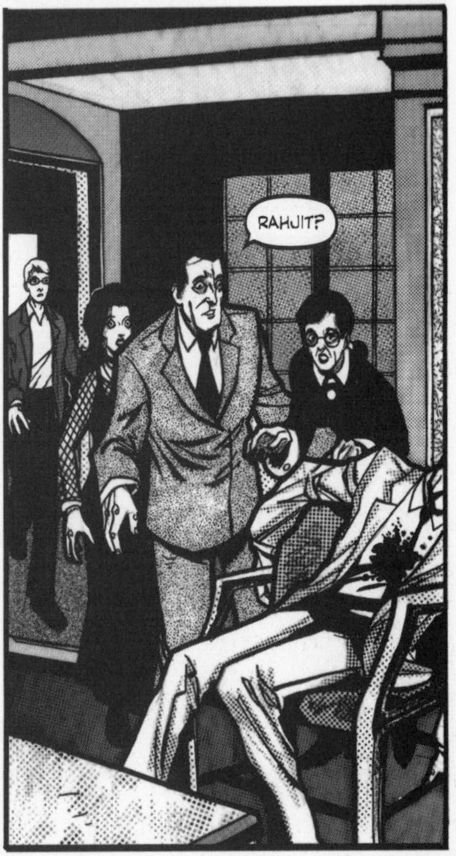
RAHJIT?

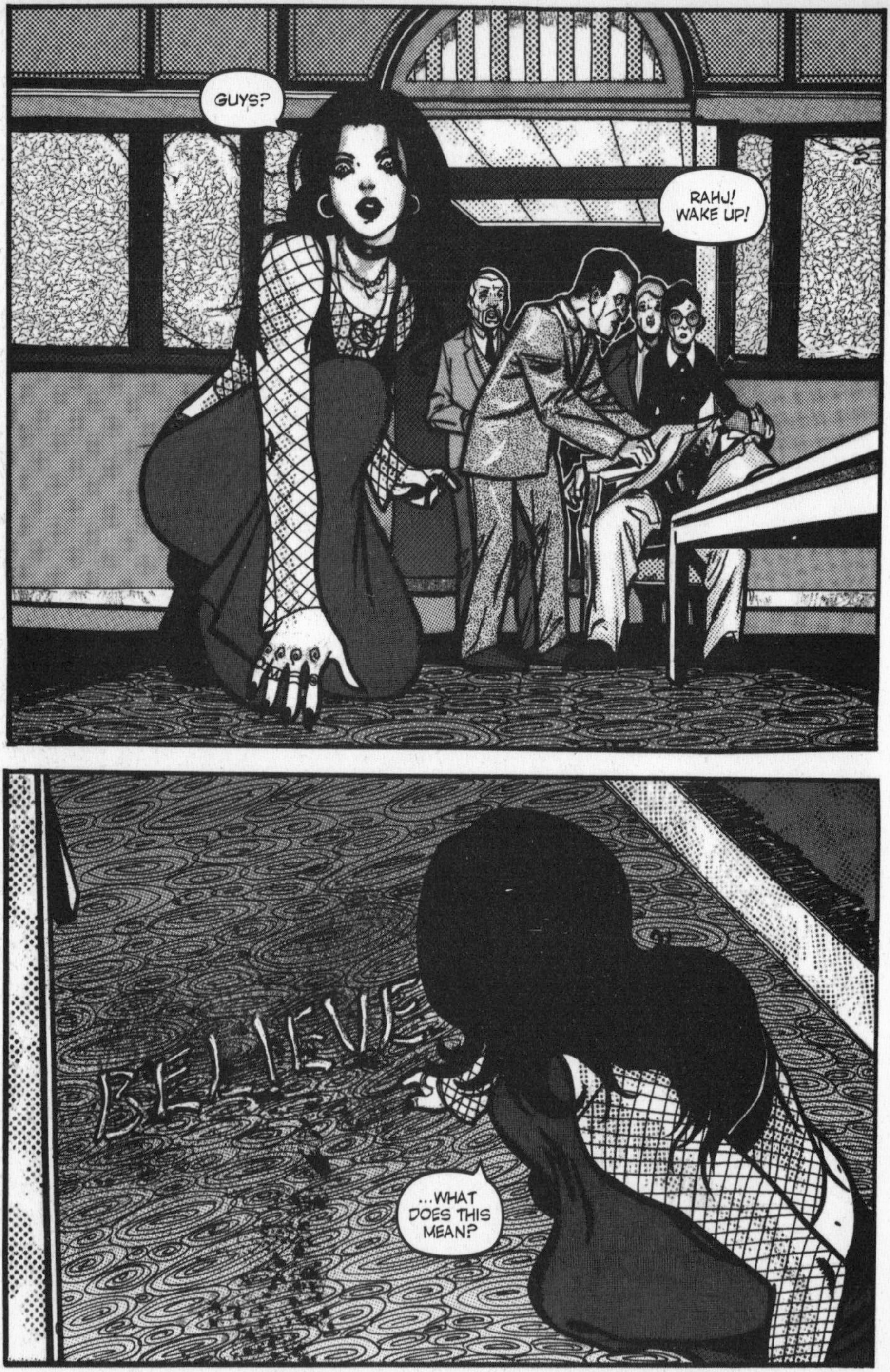
GUYS?
RAHJ! WAKE UP!
BELIEVE
...WHAT DOES THIS MEAN?

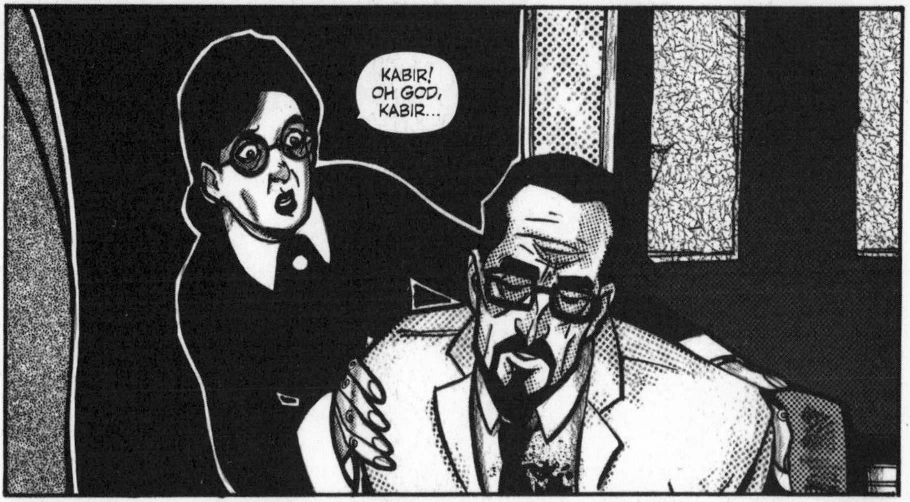
KABIR! OH GOD, KABIR...

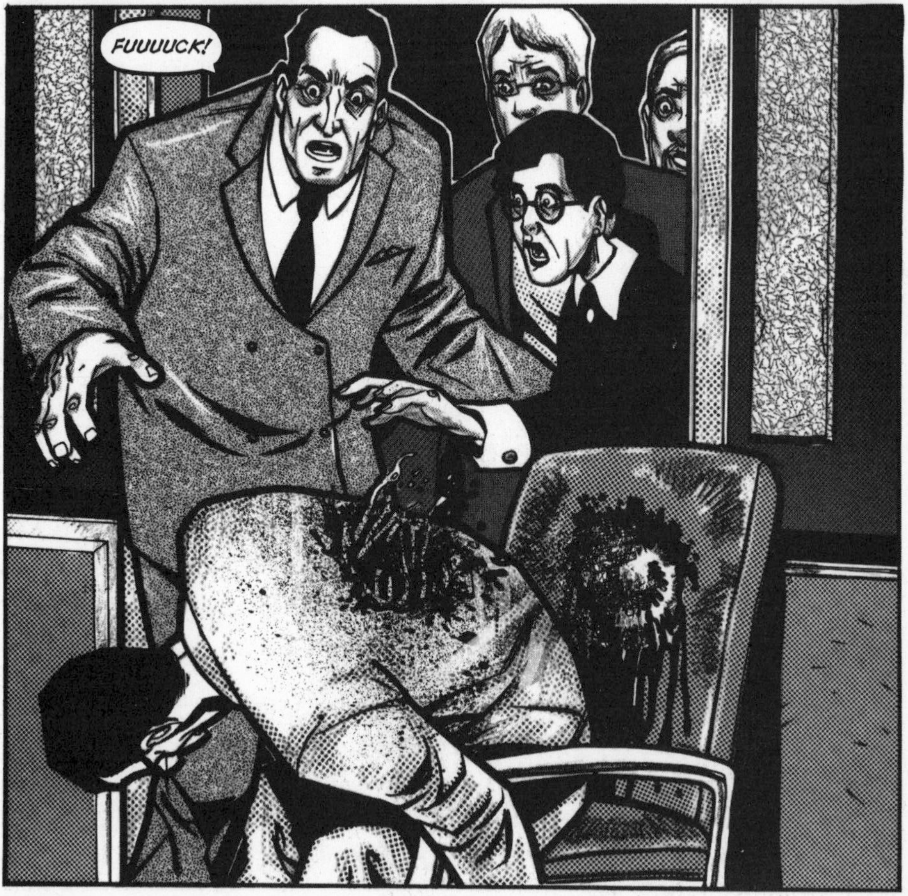
FUUUUCK!

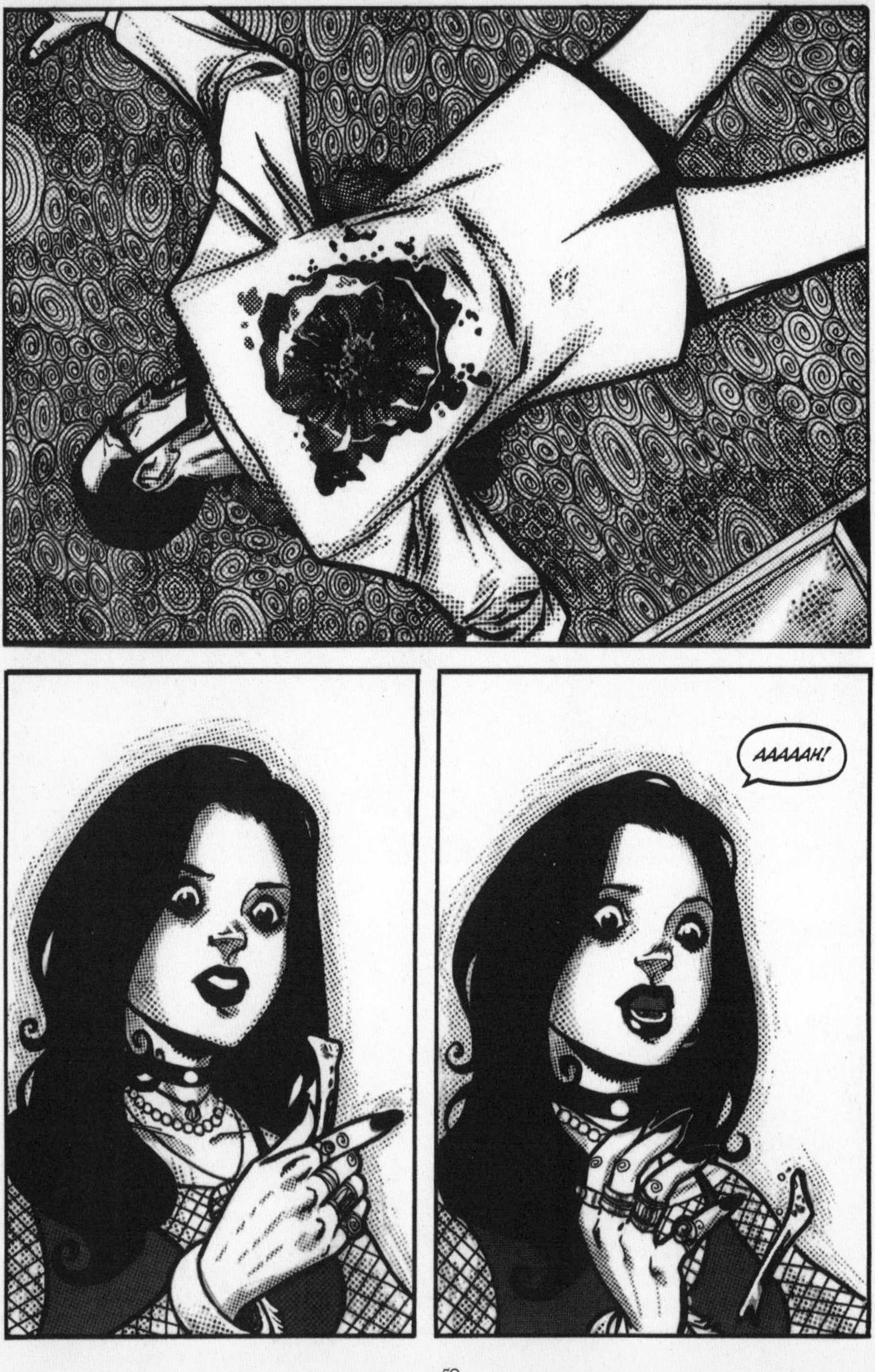
AAAAAH!

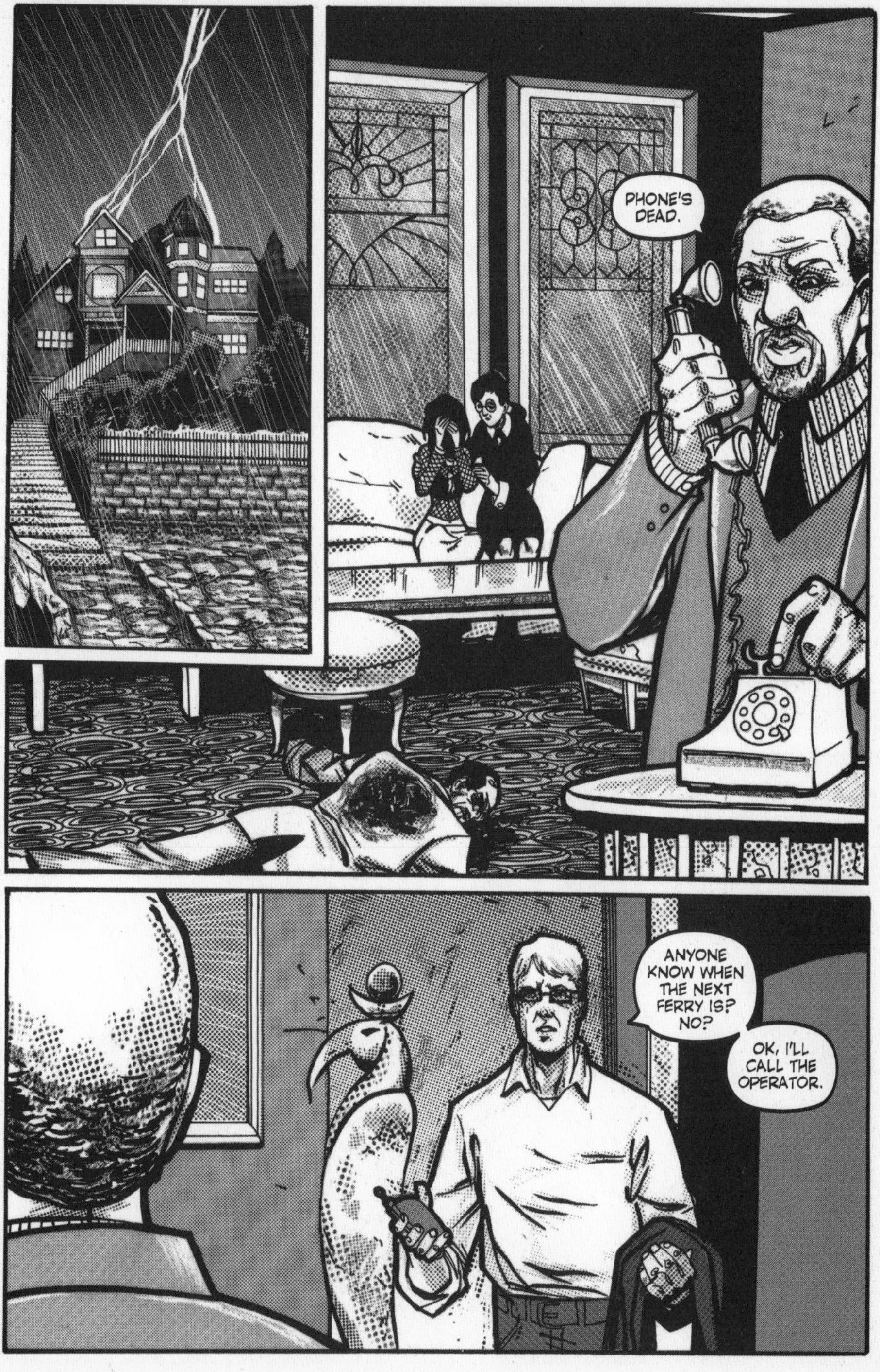
PHONE'S DEAD.
ANYONE KNOW WHEN THE NEXT FERRY IS? NO?
OK, I'LL CALL THE OPERATOR.

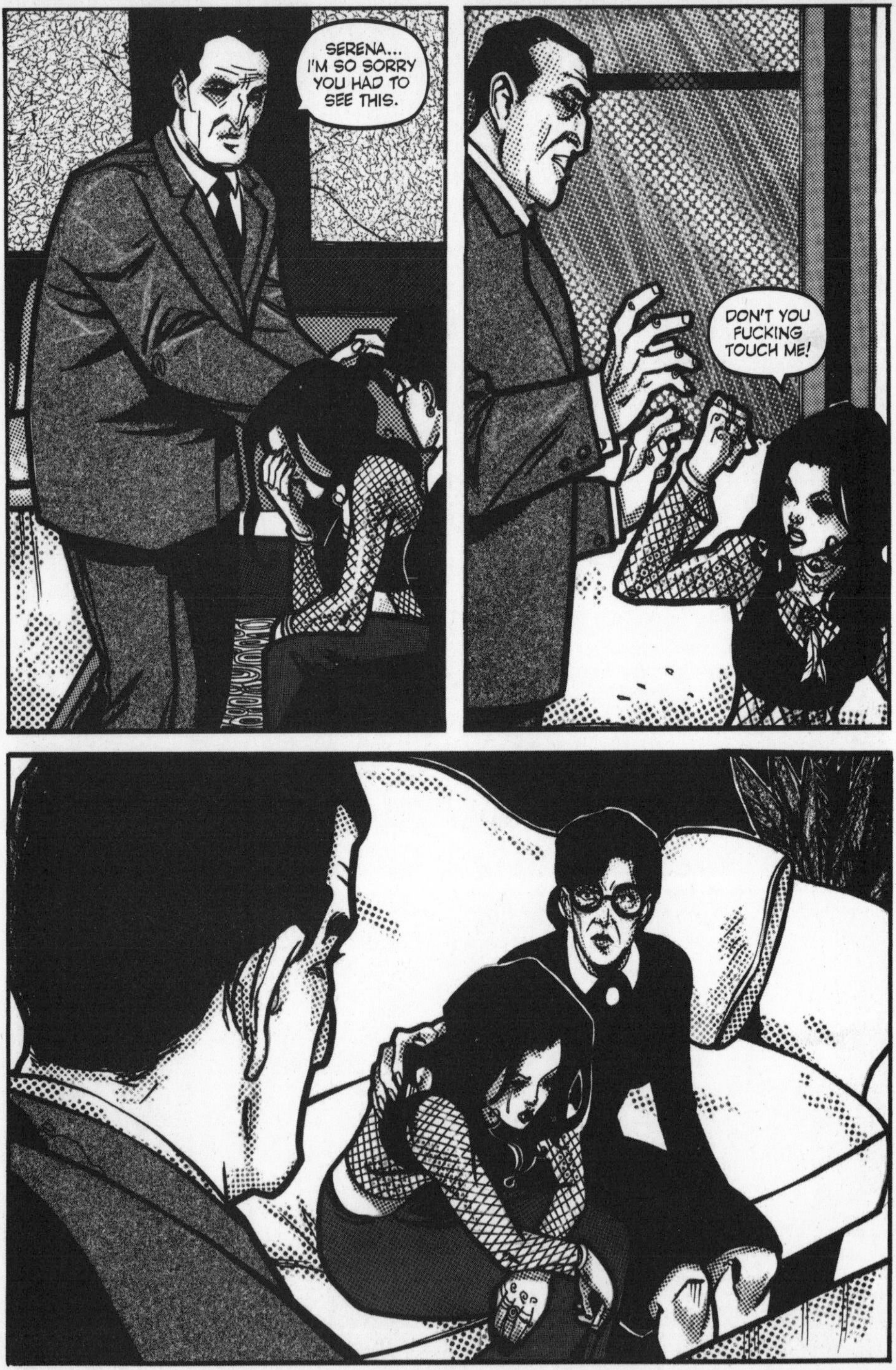
SERENA... I'M SO SORRY YOU HAD TO SEE THIS.
DON'T YOU FUCKING TOUCH ME!

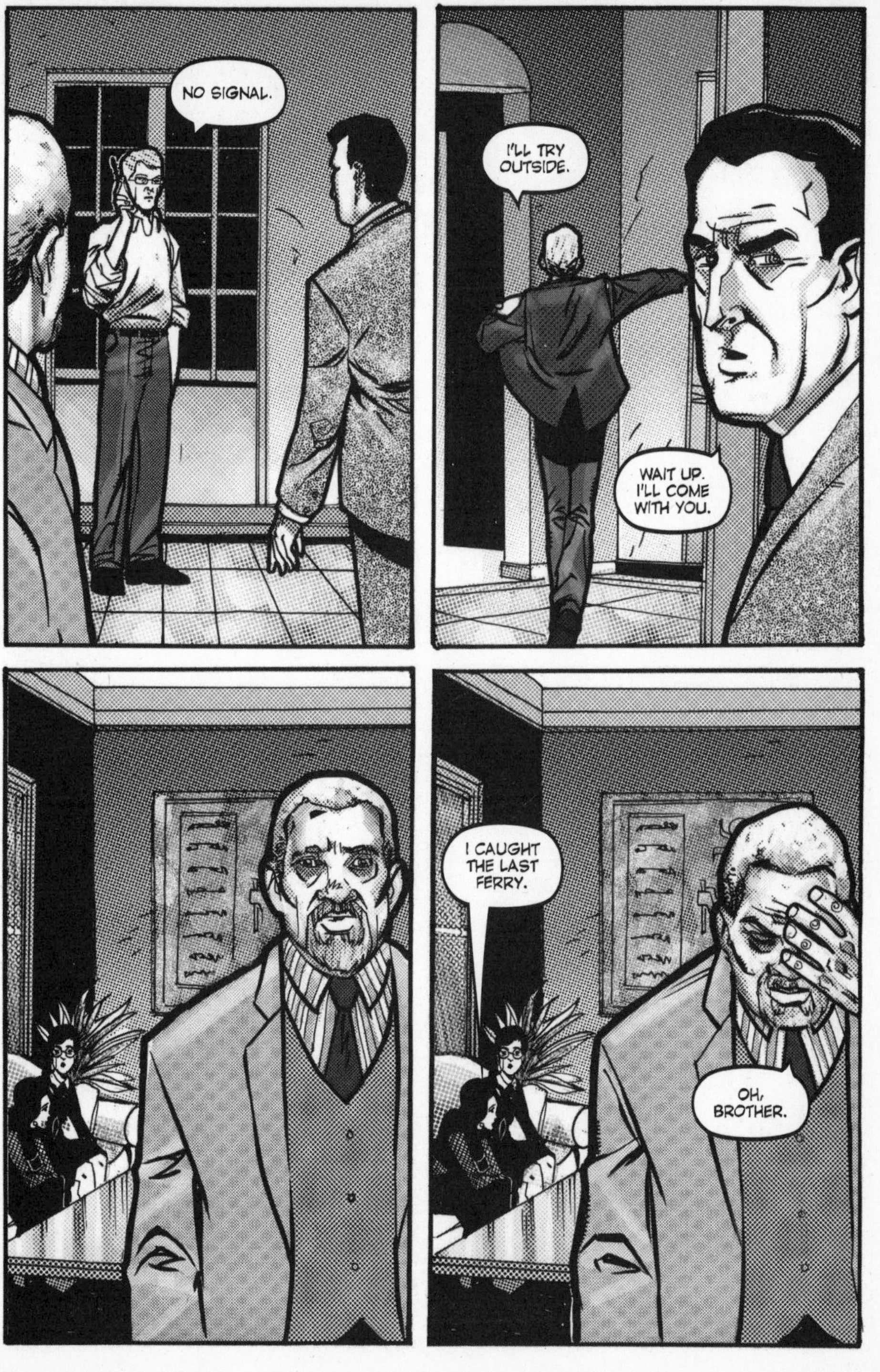
NO SIGNAL.
I'LL TRY OUTSIDE.
WAIT UP. I'LL COME WITH YOU.
I CAUGHT THE LAST FERRY.
OH, BROTHER.

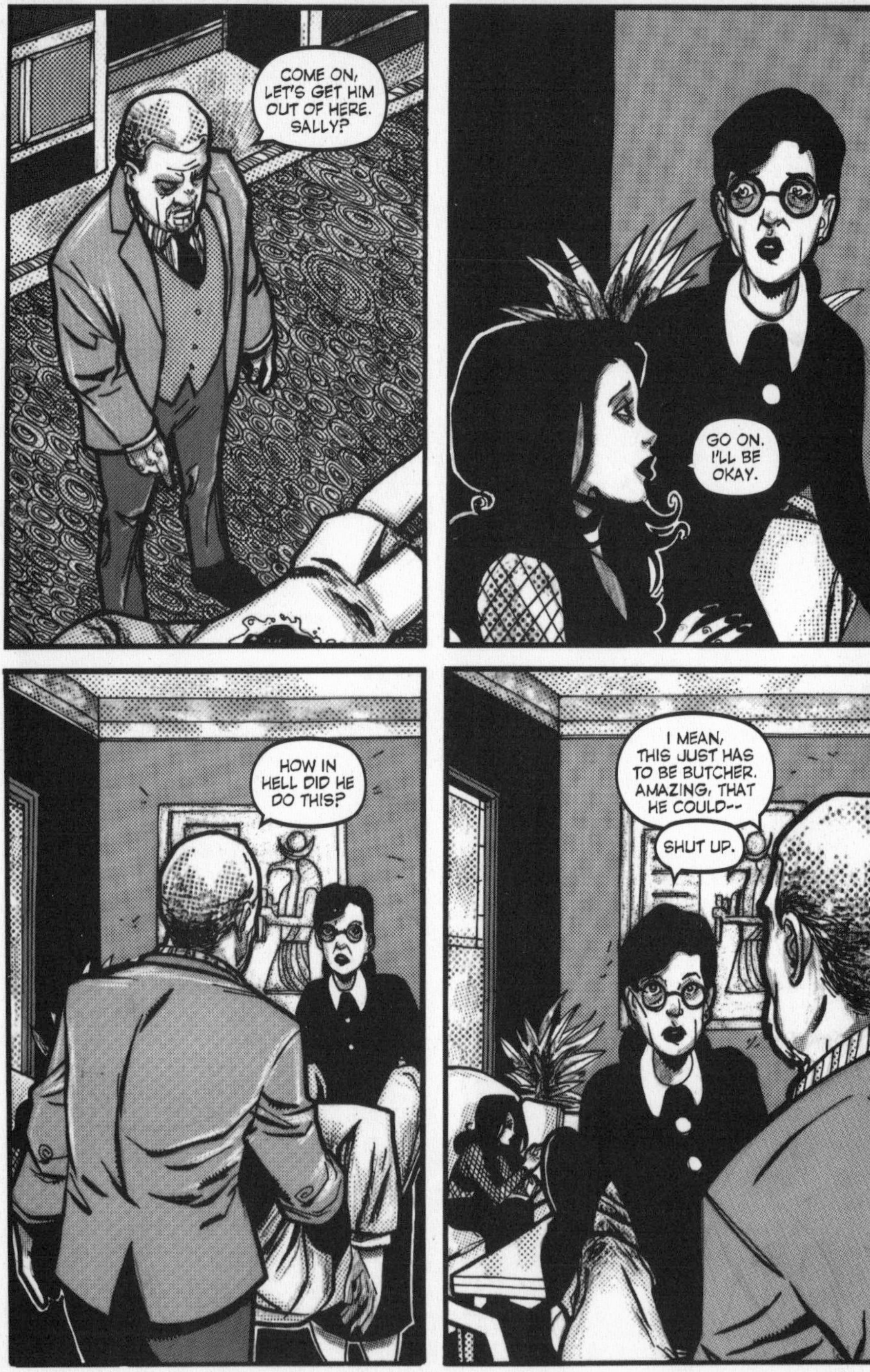
COME ON, LET'S GET HIM OUT OF HERE. SALLY?
GO ON. I'LL BE OKAY.
HOW IN HELL DID HE DO THIS?
I MEAN, THIS JUST HAS TO BE BUTCHER. AMAZING, THAT HE COULD--
SHUT UP.

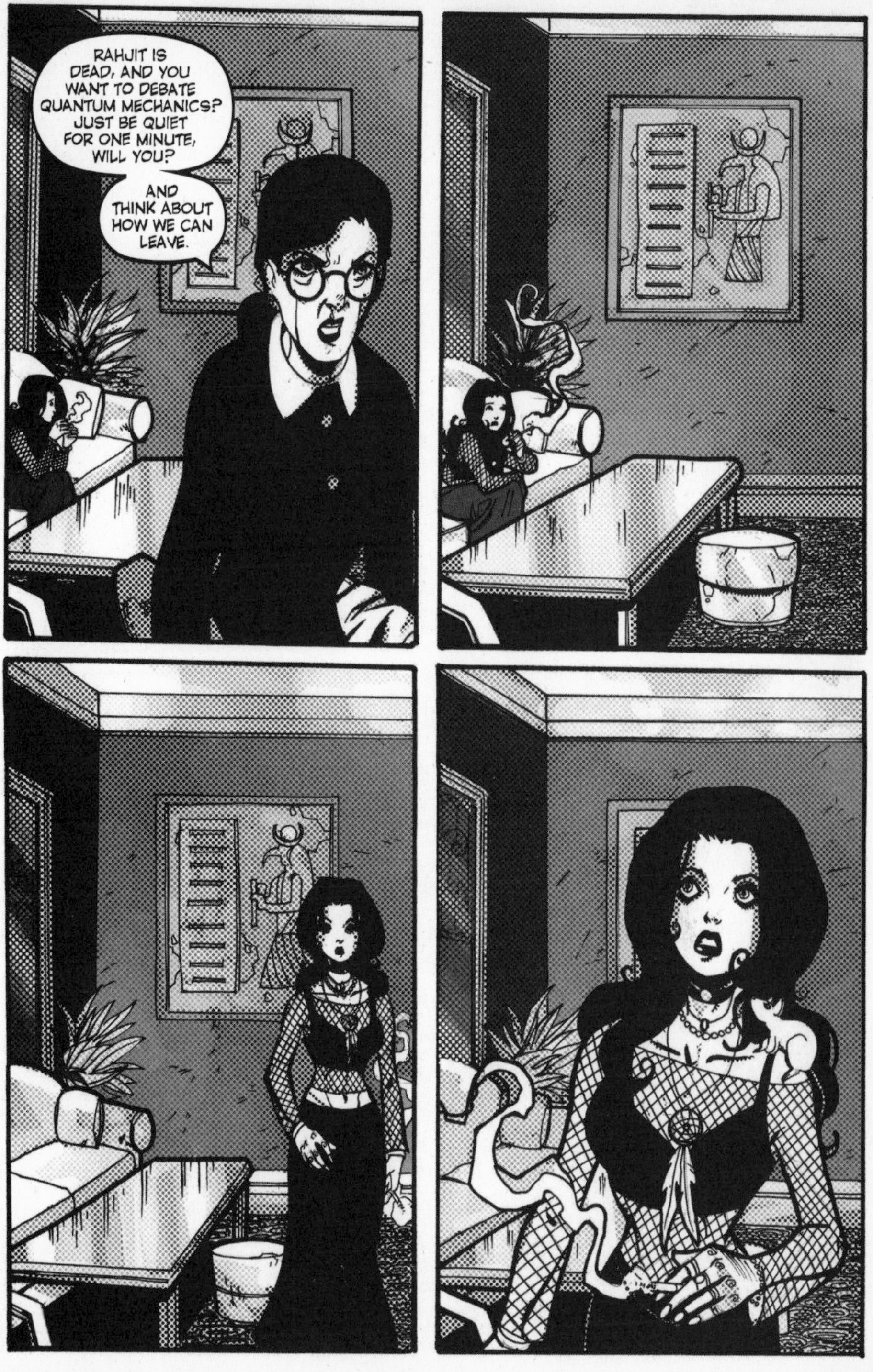
RAHJIT IS DEAD, AND YOU WANT TO DEBATE QUANTUM MECHANICS? JUST BE QUIET FOR ONE MINUTE, WILL YOU?
AND THINK ABOUT HOW WE CAN LEAVE.

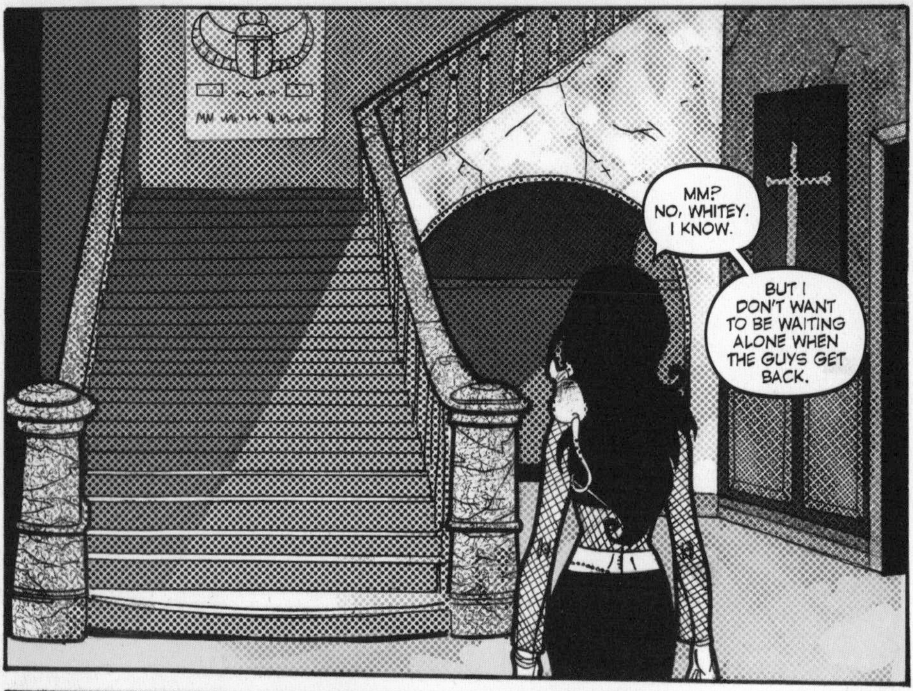
MM? NO, WHITEY. I KNOW.
BUT I DON'T WANT TO BE WAITING ALONE WHEN THE GUYS GET BACK.

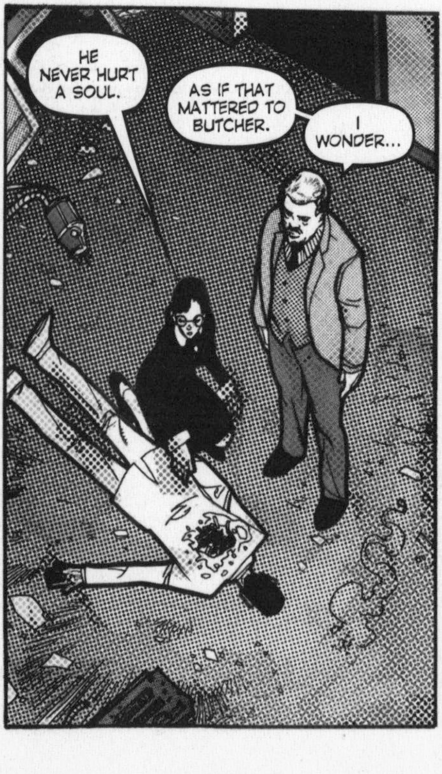
HE NEVER HURT A SOUL.
AS IF THAT MATTERED TO BUTCHER.
I WONDER...

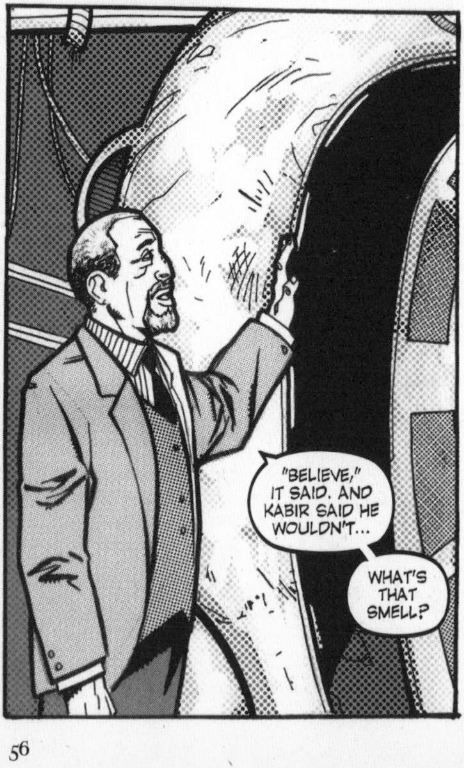
"BELIEVE," IT SAID. AND KABIR SAID HE WOULDN'T...
WHAT'S THAT SMELL?

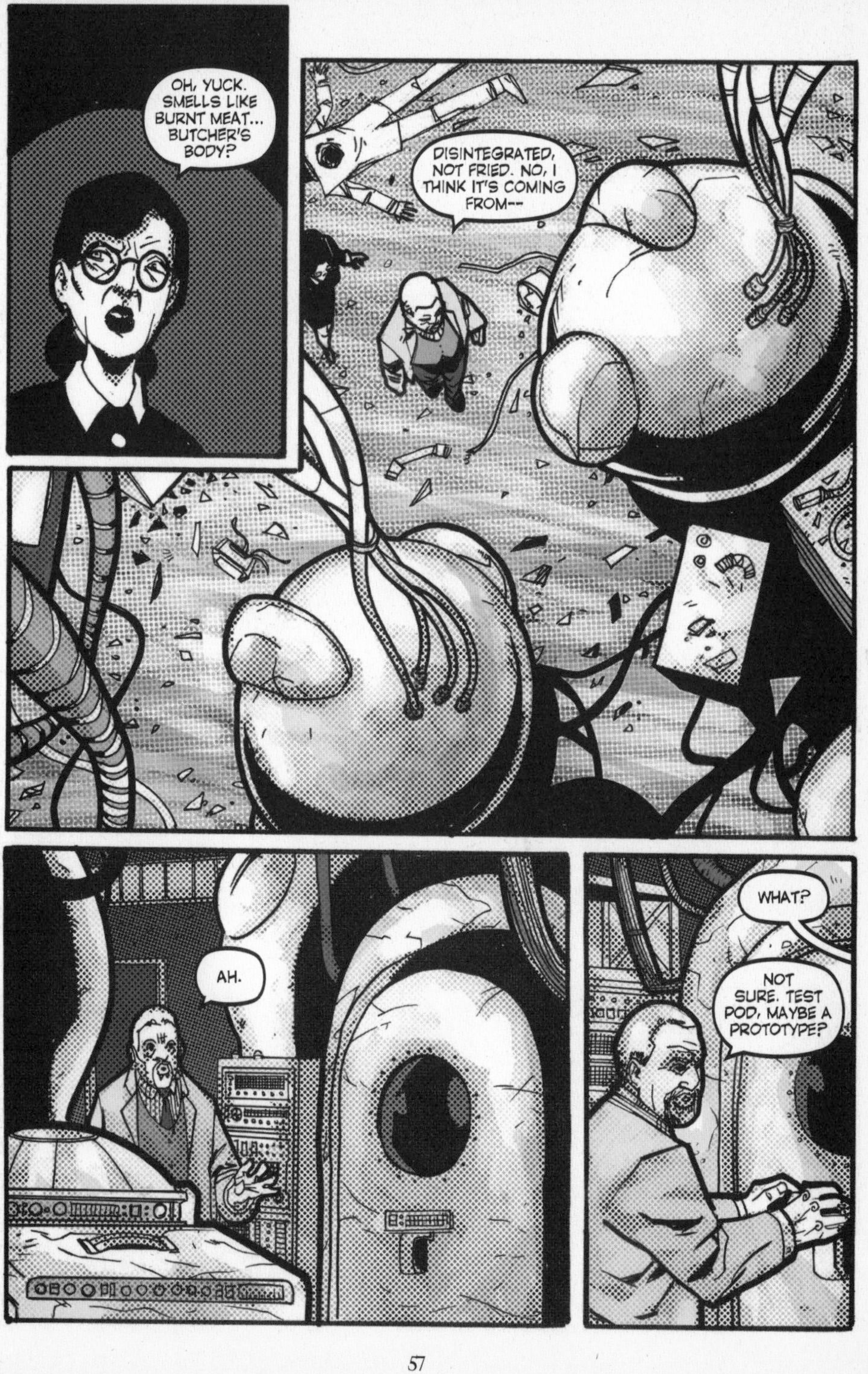
OH, YUCK. SMELLS LIKE BURNT MEAT... BUTCHER'S BODY?
DISINTEGRATED, NOT FRIED. NO, I THINK IT'S COMING FROM--
AH.
WHAT?
NOT SURE. TEST POD, MAYBE A PROTOTYPE?

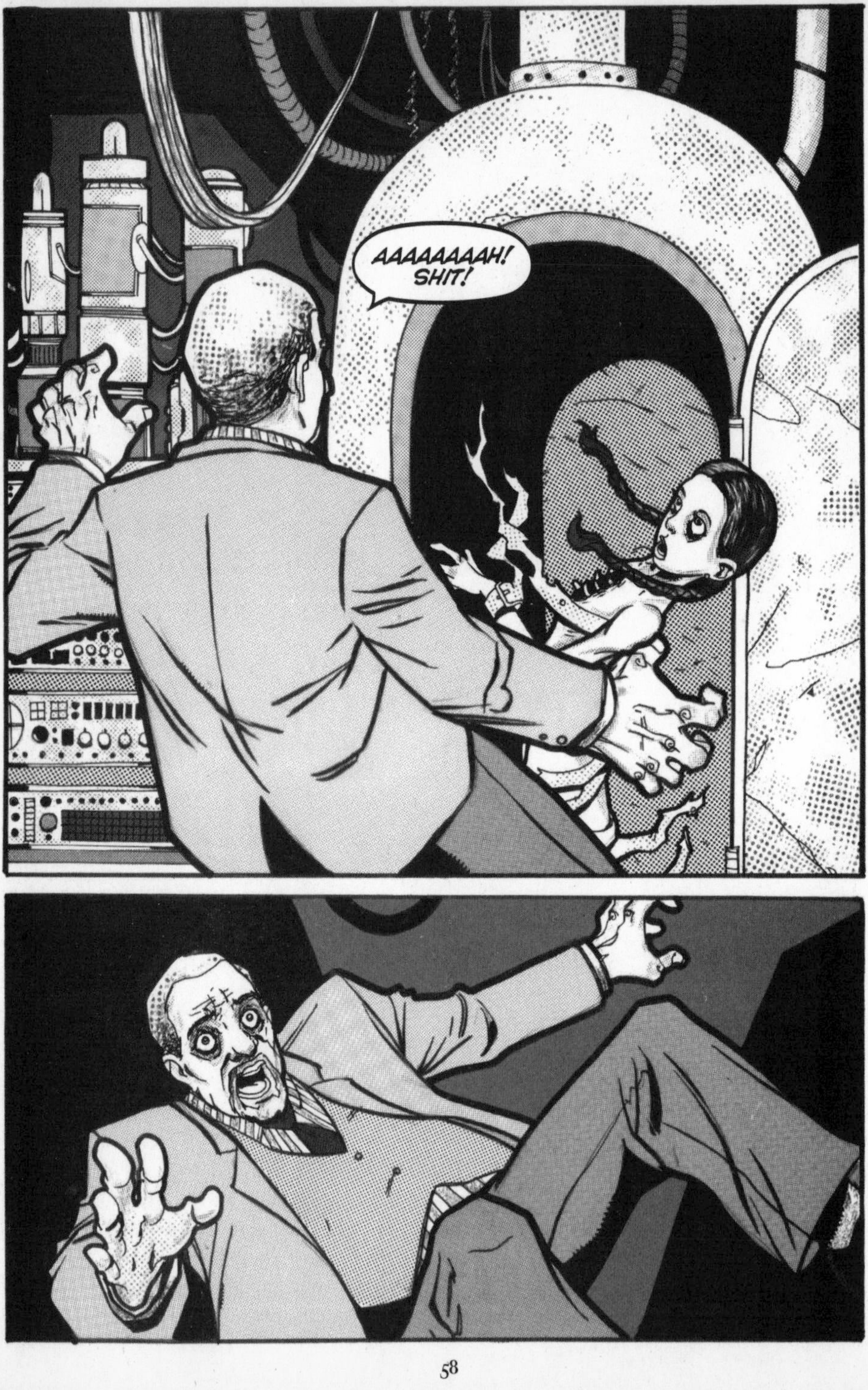
AAAAAAAAH! SHIT!

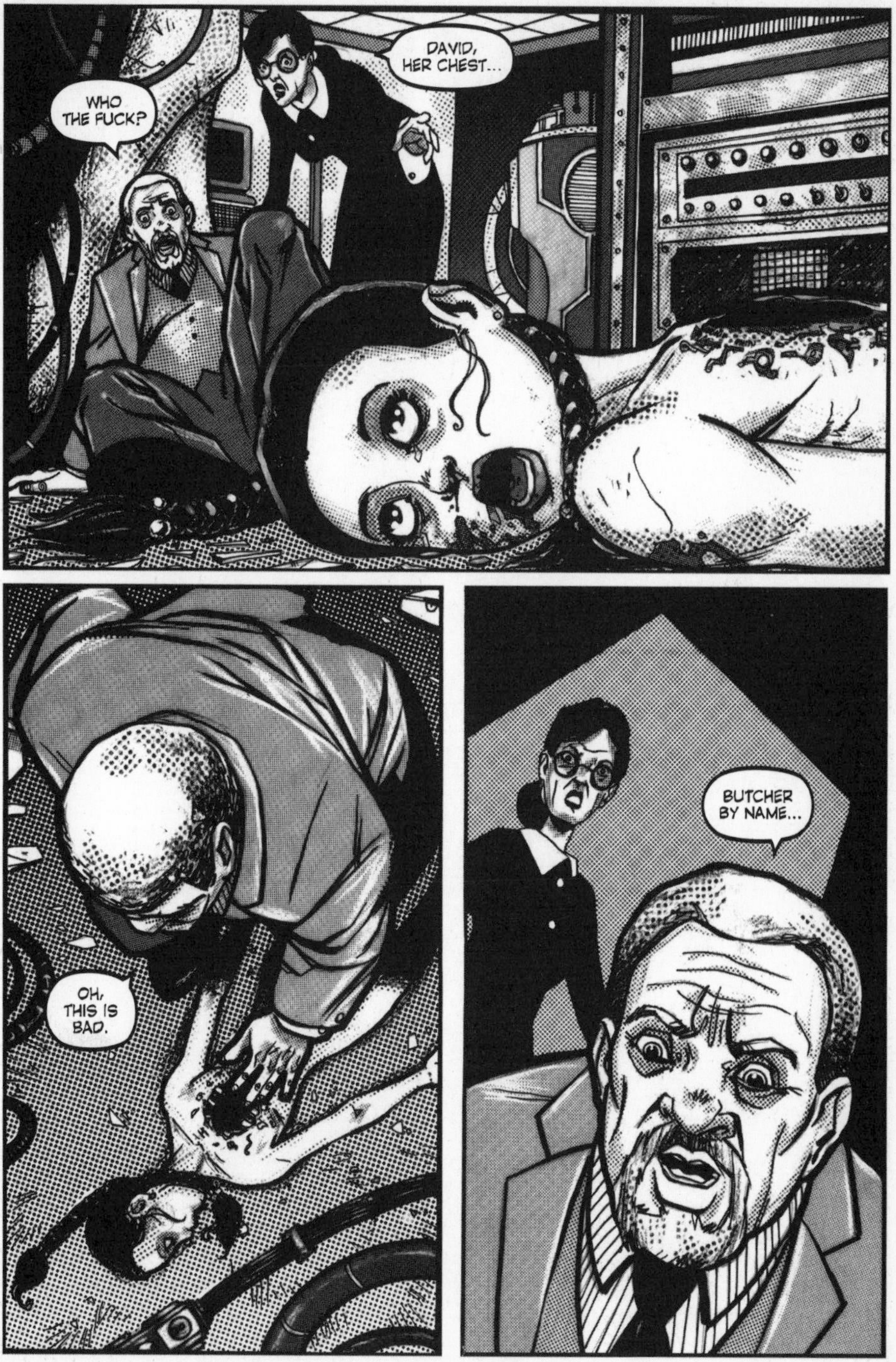
WHO THE FUCK?
DAVID, HER CHEST...
OH, THIS IS BAD.
BUTCHER BY NAME...

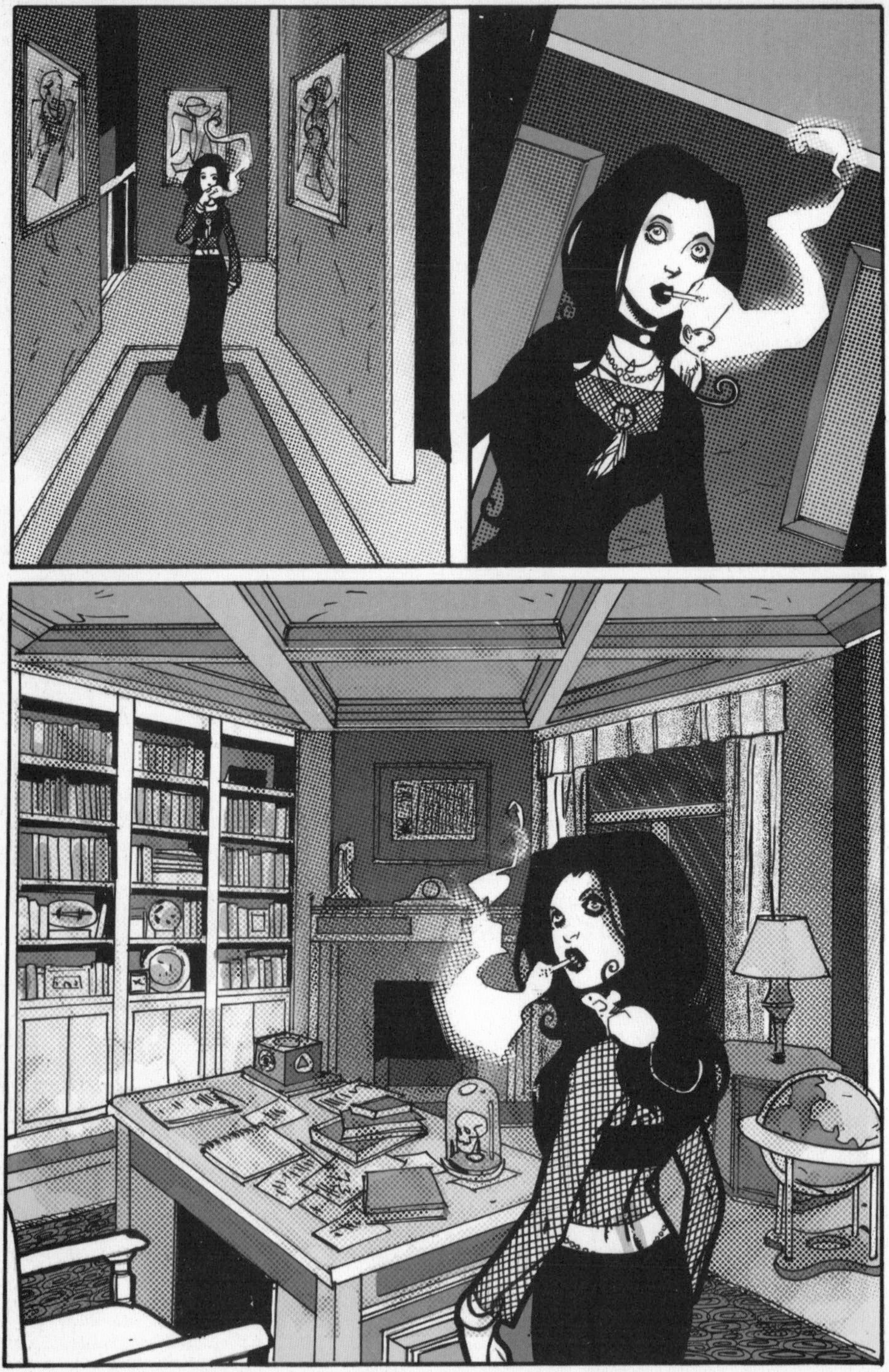

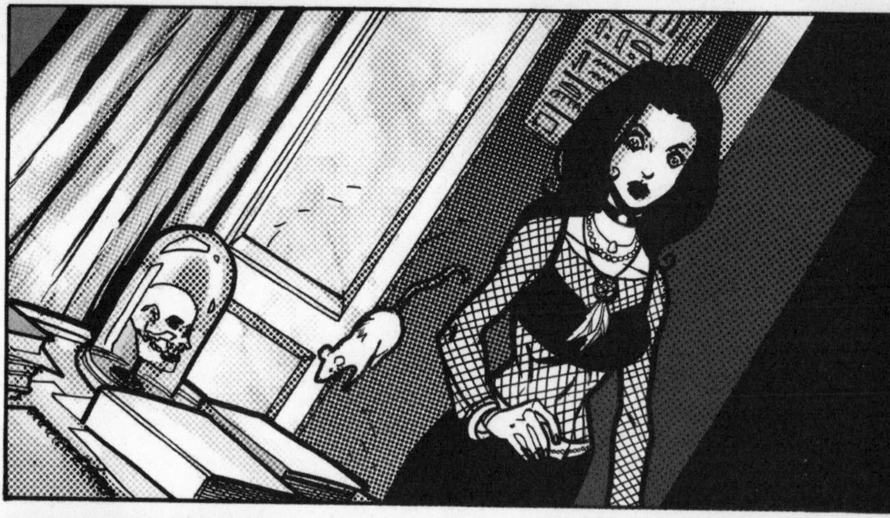

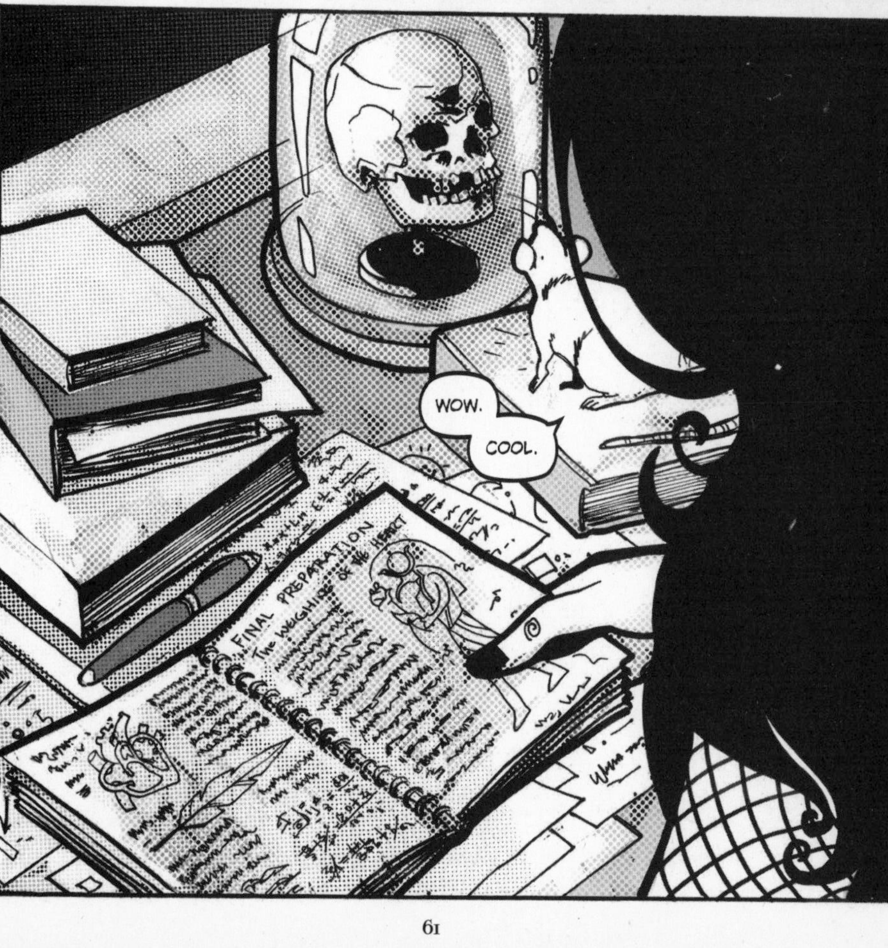
WOW.
COOL.
FINAL PREPARATION

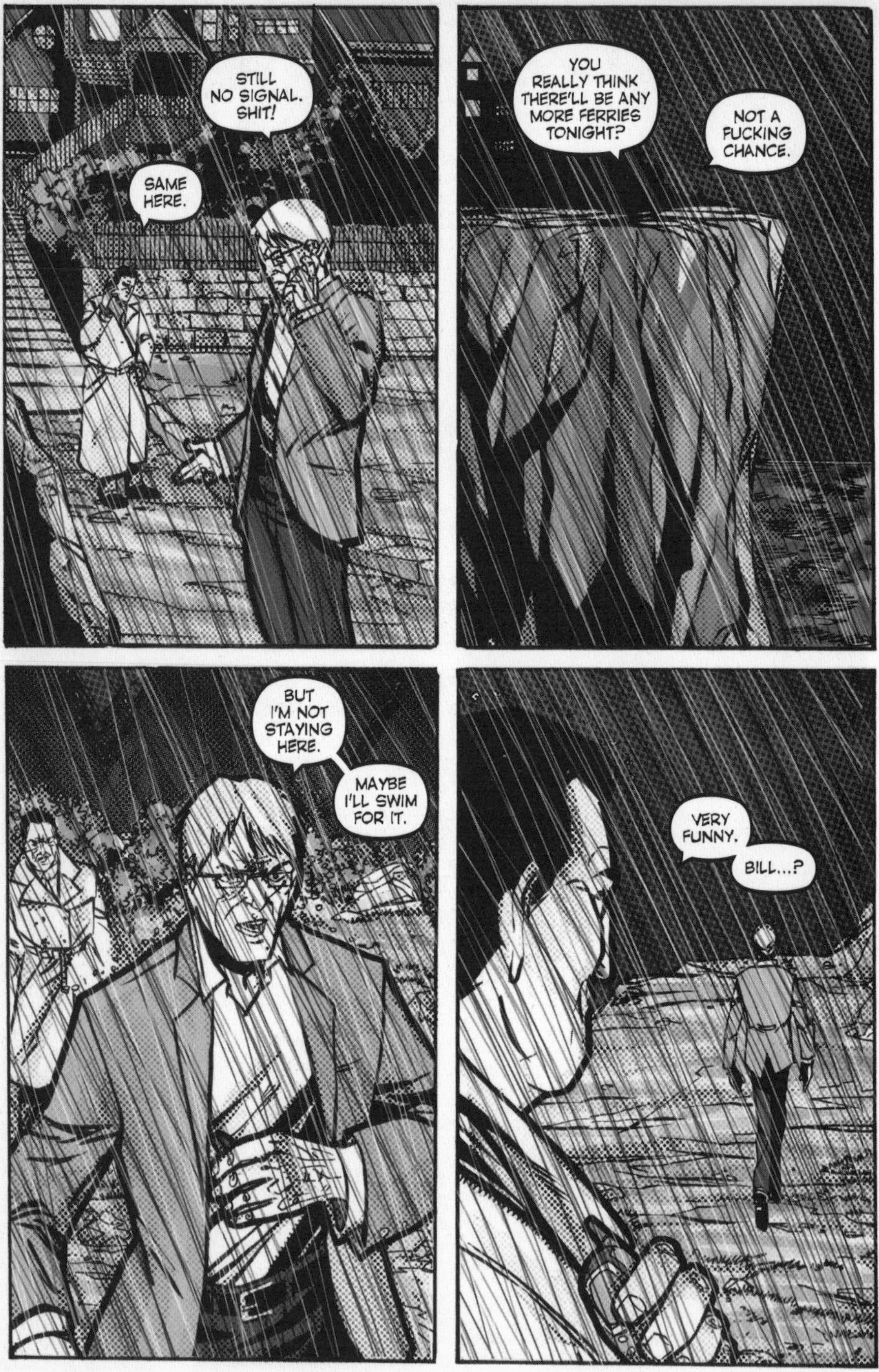
STILL NO SIGNAL. SHIT!
SAME HERE.
YOU REALLY THINK THERE'LL BE ANY MORE FERRIES TONIGHT?
NOT A FUCKING CHANCE.
BUT I'M NOT STAYING HERE.
MAYBE I'LL SWIM FOR IT.
VERY FUNNY.
BILL...?

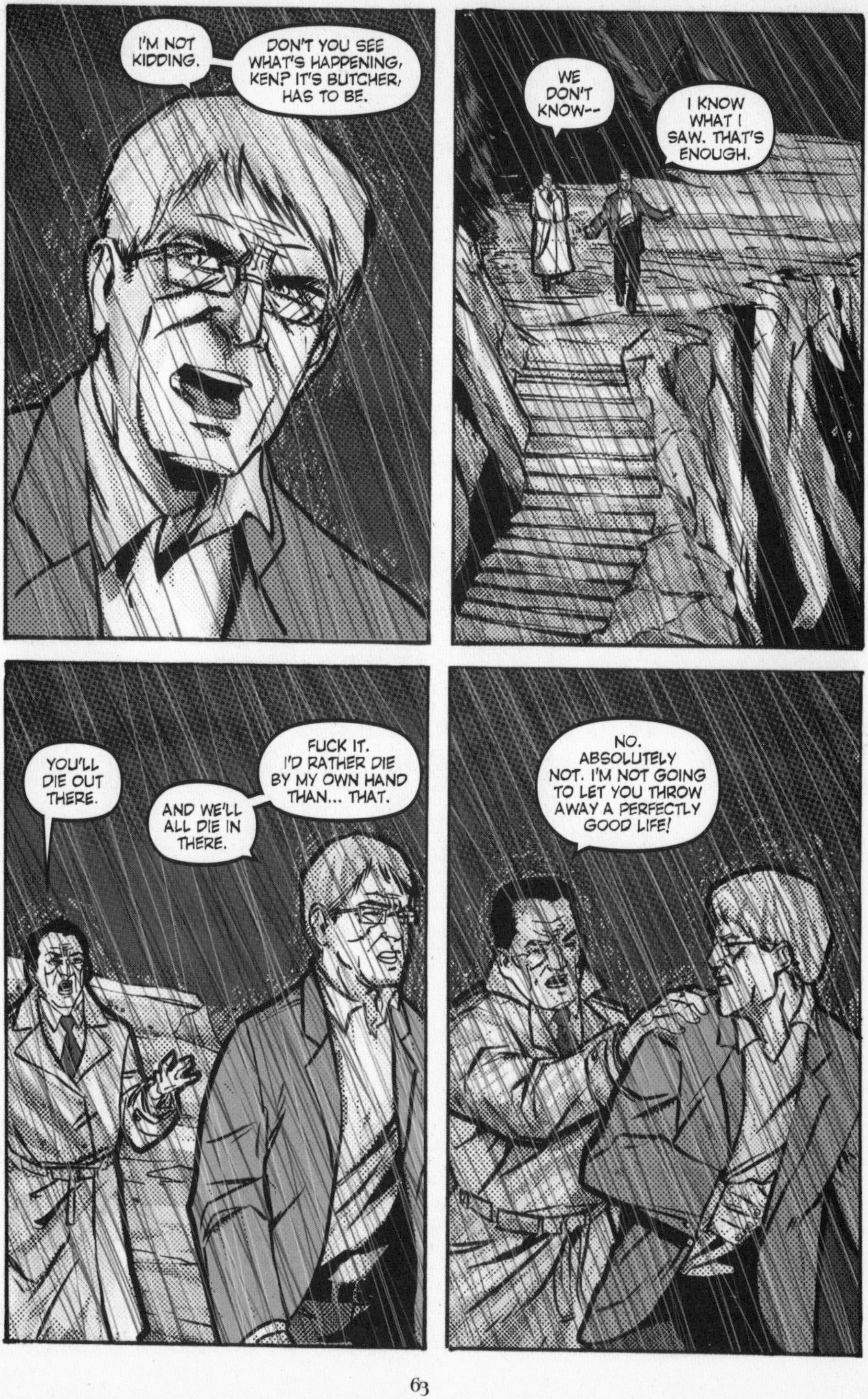
I'M NOT KIDDING.
DON'T YOU SEE WHAT'S HAPPENING, KEN? IT'S BUTCHER, HAS TO BE.
WE DON'T KNOW--
I KNOW WHAT I SAW. THAT'S ENOUGH.
YOU'LL DIE OUT THERE.
AND WE'LL ALL DIE IN THERE.
FUCK IT. I'D RATHER DIE BY MY OWN HAND THAN... THAT.
NO. ABSOLUTELY NOT. I'M NOT GOING TO LET YOU THROW AWAY A PERFECTLY GOOD LIFE!

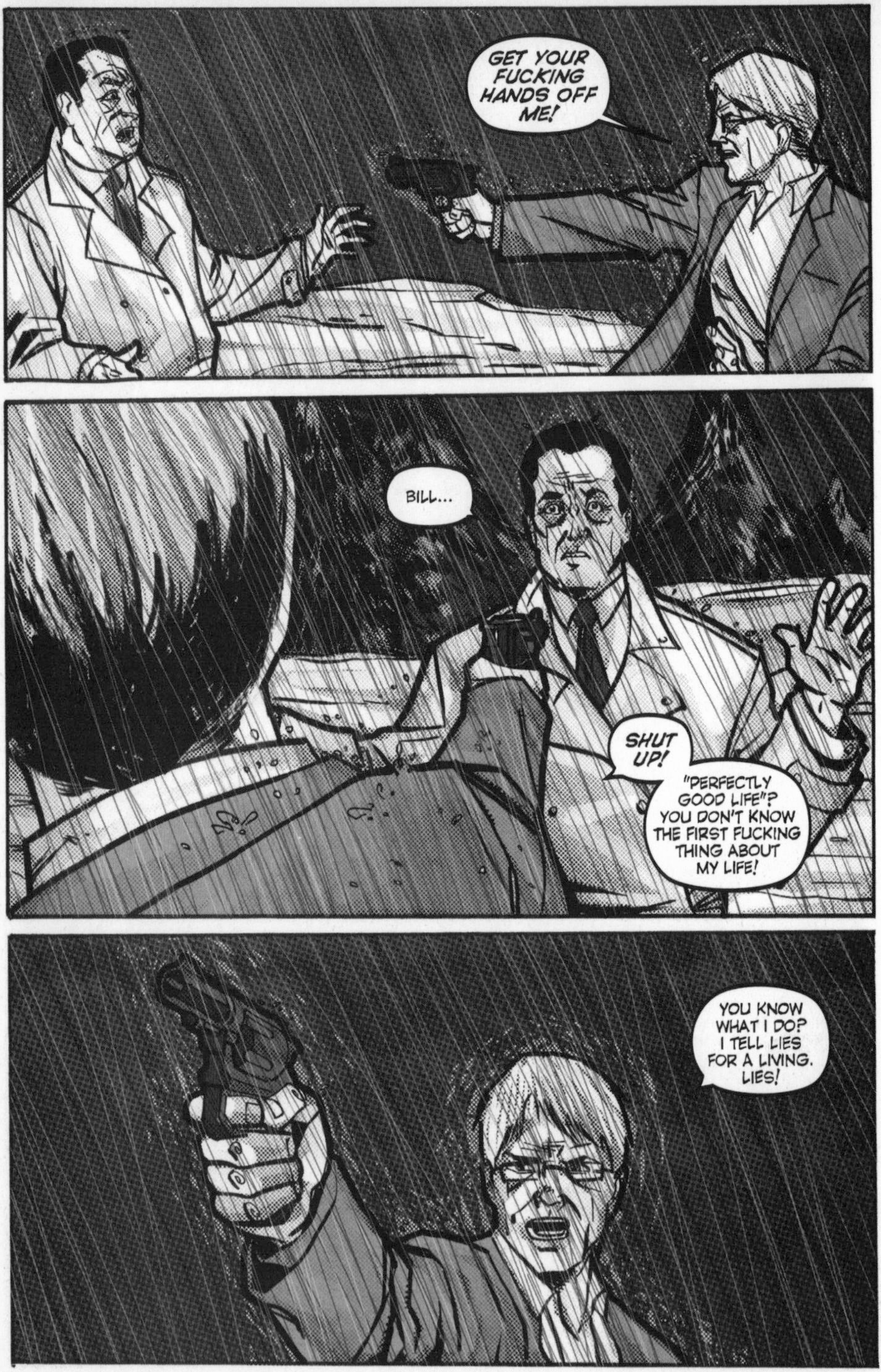
GET YOUR FUCKING HANDS OFF ME!
BILL...
SHUT UP!
"PERFECTLY GOOD LIFE"? YOU DON'T KNOW THE FIRST FUCKING THING ABOUT MY LIFE!
YOU KNOW WHAT I DO? I TELL LIES FOR A LIVING. LIES!

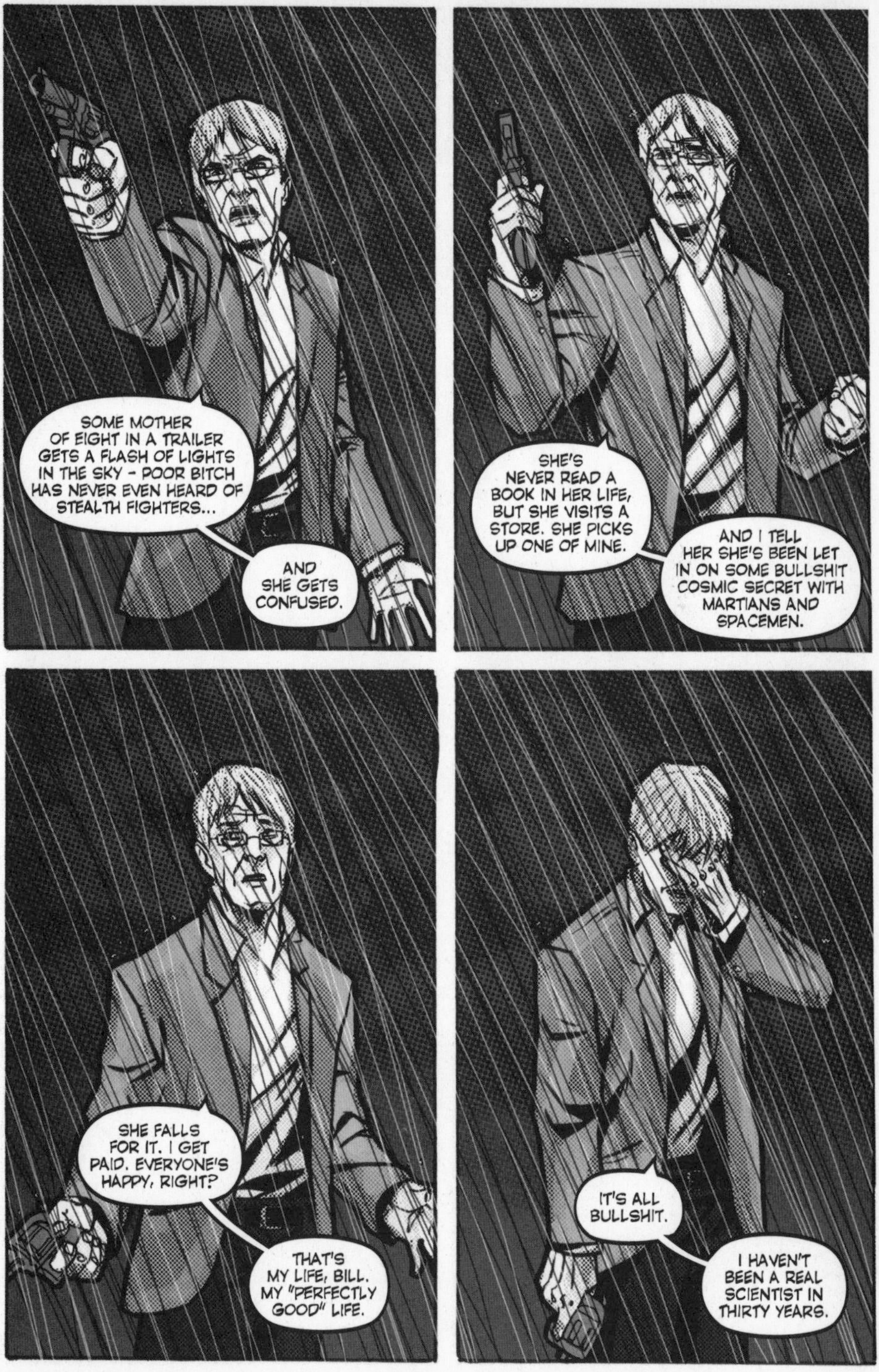
SOME MOTHER OF EIGHT IN A TRAILER GETS A FLASH OF LIGHTS IN THE SKY - POOR BITCH HAS NEVER EVEN HEARD OF STEALTH FIGHTERS...
AND SHE GETS CONFUSED.
SHE'S NEVER READ A BOOK IN HER LIFE, BUT SHE VISITS A STORE. SHE PICKS UP ONE OF MINE.
AND I TELL HER SHE'S BEEN LET IN ON SOME BULLSHIT COSMIC SECRET WITH MARTIANS AND SPACEMEN.
SHE FALLS FOR IT. I GET PAID. EVERYONE'S HAPPY, RIGHT?
THAT'S MY LIFE, BILL. MY "PERFECTLY GOOD" LIFE.
IT'S ALL BULLSHIT.
I HAVEN'T BEEN A REAL SCIENTIST IN THIRTY YEARS.

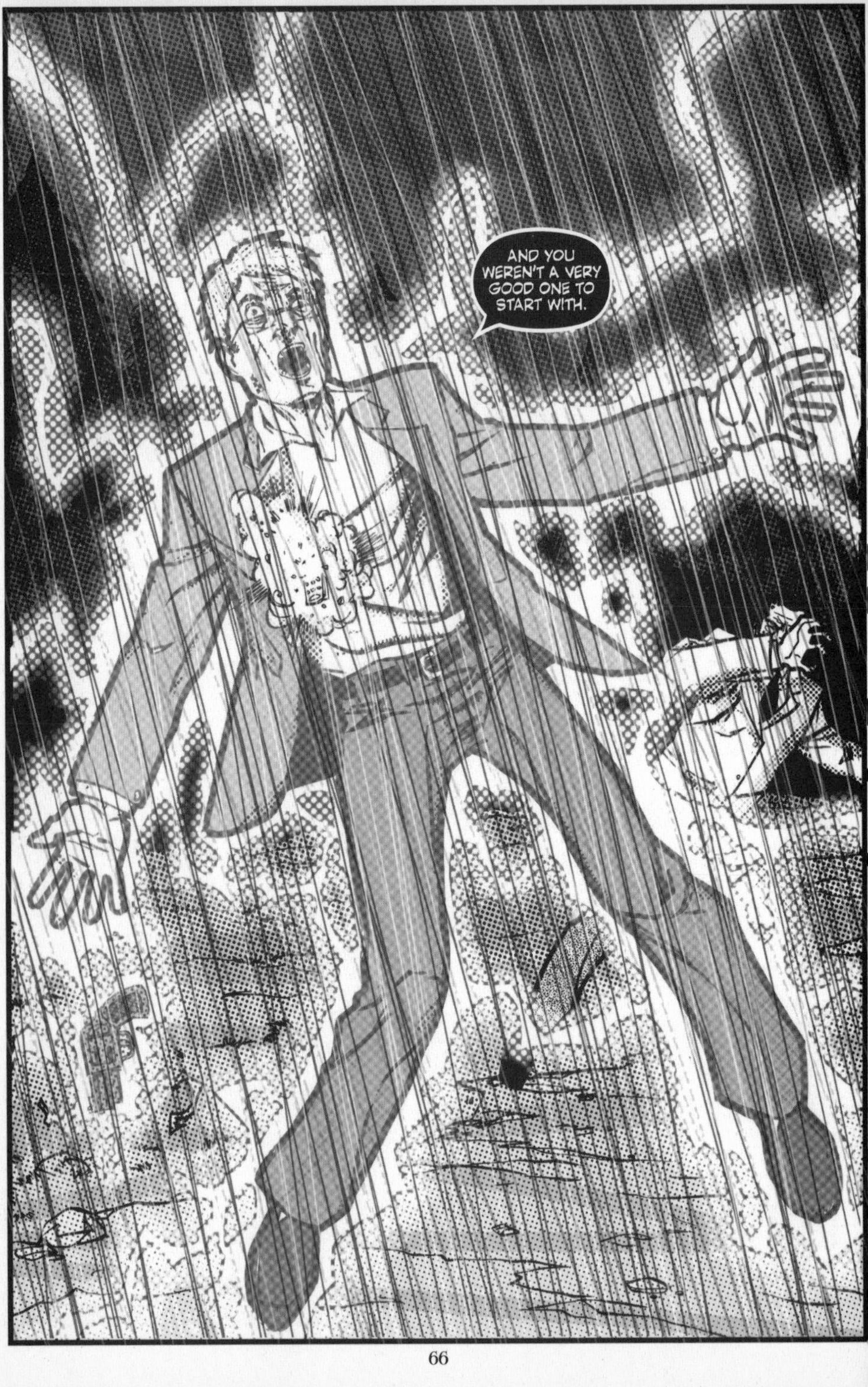
AND YOU WEREN'T A VERY GOOD ONE TO START WITH.

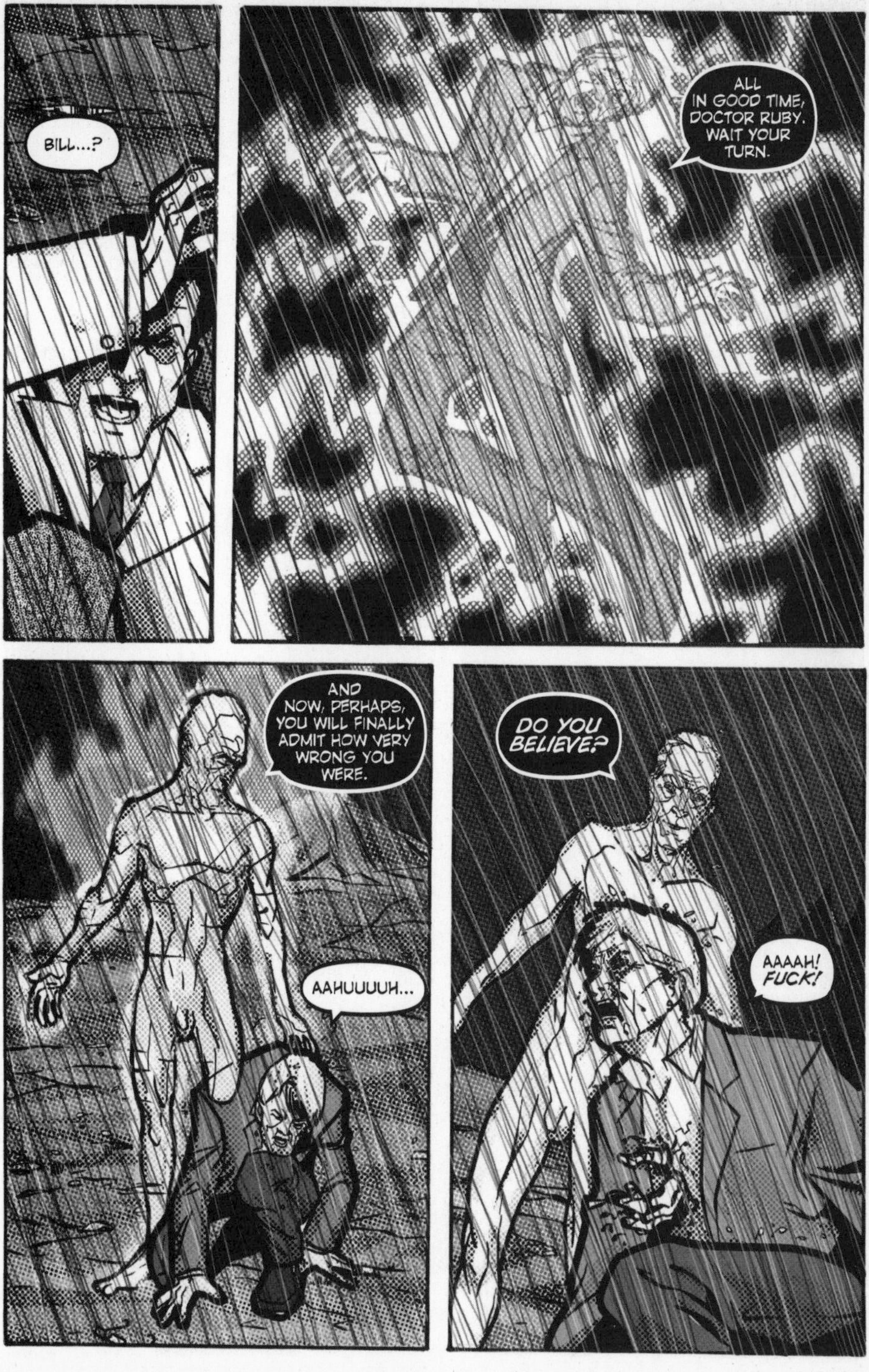
BILL...?
ALL IN GOOD TIME, DOCTOR RUBY. WAIT YOUR TURN.
AND NOW, PERHAPS, YOU WILL FINALLY ADMIT HOW VERY WRONG YOU WERE.
AAHUUUUH...
DO YOU BELIEVE?
AAAAH! FUCK!

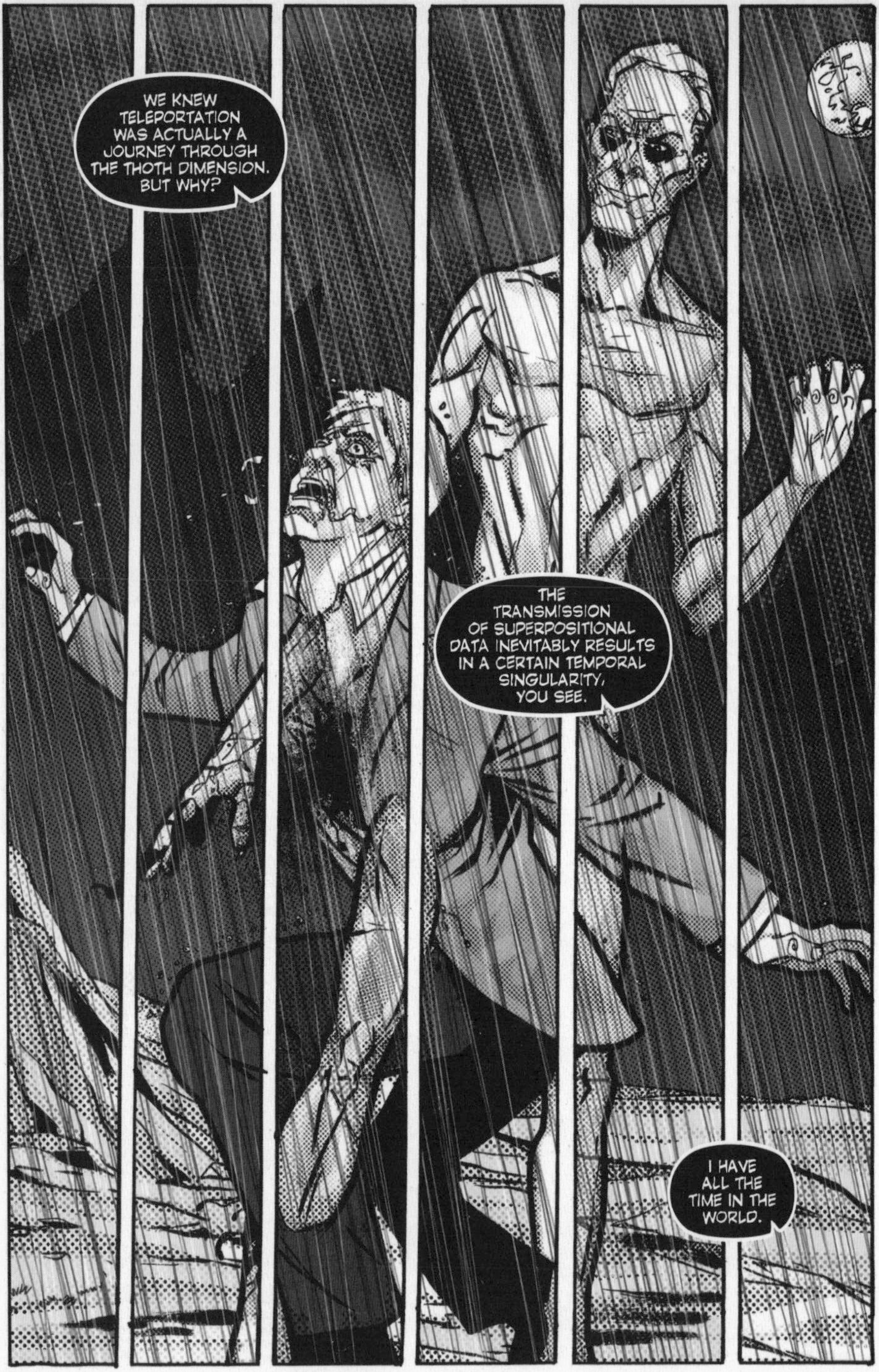
WE KNEW TELEPORTATION WAS ACTUALLY A JOURNEY THROUGH THE THOTH DIMENSION. BUT WHY?
THE TRANSMISSION OF SUPERPOSITIONAL DATA INEVITABLY RESULTS IN A CERTAIN TEMPORAL SINGULARITY, YOU SEE.
I HAVE ALL THE TIME IN THE WORLD.

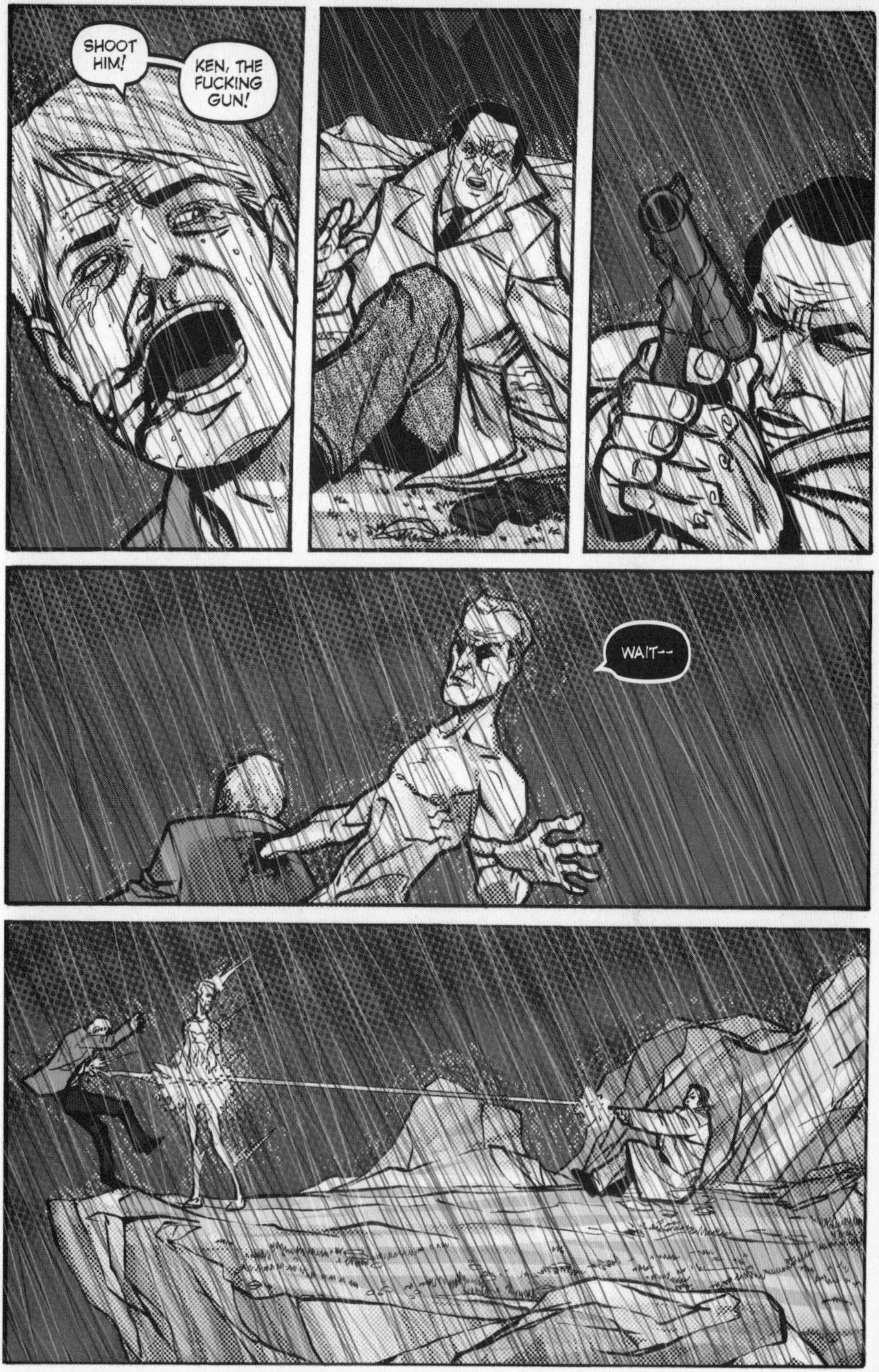
SHOOT HIM!
KEN, THE FUCKING GUN!
WAIT--

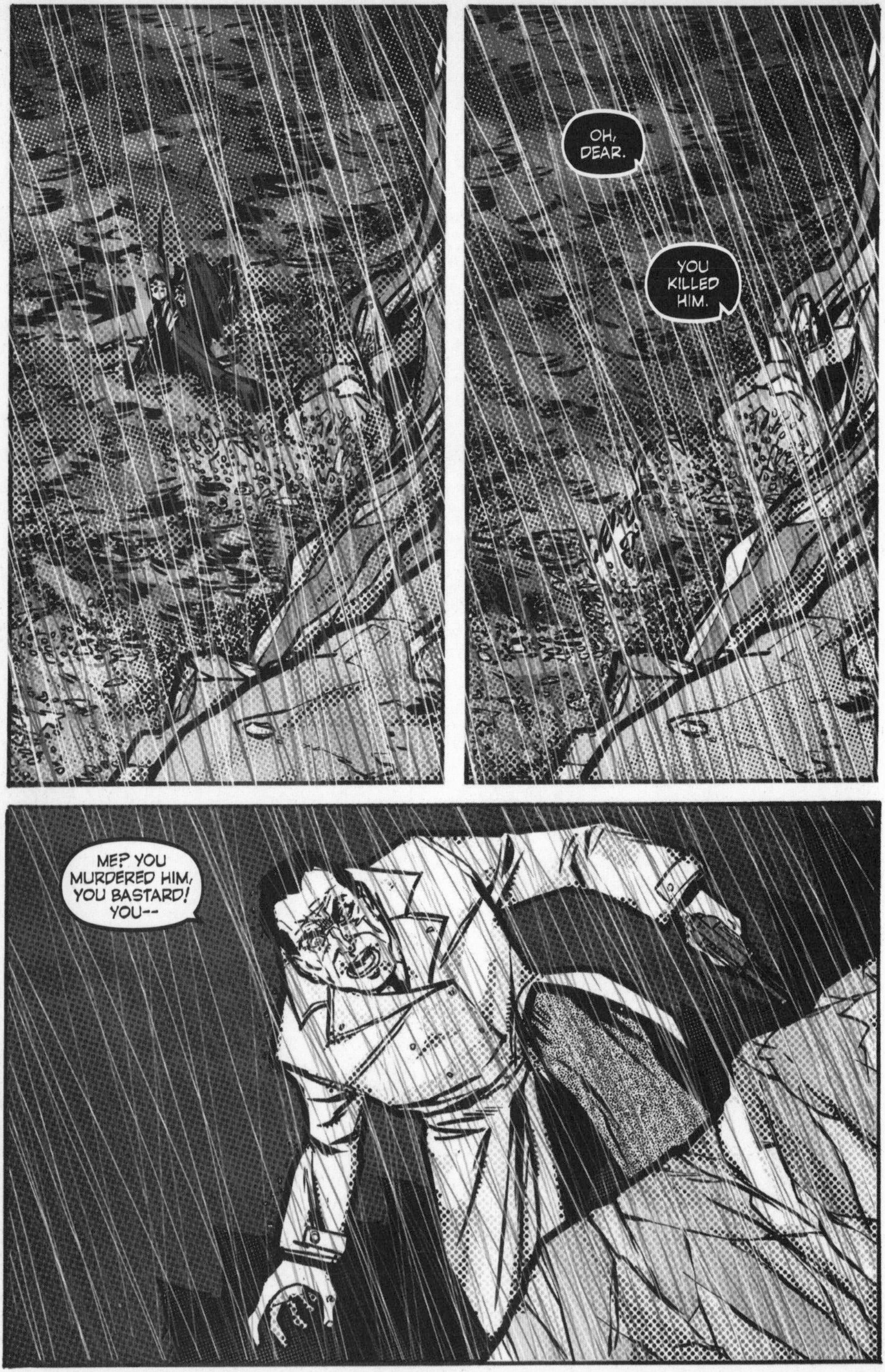
OH, DEAR.
YOU KILLED HIM.
ME? YOU MURDERED HIM, YOU BASTARD! YOU--

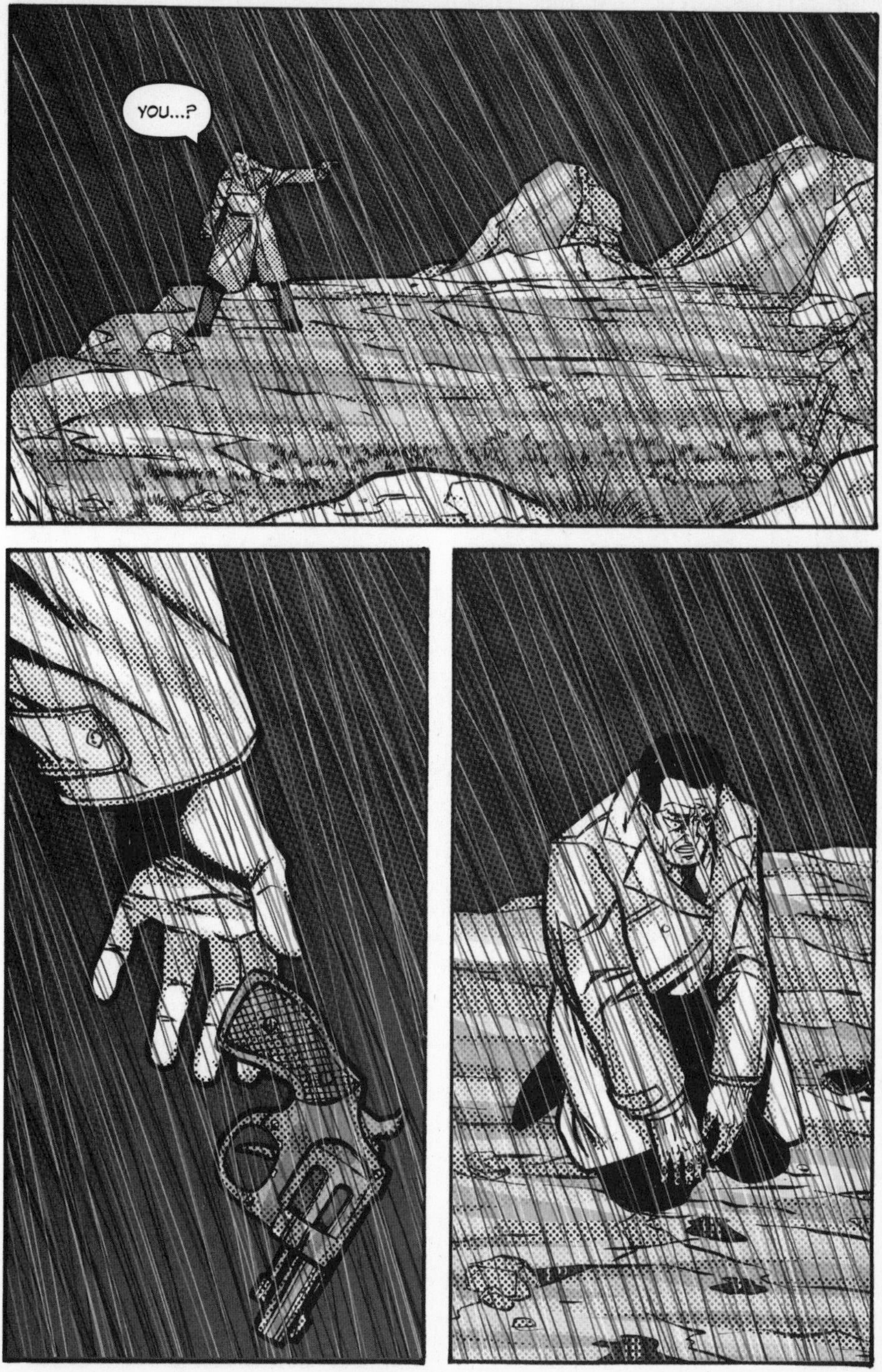
YOU...?

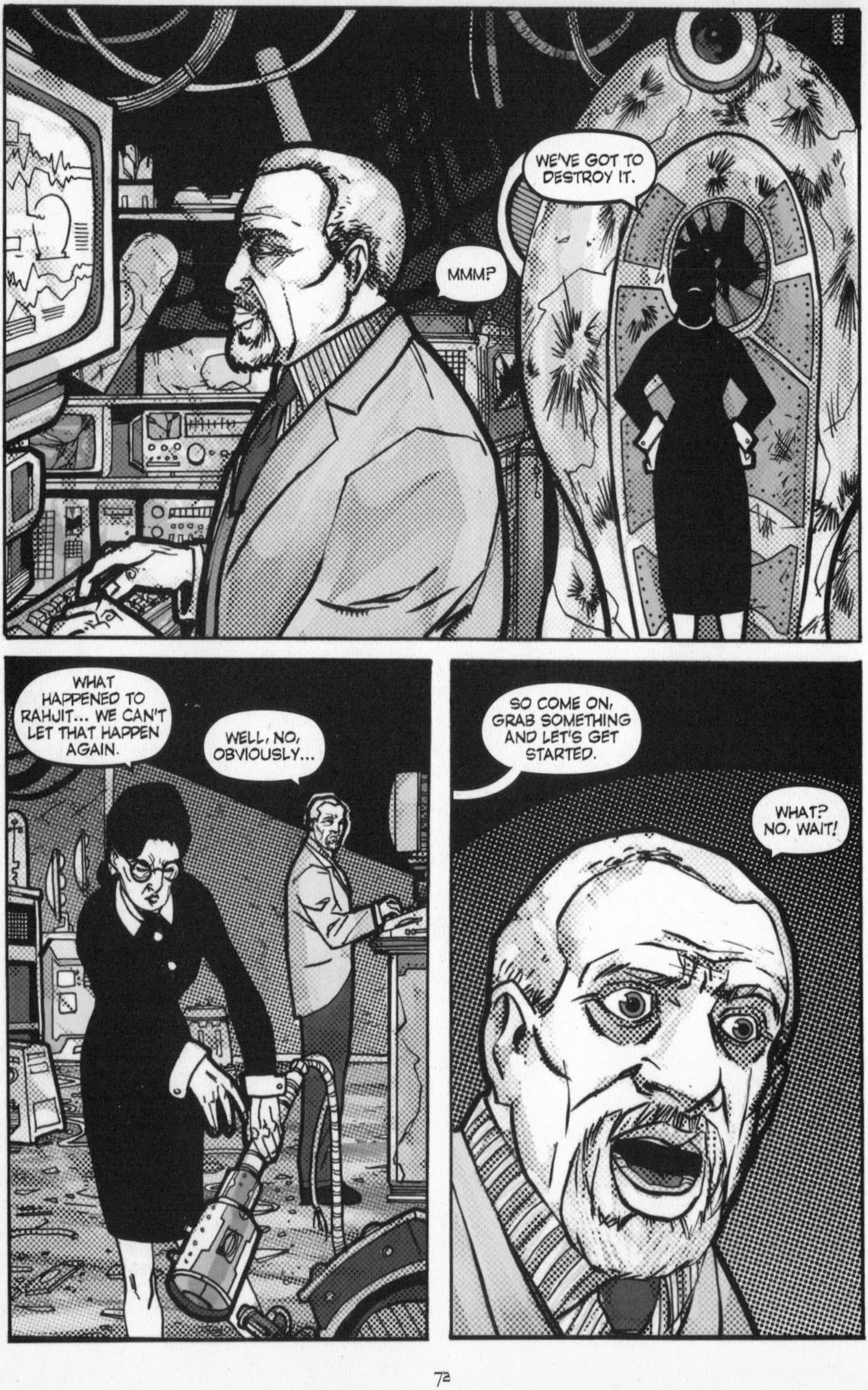
WE'VE GOT TO DESTROY IT.
MMM?
WHAT HAPPENED TO RAHJIT... WE CAN'T LET THAT HAPPEN AGAIN.
WELL, NO, OBVIOUSLY...
SO COME ON, GRAB SOMETHING AND LET'S GET STARTED.
WHAT? NO, WAIT!

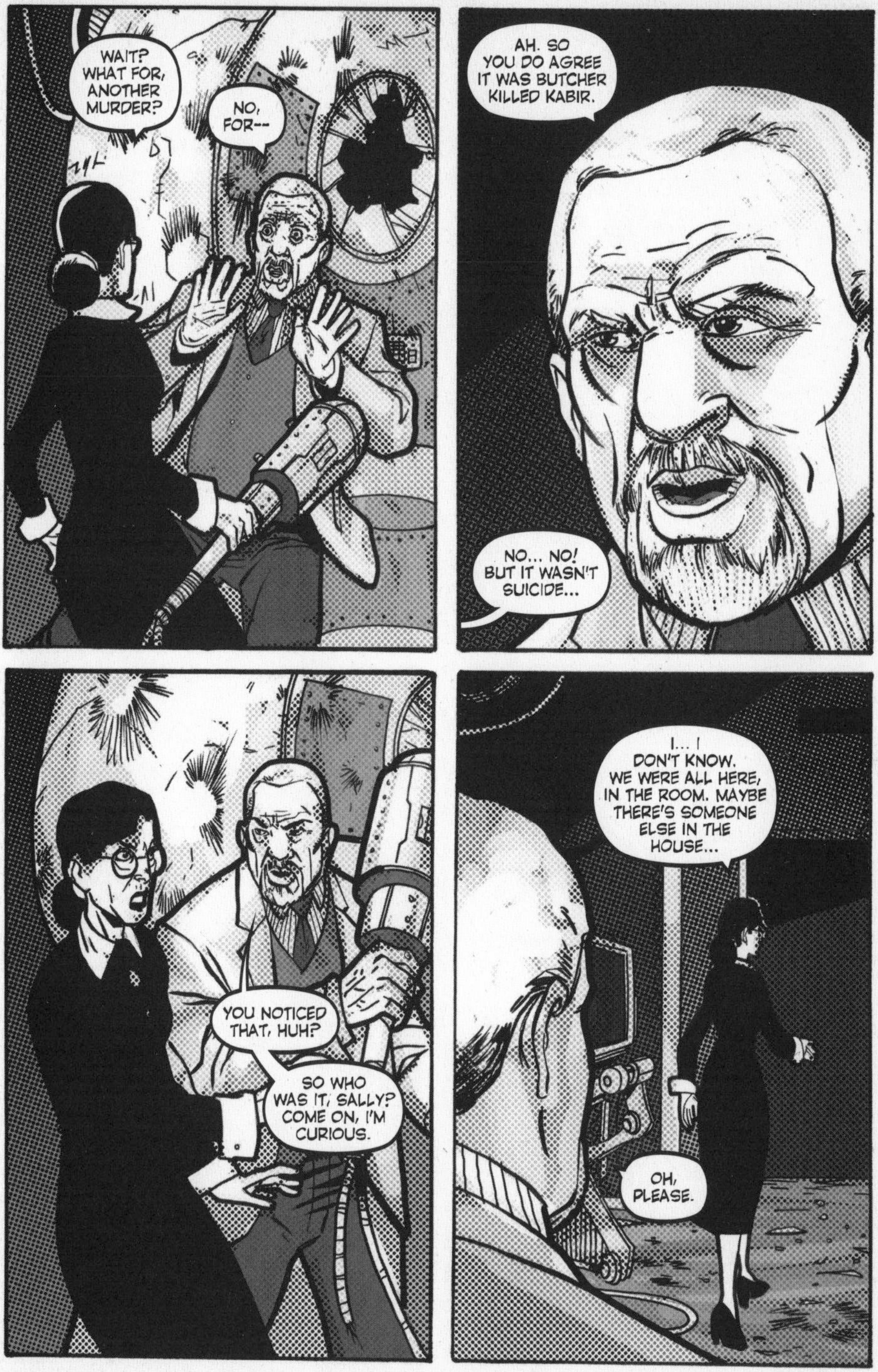
WAIT? WHAT FOR, ANOTHER MURDER?
NO, FOR--
AH. SO YOU DO AGREE IT WAS BUTCHER KILLED KABIR.
NO... NO! BUT IT WASN'T SUICIDE...
YOU NOTICED THAT, HUH?
SO WHO WAS IT, SALLY? COME ON, I'M CURIOUS.
I... I DON'T KNOW. WE WERE ALL HERE, IN THE ROOM. MAYBE THERE'S SOMEONE ELSE IN THE HOUSE...
OH, PLEASE.

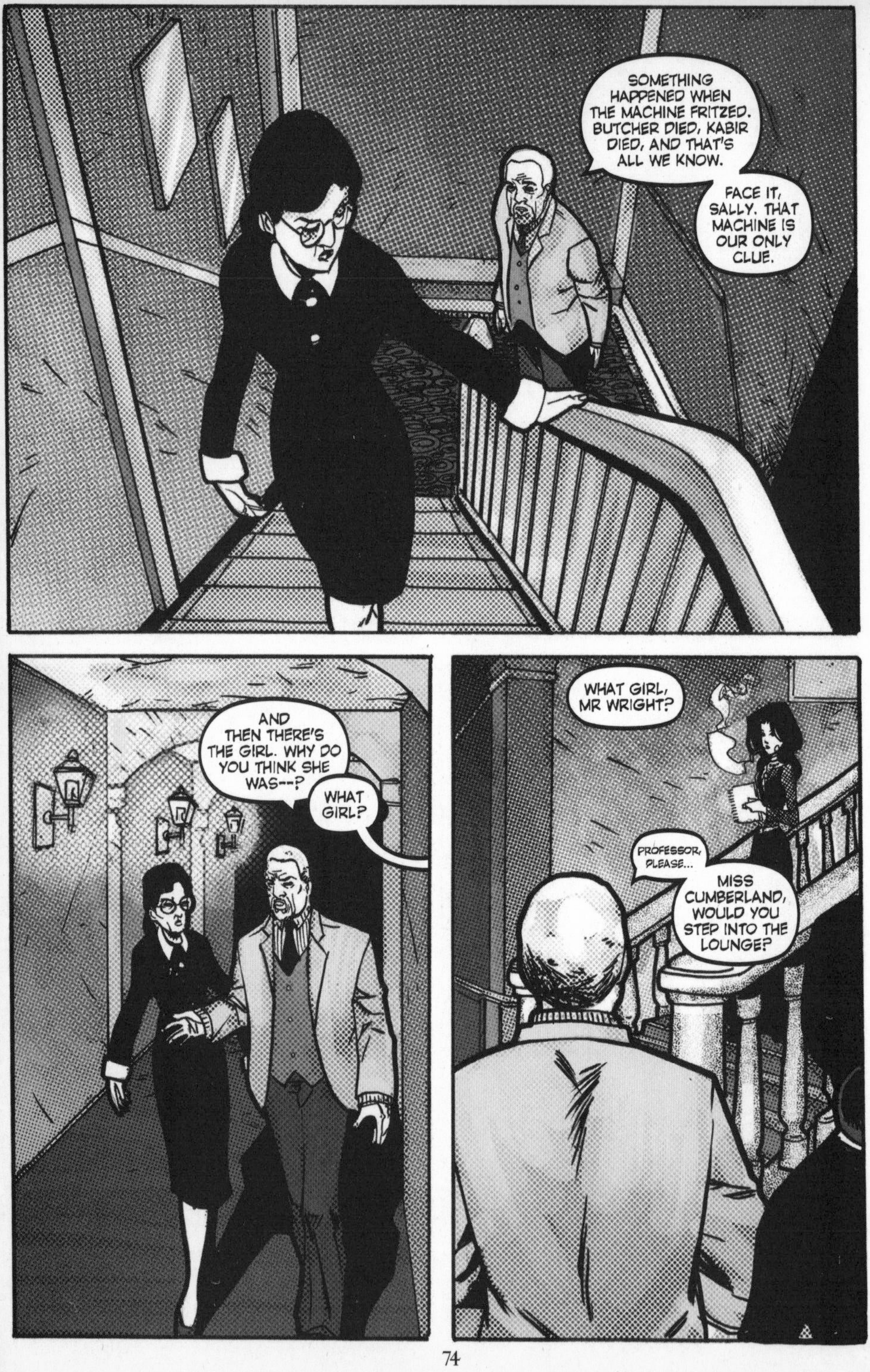
SOMETHING HAPPENED WHEN THE MACHINE FRITZED. BUTCHER DIED, KABIR DIED, AND THAT'S ALL WE KNOW.
FACE IT, SALLY. THAT MACHINE IS OUR ONLY CLUE.
AND THEN THERE'S THE GIRL. WHY DO YOU THINK SHE WAS--?
WHAT GIRL?
WHAT GIRL, MR WRIGHT?
PROFESSOR, PLEASE...
MISS CUMBERLAND, WOULD YOU STEP INTO THE LOUNGE?

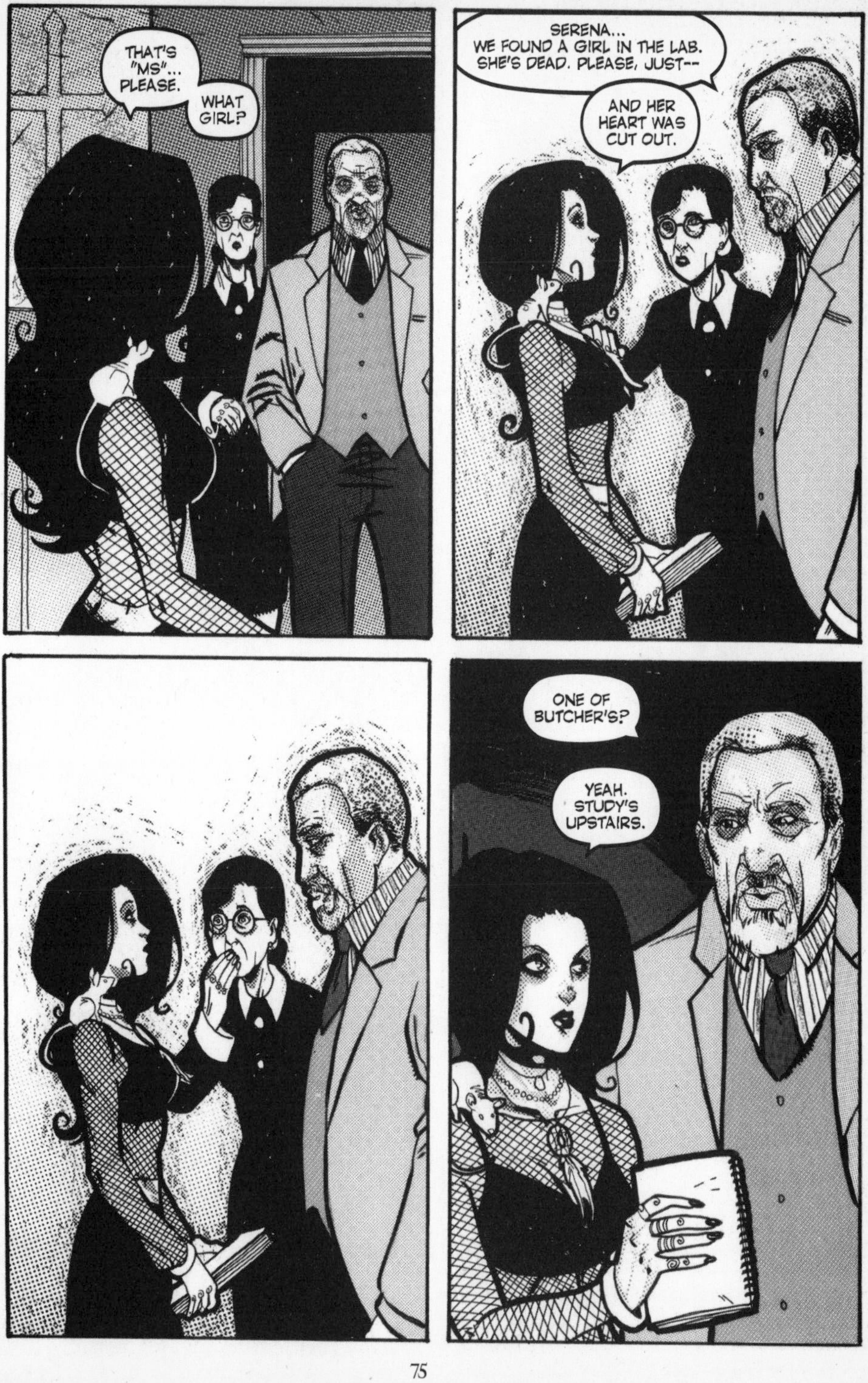
THAT'S "MS"... PLEASE.
WHAT GIRL?
SERENA... WE FOUND A GIRL IN THE LAB. SHE'S DEAD. PLEASE, JUST--
AND HER HEART WAS CUT OUT.
ONE OF BUTCHER'S?
YEAH. STUDY'S UPSTAIRS.

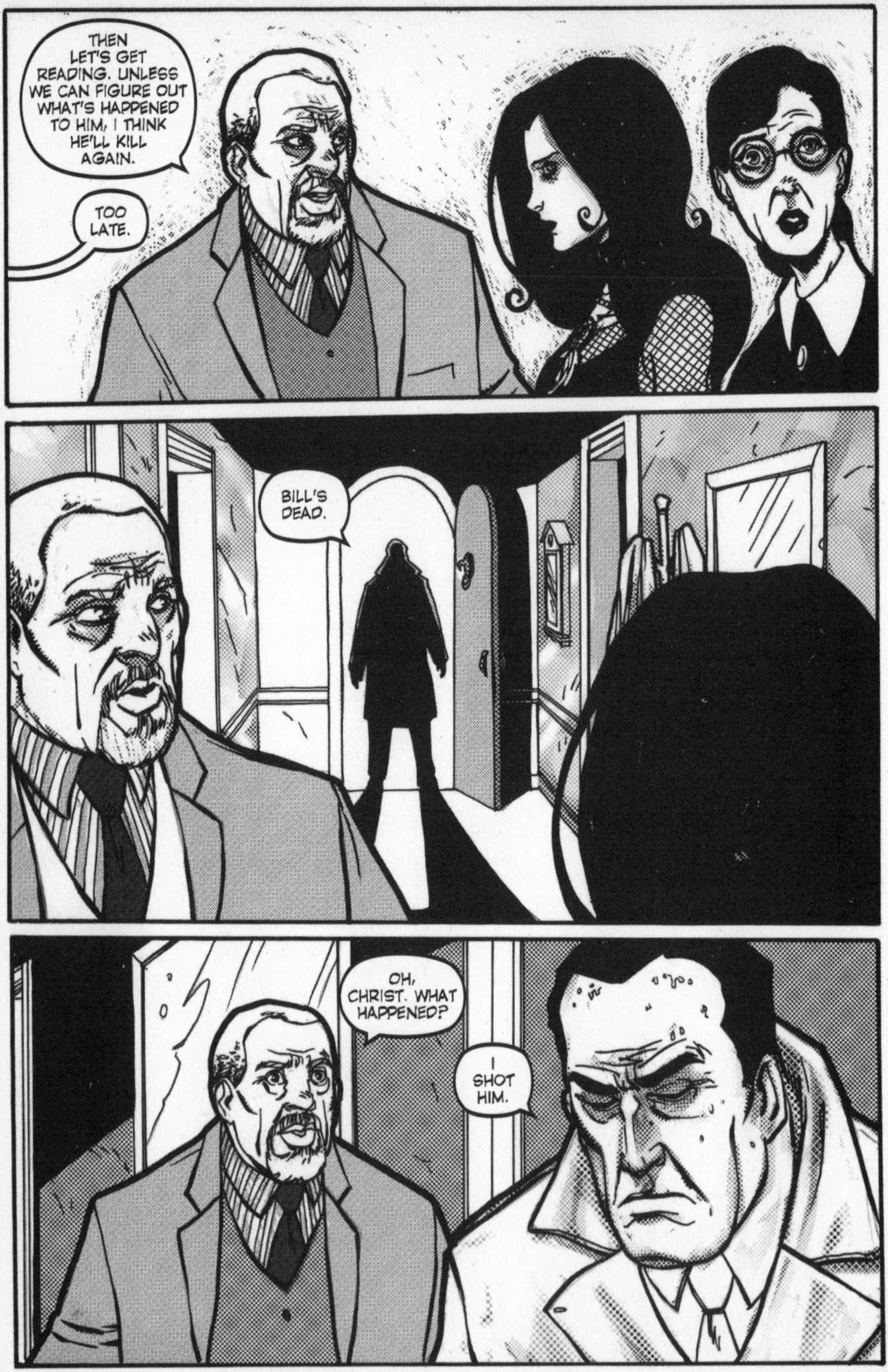
THEN LET'S GET READING. UNLESS WE CAN FIGURE OUT WHAT'S HAPPENED TO HIM, I THINK HE'LL KILL AGAIN.
TOO LATE.
BILL'S DEAD.
OH, CHRIST. WHAT HAPPENED?
I SHOT HIM.

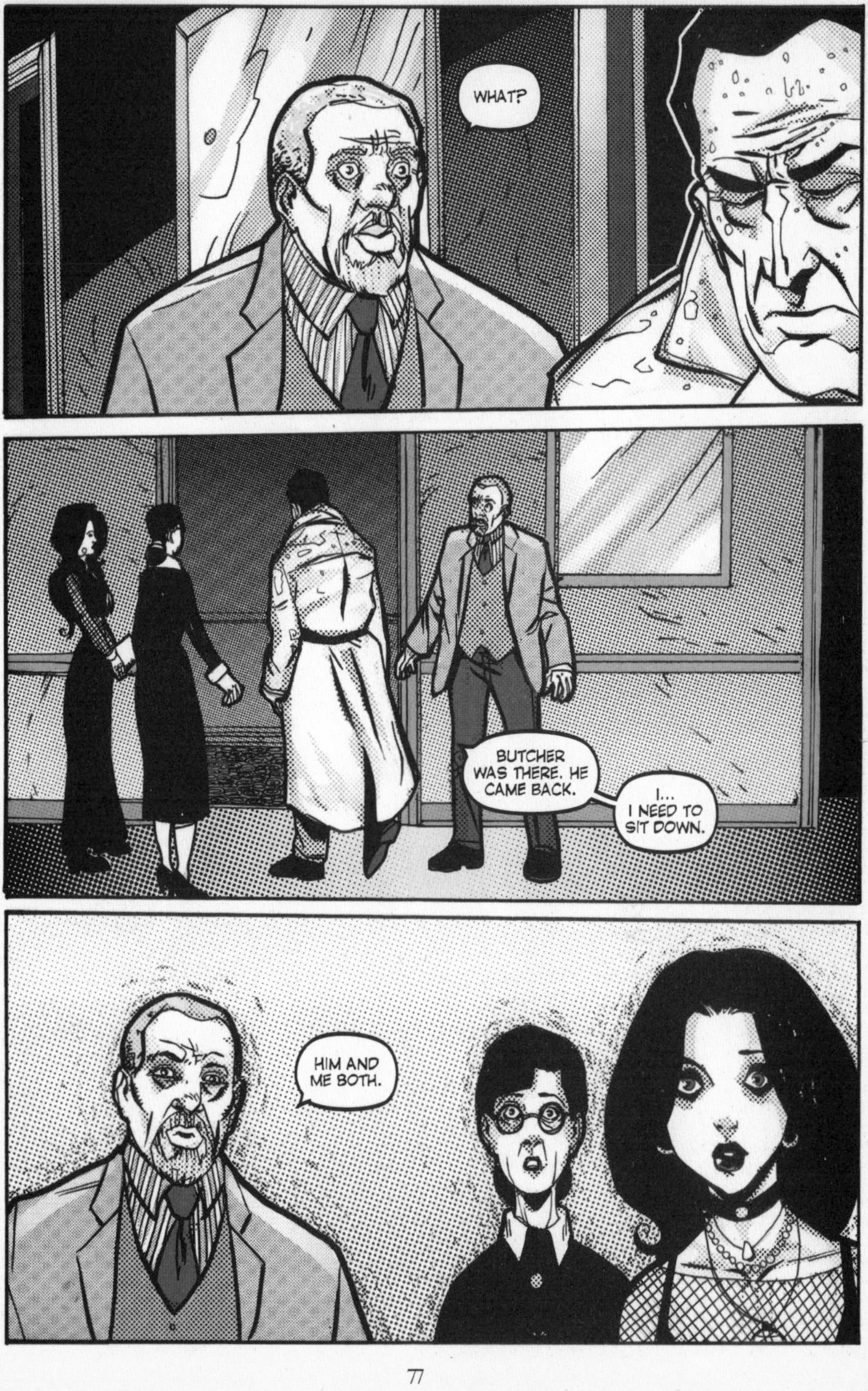
WHAT?
BUTCHER WAS THERE. HE CAME BACK.
I... I NEED TO SIT DOWN.
HIM AND ME BOTH.

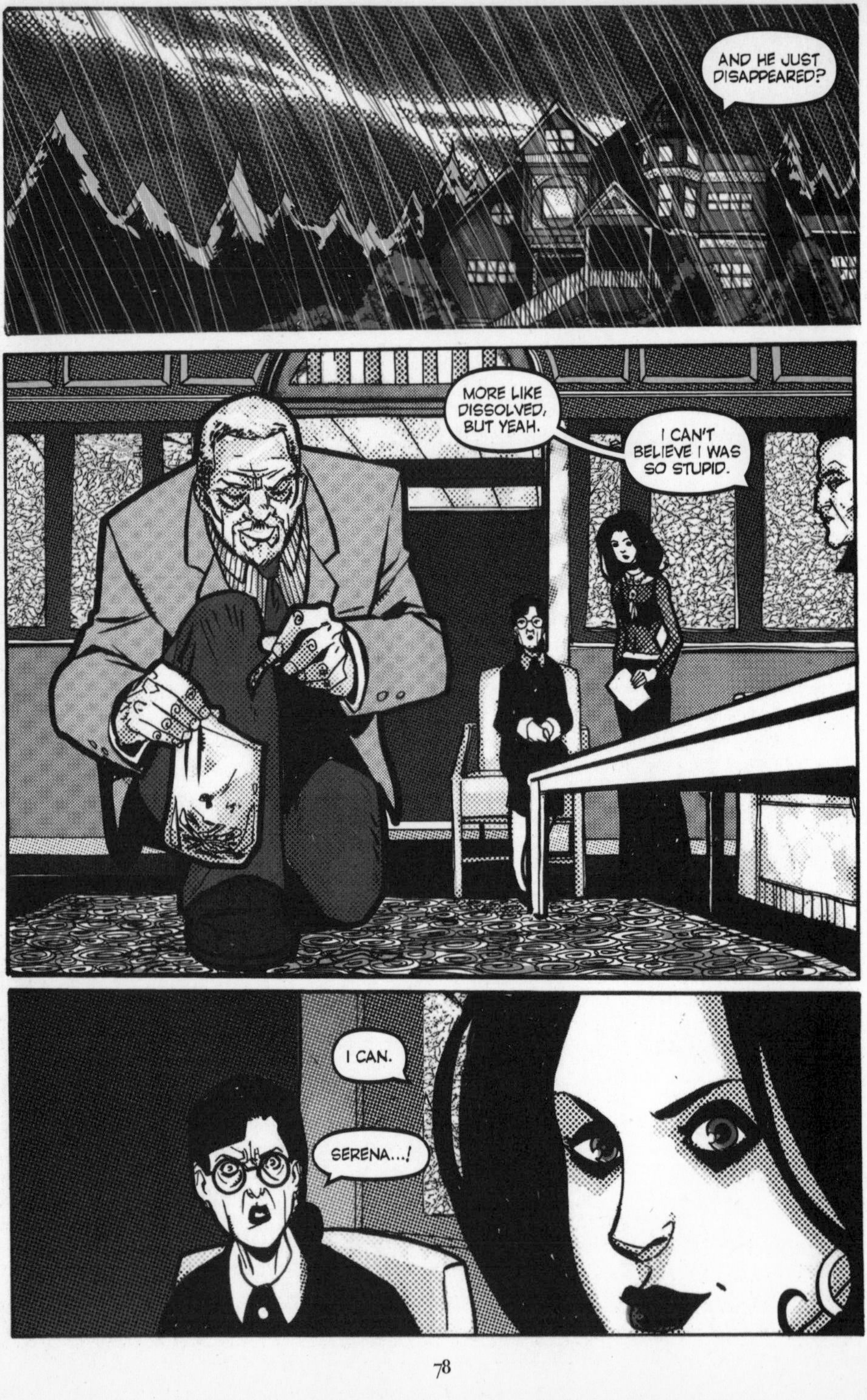
AND HE JUST DISAPPEARED?
MORE LIKE DISSOLVED, BUT YEAH.
I CAN'T BELIEVE I WAS SO STUPID.
I CAN.
SERENA...!

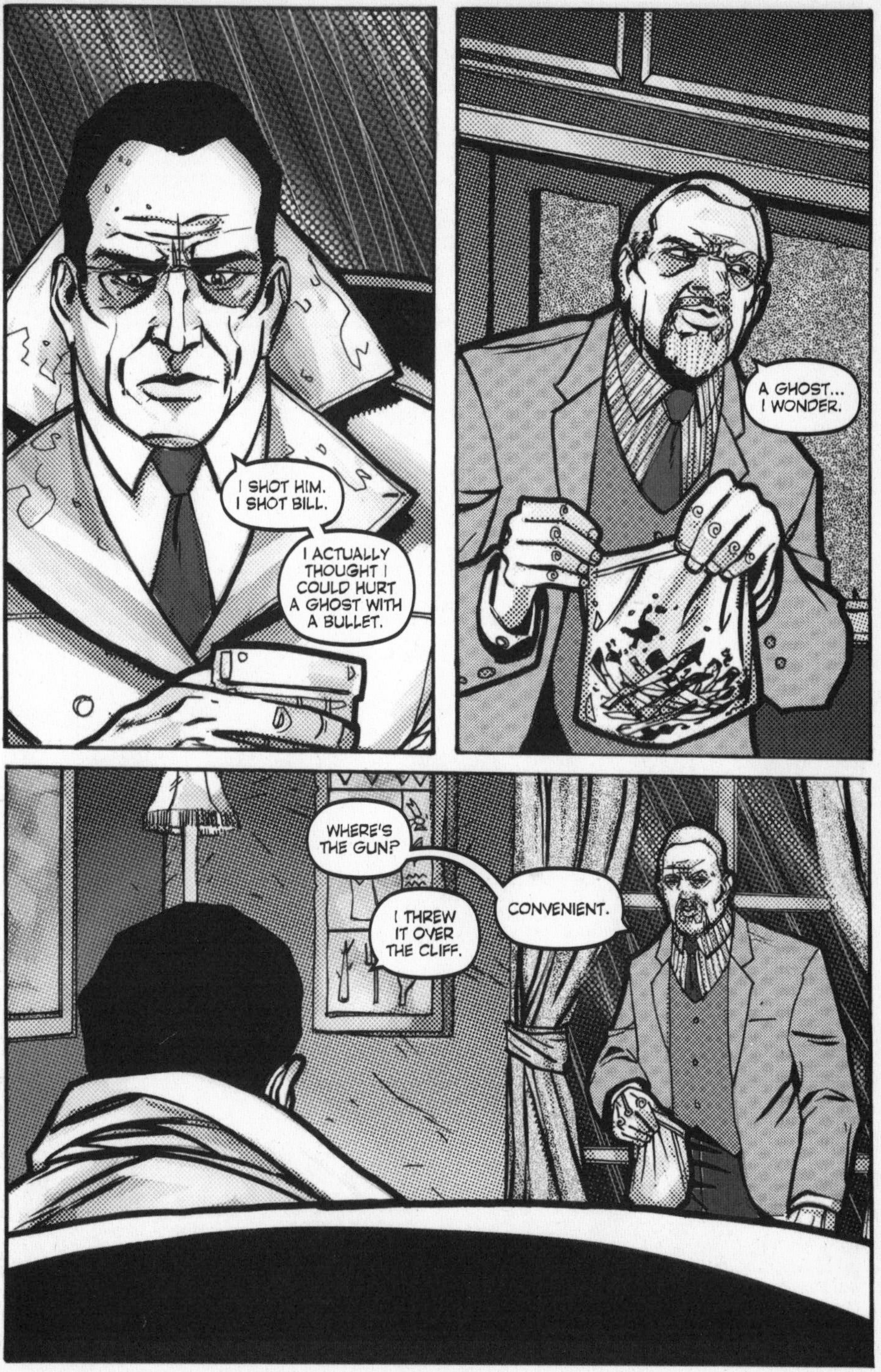
I SHOT HIM. I SHOT BILL.
I ACTUALLY THOUGHT I COULD HURT A GHOST WITH A BULLET.
A GHOST... I WONDER.
WHERE'S THE GUN?
I THREW IT OVER THE CLIFF.
CONVENIENT.

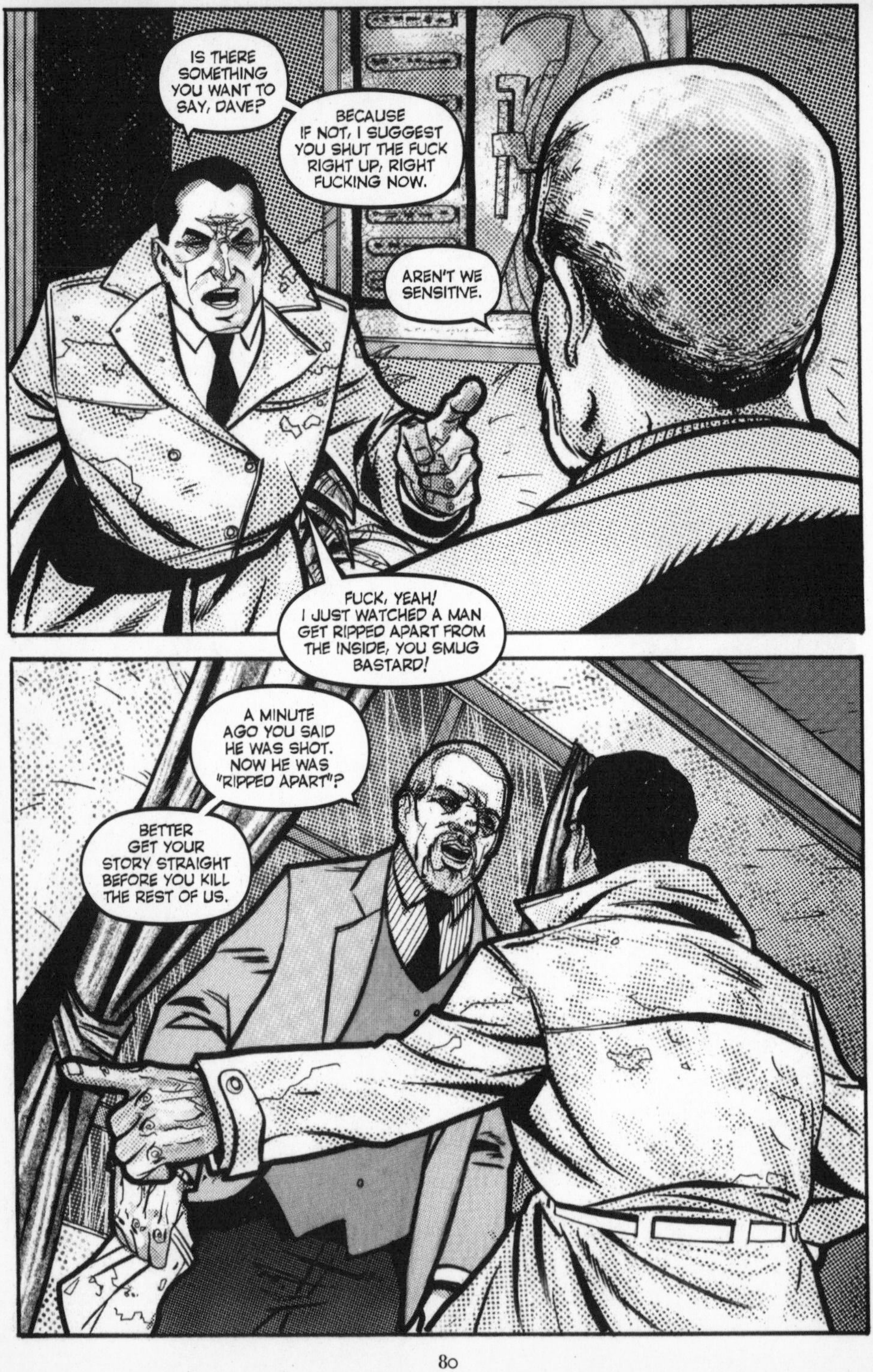
IS THERE SOMETHING YOU WANT TO SAY, DAVE?
BECAUSE IF NOT, I SUGGEST YOU SHUT THE FUCK RIGHT UP, RIGHT FUCKING NOW.
AREN'T WE SENSITIVE.
FUCK, YEAH! I JUST WATCHED A MAN GET RIPPED APART FROM THE INSIDE, YOU SMUG BASTARD!
A MINUTE AGO YOU SAID HE WAS SHOT. NOW HE WAS "RIPPED APART"?
BETTER GET YOUR STORY STRAIGHT BEFORE YOU KILL THE REST OF US.

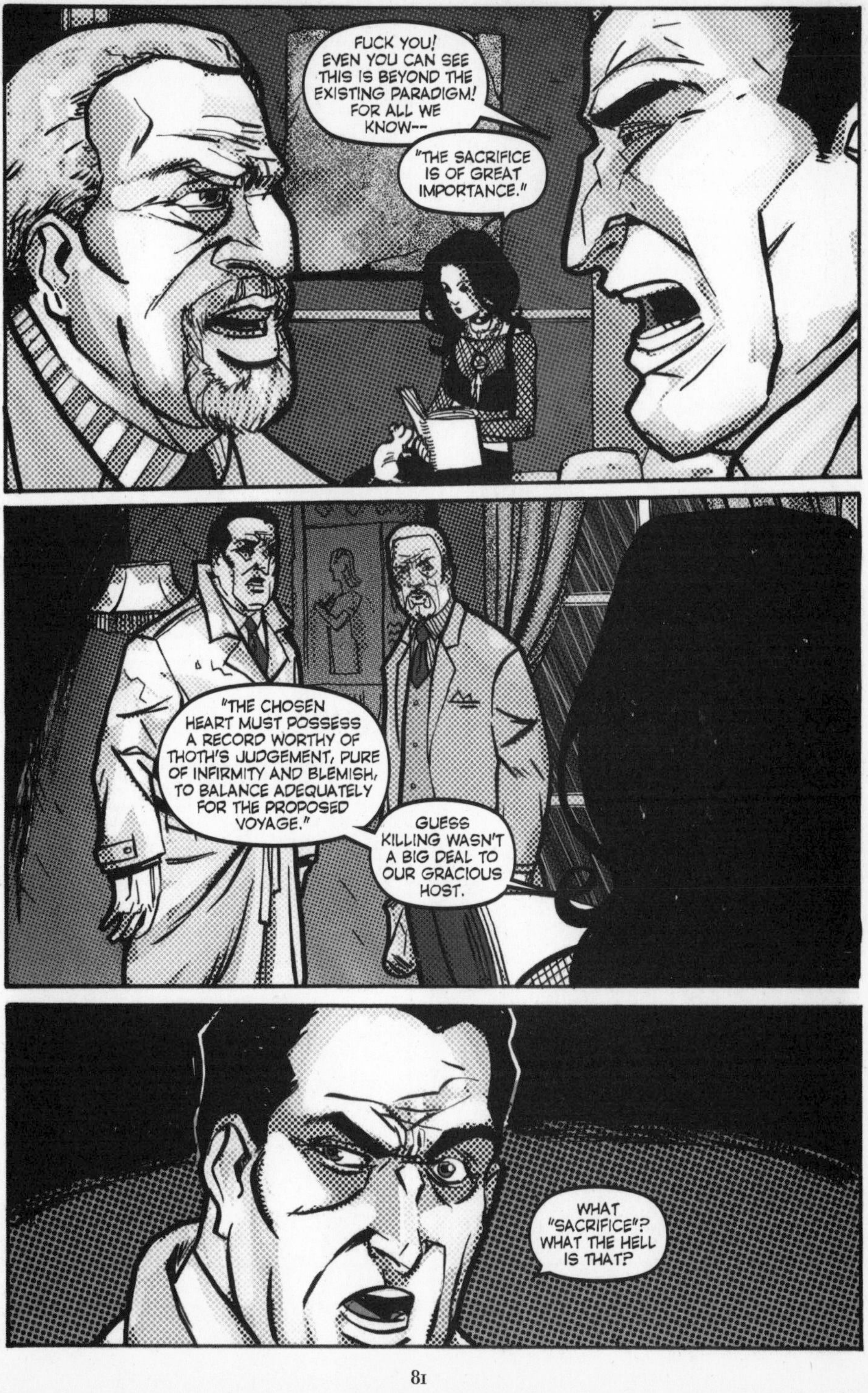
FUCK YOU! EVEN YOU CAN SEE THIS IS BEYOND THE EXISTING PARADIGM! FOR ALL WE KNOW--
"THE SACRIFICE IS OF GREAT IMPORTANCE."
"THE CHOSEN HEART MUST POSSESS A RECORD WORTHY OF THOTH'S JUDGEMENT, PURE OF INFIRMITY AND BLEMISH, TO BALANCE ADEQUATELY FOR THE PROPOSED VOYAGE."
GUESS KILLING WASN'T A BIG DEAL TO OUR GRACIOUS HOST.
WHAT "SACRIFICE"? WHAT THE HELL IS THAT?

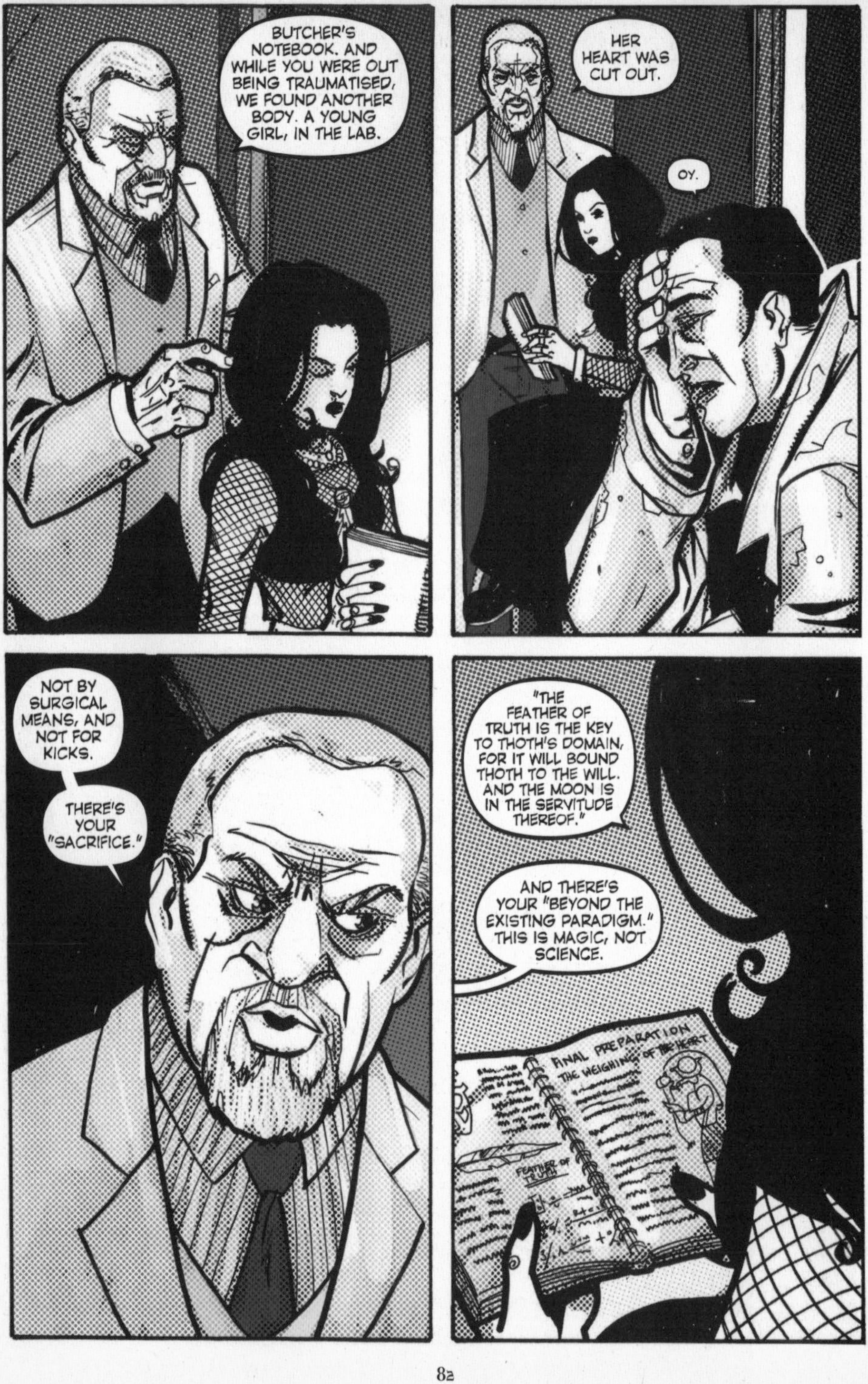
BUTCHER'S NOTEBOOK. AND WHILE YOU WERE OUT BEING TRAUMATISED, WE FOUND ANOTHER BODY. A YOUNG GIRL, IN THE LAB.
HER HEART WAS CUT OUT.
OY.
NOT BY SURGICAL MEANS, AND NOT FOR KICKS.
THERE'S YOUR "SACRIFICE."
"THE FEATHER OF TRUTH IS THE KEY TO THOTH'S DOMAIN, FOR IT WILL BOUND THOTH TO THE WILL. AND THE MOON IS IN THE SERVITUDE THEREOF."
AND THERE'S YOUR "BEYOND THE EXISTING PARADIGM." THIS IS MAGIC, NOT SCIENCE.
FINAL PREPARATION
THE WEIGHING OF THE HEART
FEATHER OF TRUTH

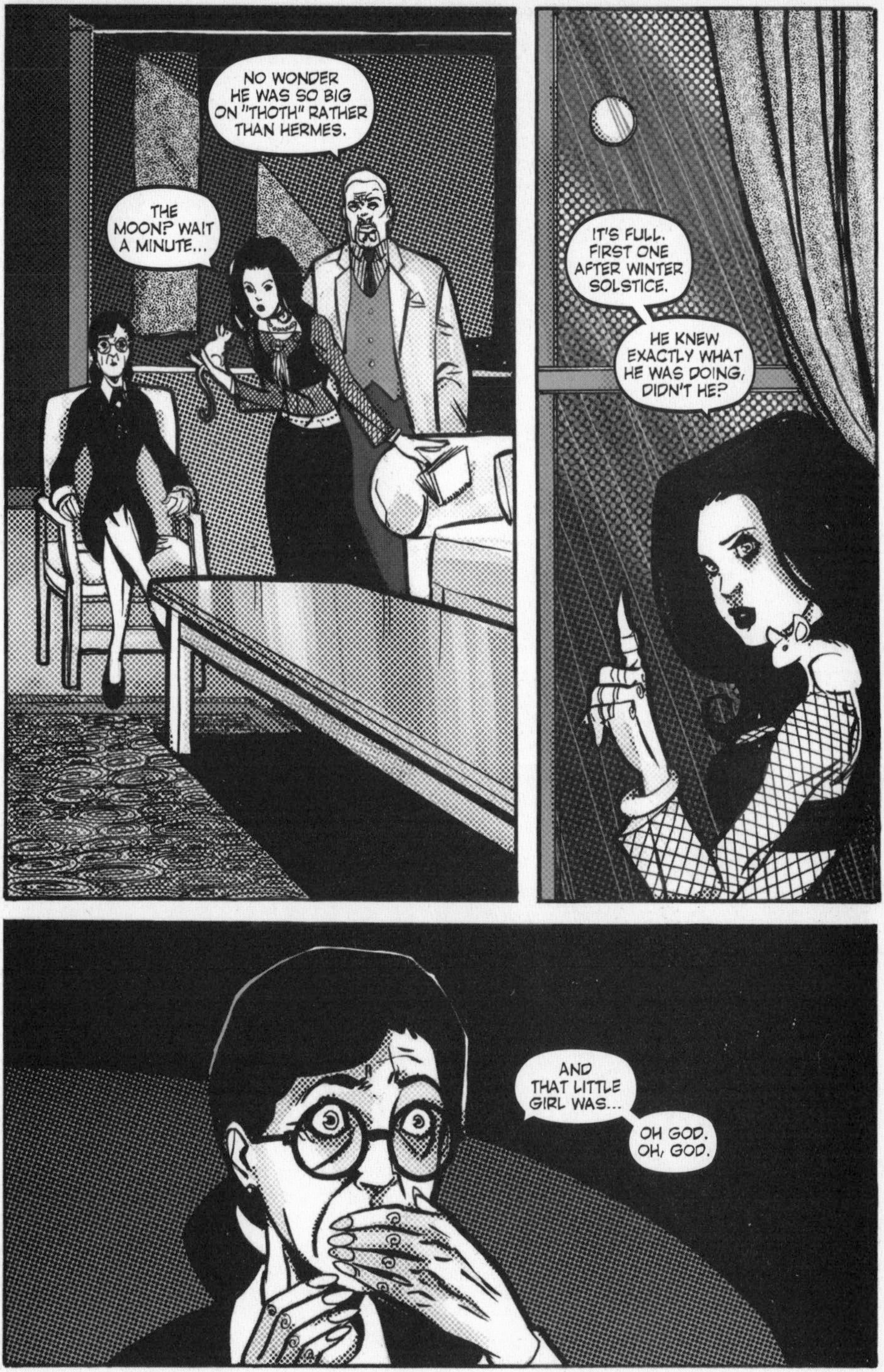
NO WONDER HE WAS SO BIG ON "THOTH" RATHER THAN HERMES.
THE MOON? WAIT A MINUTE...
IT'S FULL. FIRST ONE AFTER WINTER SOLSTICE.
HE KNEW EXACTLY WHAT HE WAS DOING, DIDN'T HE?
AND THAT LITTLE GIRL WAS...
OH GOD. OH, GOD.

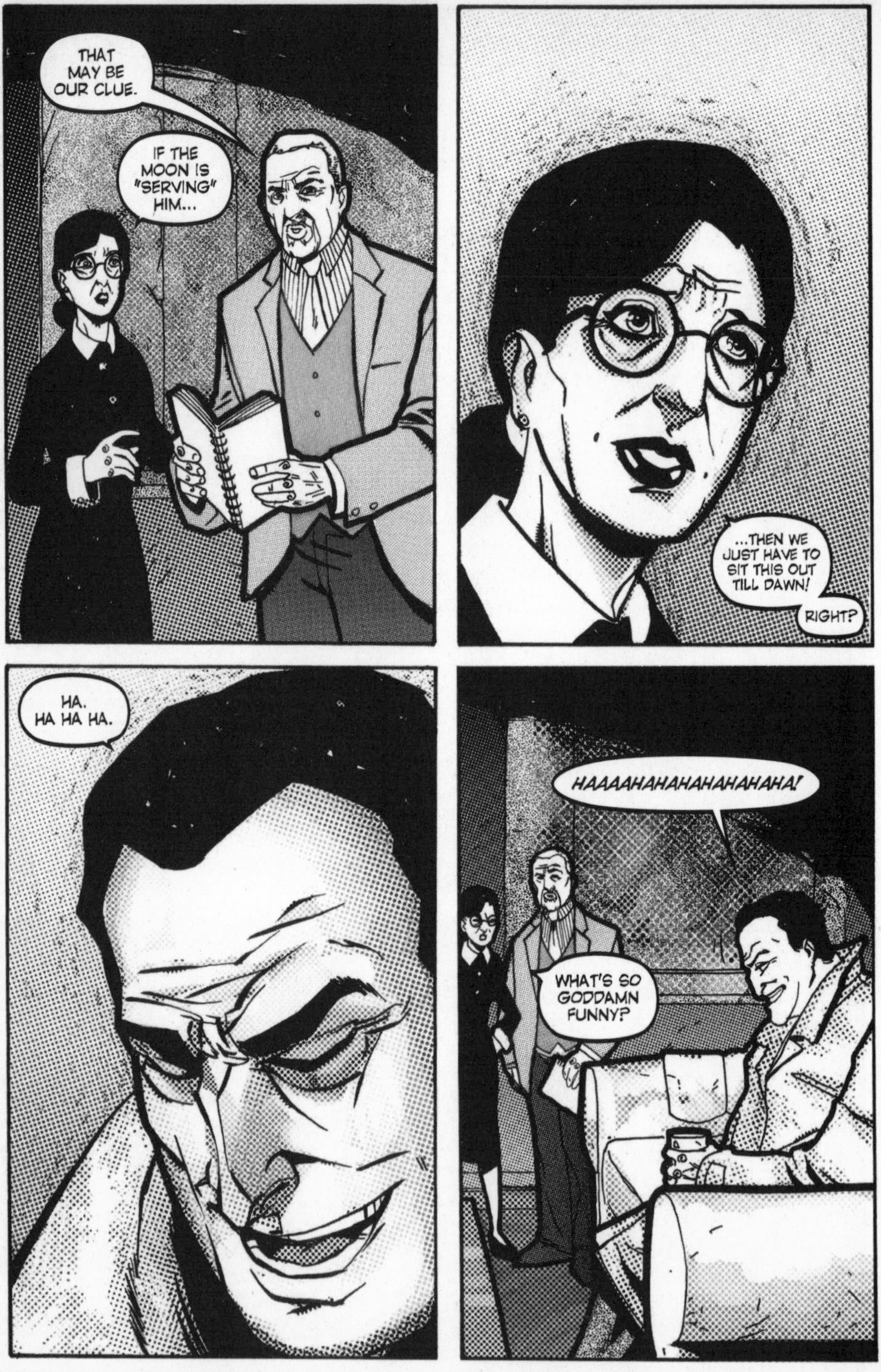
THAT MAY BE OUR CLUE.
IF THE MOON IS "SERVING" HIM...
...THEN WE JUST HAVE TO SIT THIS OUT TILL DAWN!
RIGHT?
HA. HA HA HA.
HAAAAHAHAHAHAHAHAHA!
WHAT'S SO GODDAMN FUNNY?

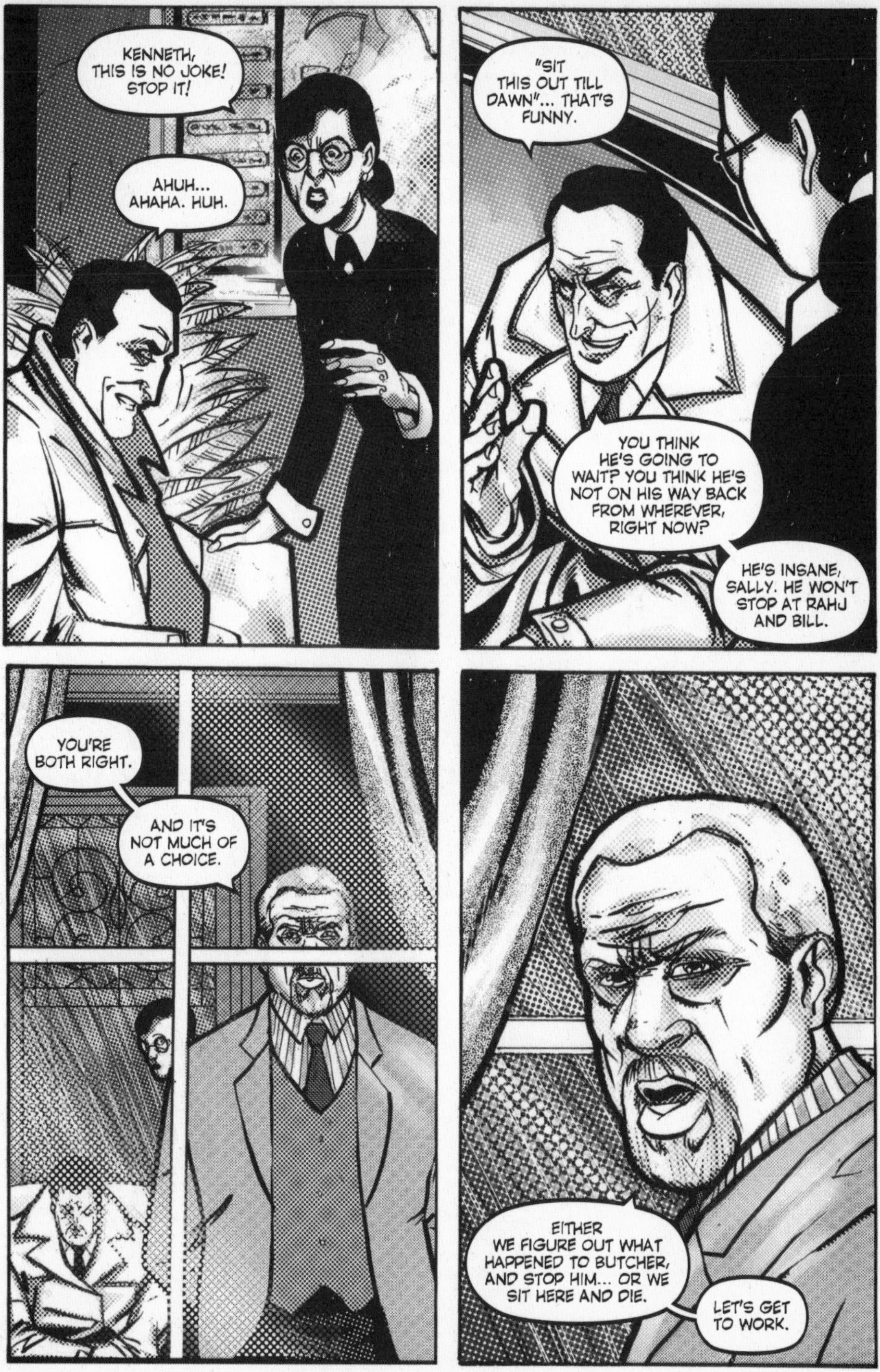
KENNETH, THIS IS NO JOKE! STOP IT!
AHUH... AHAHA. HUH.
"SIT THIS OUT TILL DAWN"... THAT'S FUNNY.
YOU THINK HE'S GOING TO WAIT? YOU THINK HE'S NOT ON HIS WAY BACK FROM WHEREVER, RIGHT NOW?
HE'S INSANE, SALLY. HE WON'T STOP AT RAHJ AND BILL.
YOU'RE BOTH RIGHT.
AND IT'S NOT MUCH OF A CHOICE.
EITHER WE FIGURE OUT WHAT HAPPENED TO BUTCHER, AND STOP HIM... OR WE SIT HERE AND DIE.
LET'S GET TO WORK.

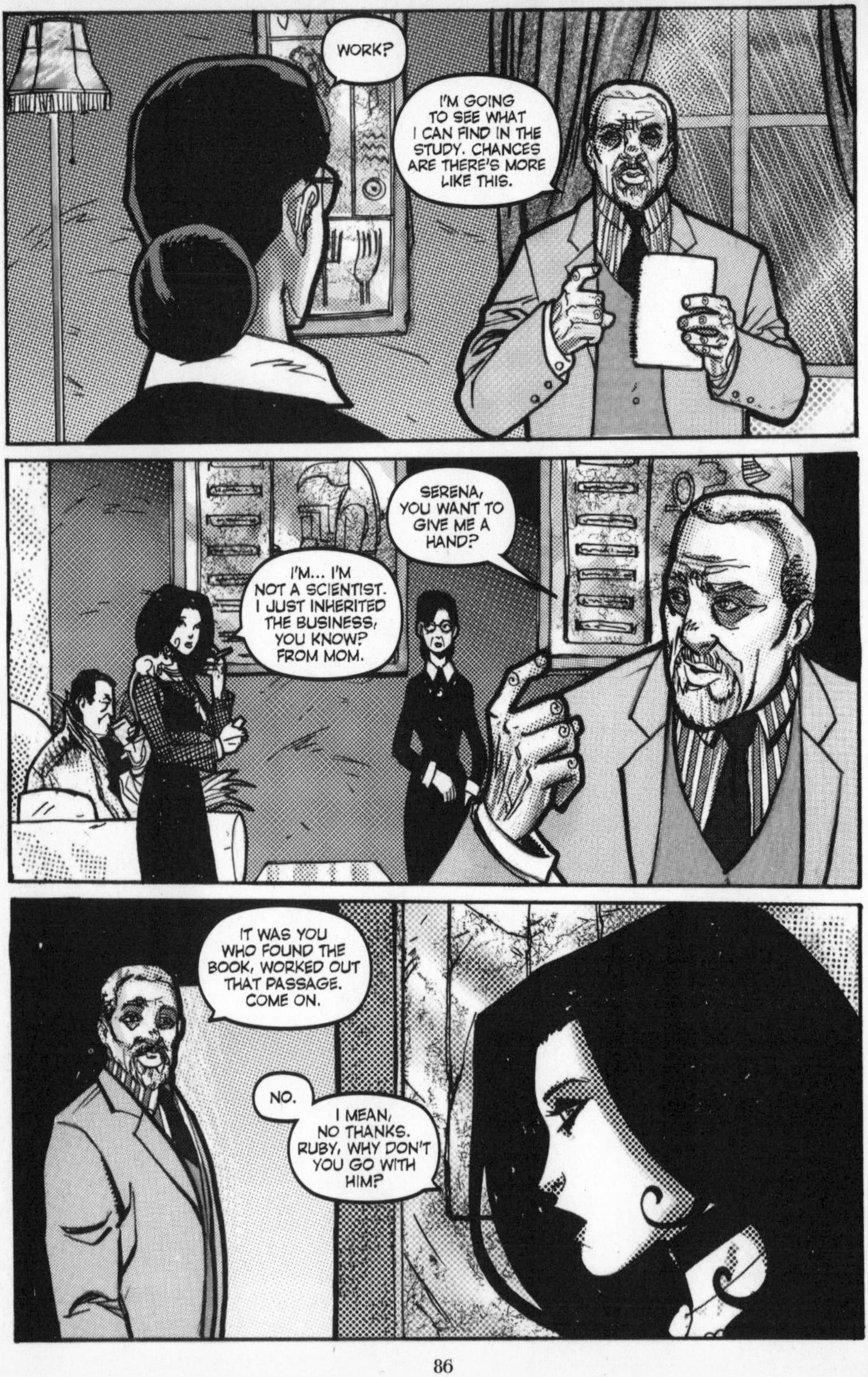
WORK?
I'M GOING TO SEE WHAT I CAN FIND IN THE STUDY. CHANCES ARE THERE'S MORE LIKE THIS.
SERENA, YOU WANT TO GIVE ME A HAND?
I'M... I'M NOT A SCIENTIST. I JUST INHERITED THE BUSINESS, YOU KNOW? FROM MOM.
IT WAS YOU WHO FOUND THE BOOK, WORKED OUT THAT PASSAGE. COME ON.
NO.
I MEAN, NO THANKS. RUBY, WHY DON'T YOU GO WITH HIM?

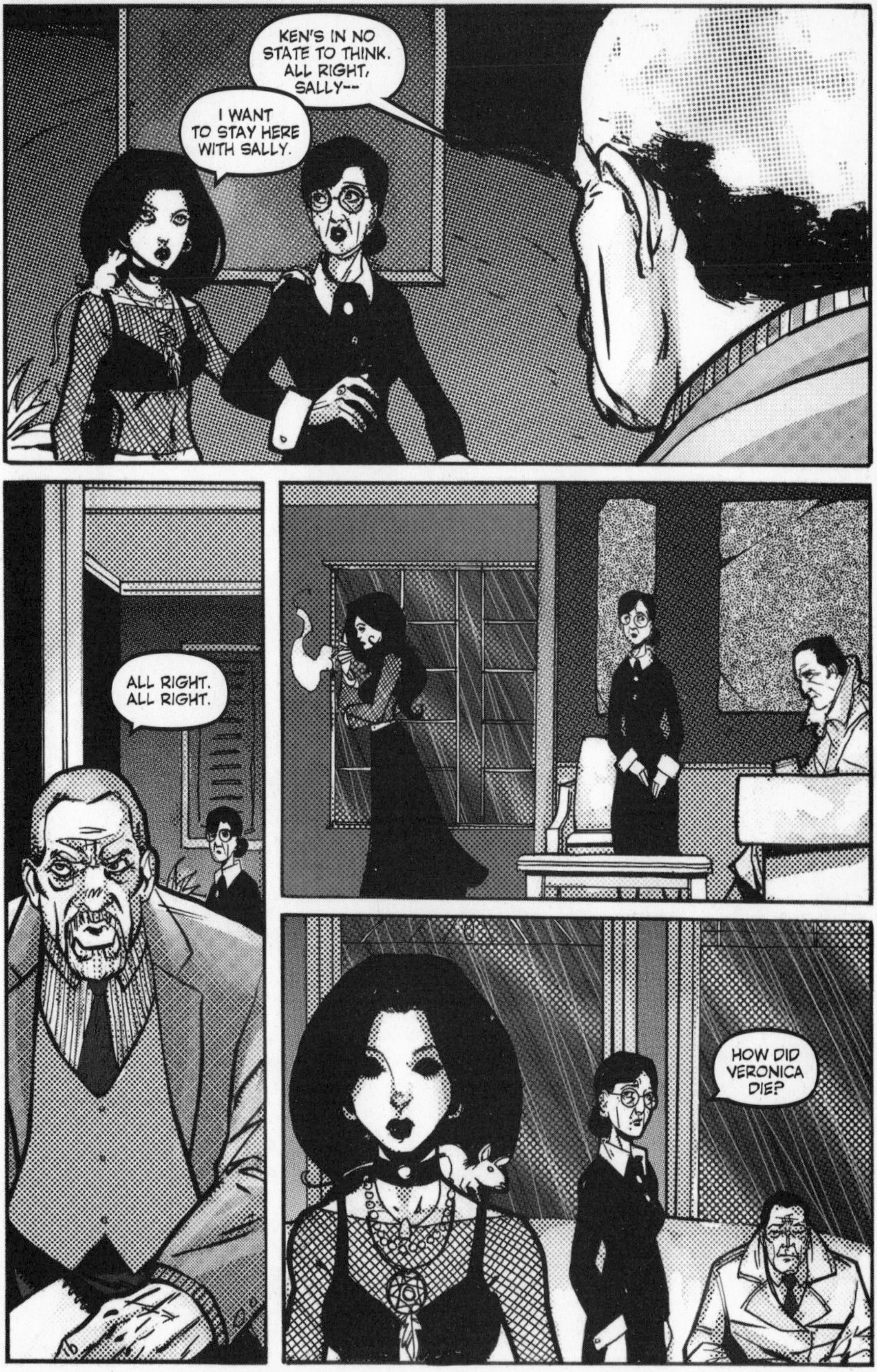
I WANT TO STAY HERE WITH SALLY.
KEN'S IN NO STATE TO THINK. ALL RIGHT, SALLY--
ALL RIGHT. ALL RIGHT.
HOW DID VERONICA DIE?

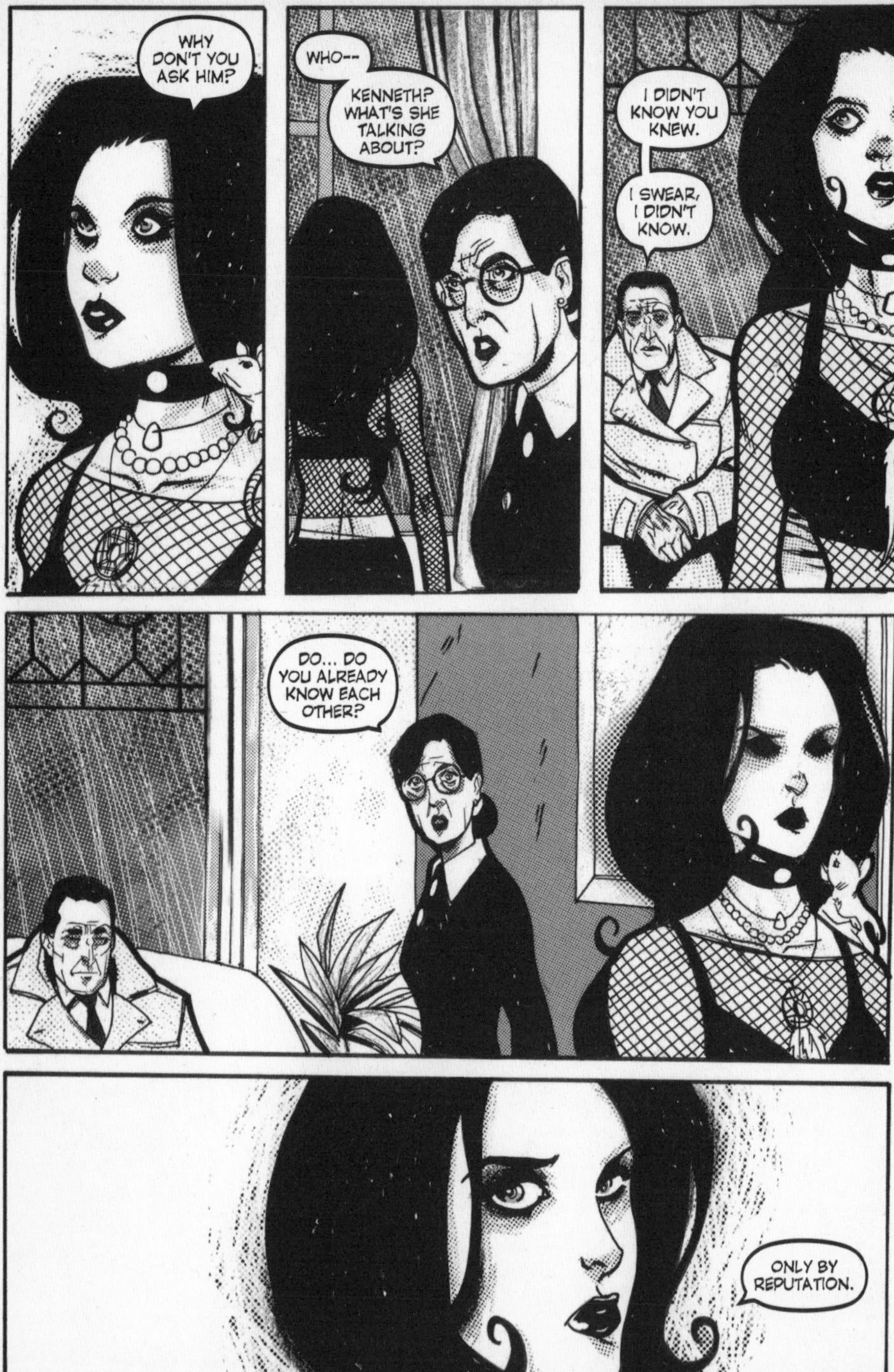
WHY DON'T YOU ASK HIM?
WHO--
KENNETH? WHAT'S SHE TALKING ABOUT?
I DIDN'T KNOW YOU KNEW.
I SWEAR, I DIDN'T KNOW.
DO... DO YOU ALREADY KNOW EACH OTHER?
ONLY BY REPUTATION.

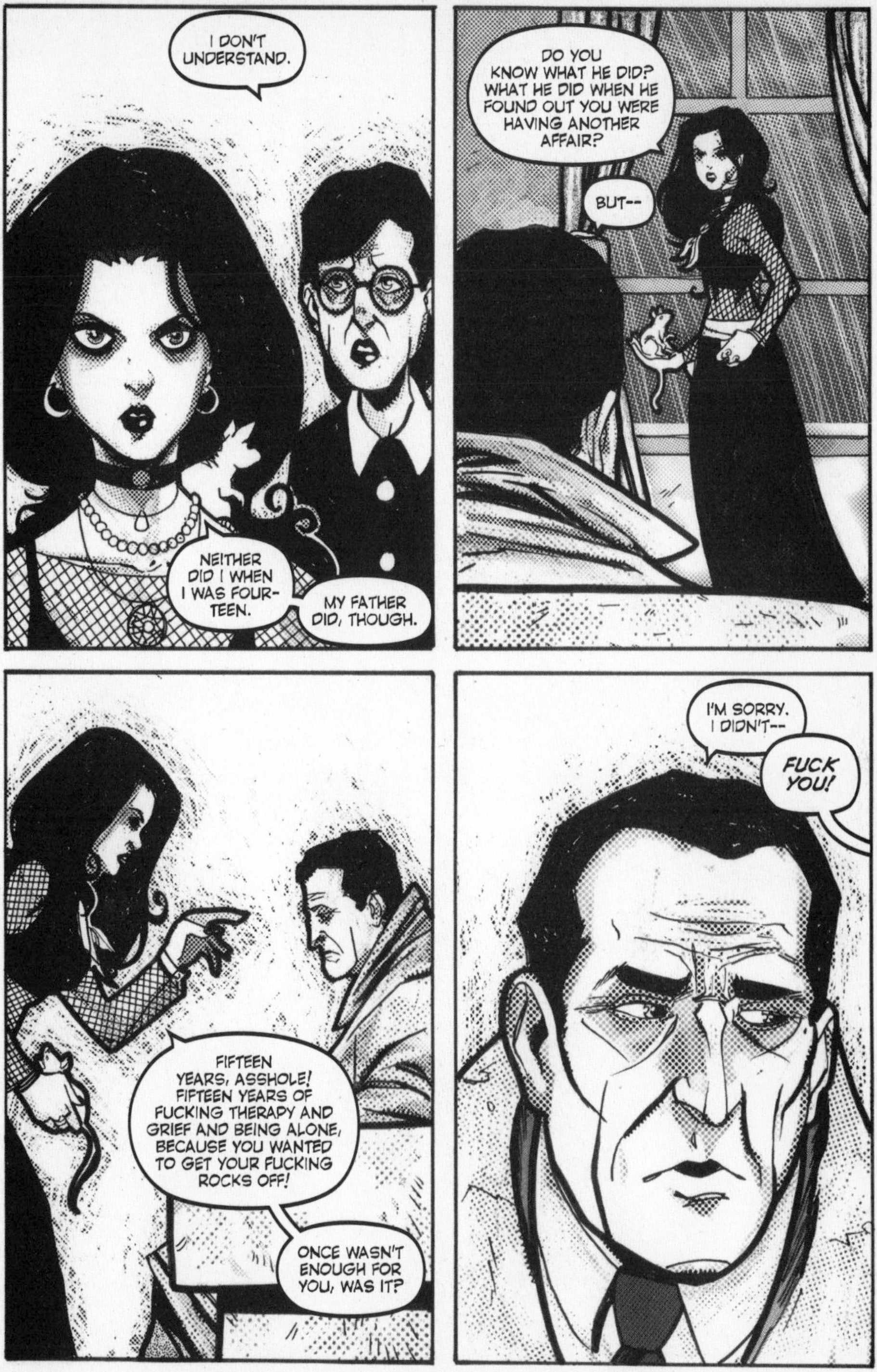
I DON'T UNDERSTAND.
NEITHER DID I WHEN I WAS FOURTEEN.
MY FATHER DID, THOUGH.
DO YOU KNOW WHAT HE DID? WHAT HE DID WHEN HE FOUND OUT YOU WERE HAVING ANOTHER AFFAIR?
BUT--
FIFTEEN YEARS, ASSHOLE! FIFTEEN YEARS OF FUCKING THERAPY AND GRIEF AND BEING ALONE, BECAUSE YOU WANTED TO GET YOUR FUCKING ROCKS OFF!
ONCE WASN'T ENOUGH FOR YOU, WAS IT?
I'M SORRY. I DIDN'T--
FUCK YOU!

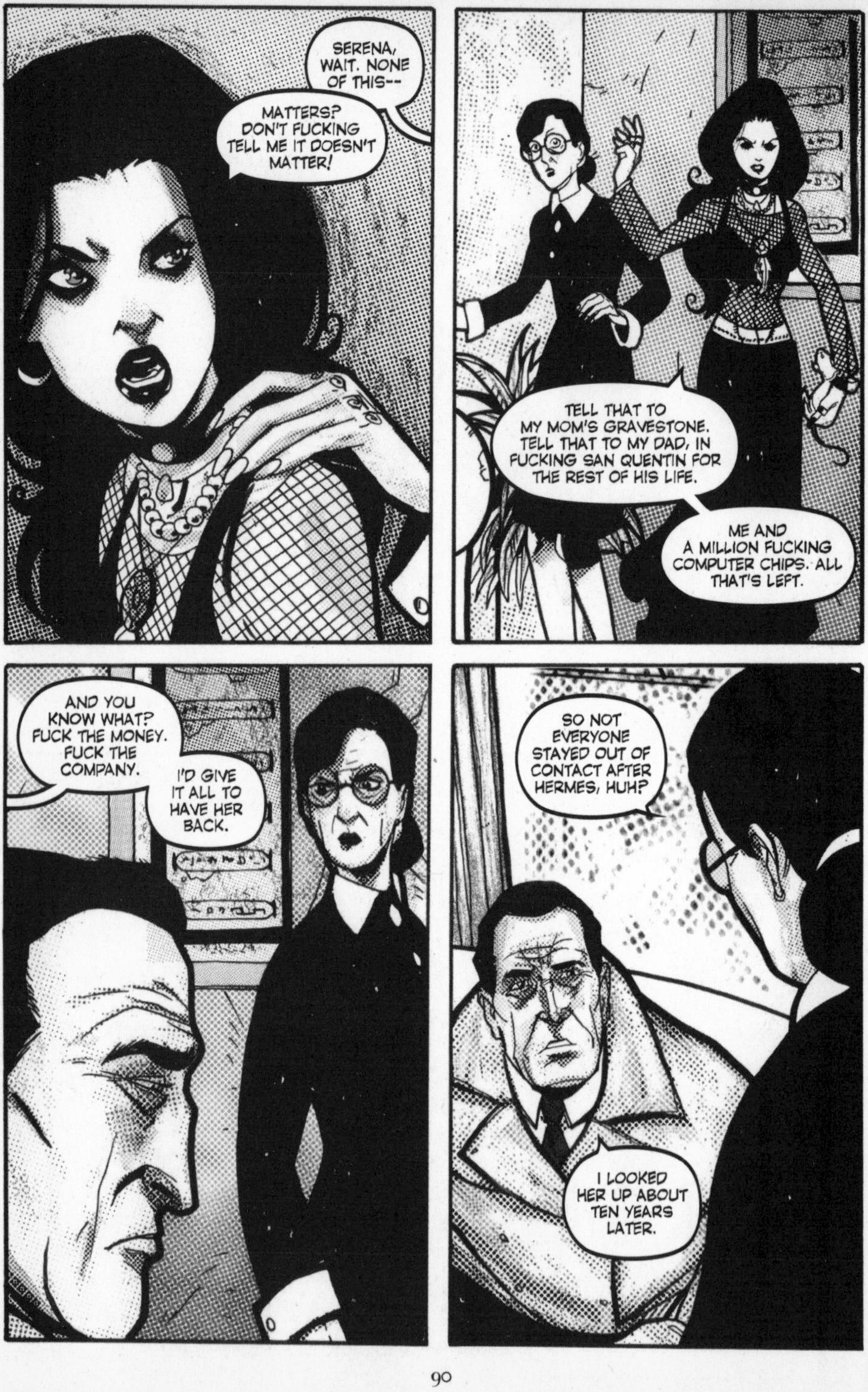
SERENA, WAIT. NONE OF THIS--
MATTERS? DON'T FUCKING TELL ME IT DOESN'T MATTER!
TELL THAT TO MY MOM'S GRAVESTONE. TELL THAT TO MY DAD, IN FUCKING SAN QUENTIN FOR THE REST OF HIS LIFE.
ME AND A MILLION FUCKING COMPUTER CHIPS. ALL THAT'S LEFT.
AND YOU KNOW WHAT? FUCK THE MONEY. FUCK THE COMPANY.
I'D GIVE IT ALL TO HAVE HER BACK.
SO NOT EVERYONE STAYED OUT OF CONTACT AFTER HERMES, HUH?
I LOOKED HER UP ABOUT TEN YEARS LATER.

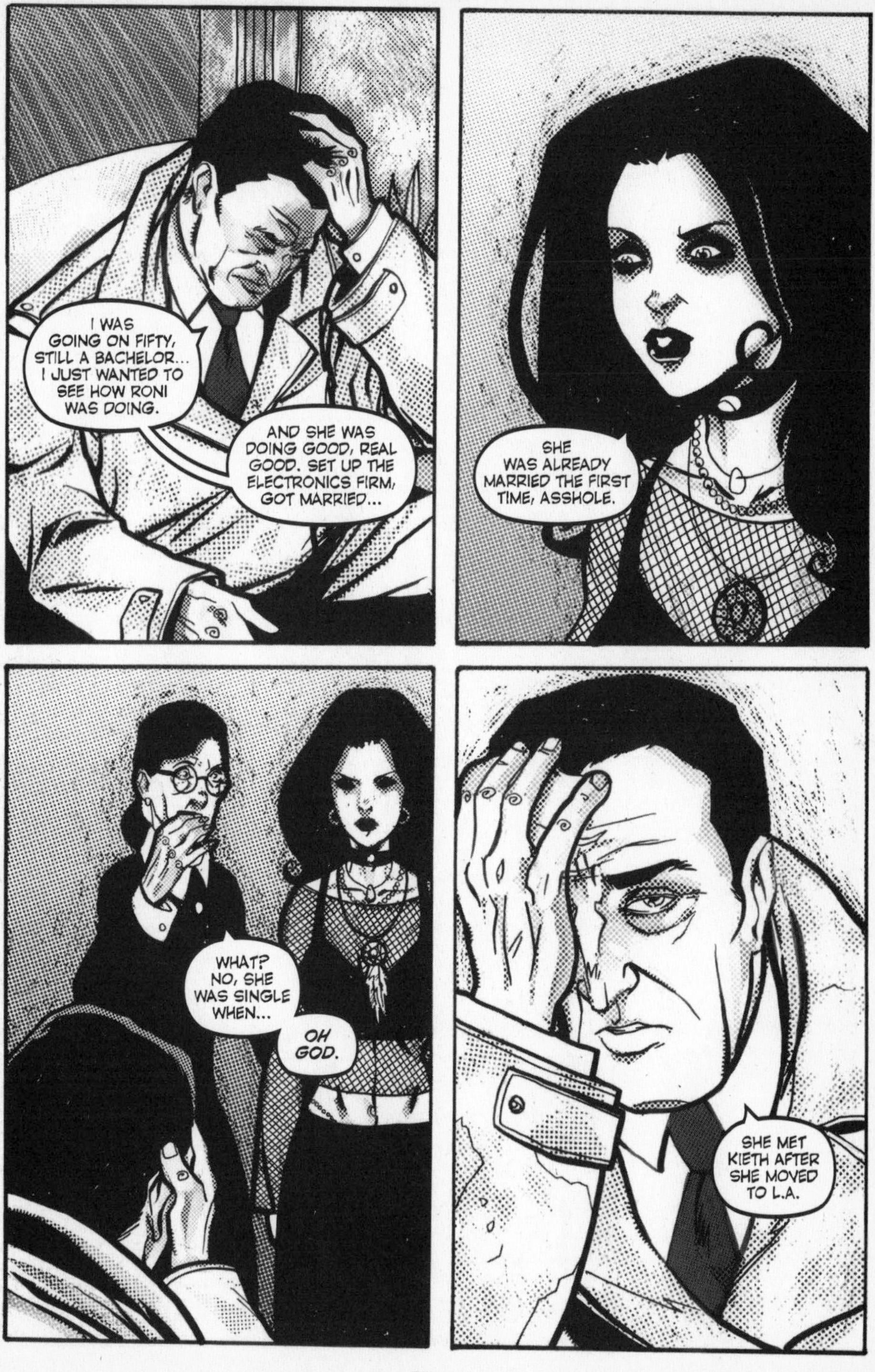
I WAS GOING ON FIFTY, STILL A BACHELOR... I JUST WANTED TO SEE HOW RONI WAS DOING.
AND SHE WAS DOING GOOD, REAL GOOD. SET UP THE ELECTRONICS FIRM, GOT MARRIED...
SHE WAS ALREADY MARRIED THE FIRST TIME, ASSHOLE.
WHAT? NO, SHE WAS SINGLE WHEN...
OH GOD.
SHE MET KIETH AFTER SHE MOVED TO L.A.

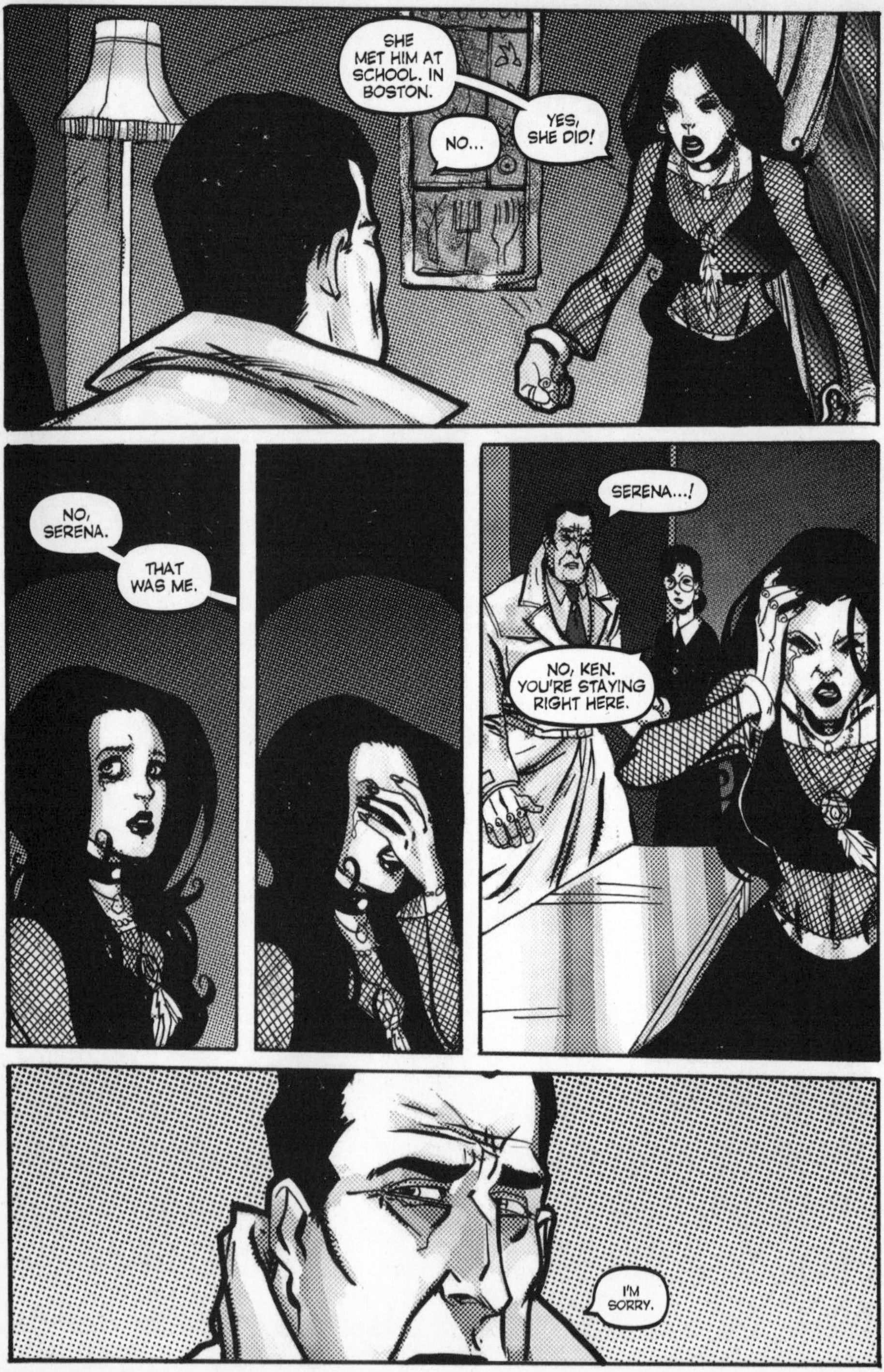
SHE MET HIM AT SCHOOL. IN BOSTON.
NO...
YES, SHE DID!
NO, SERENA.
THAT WAS ME.
SERENA...!
NO, KEN. YOU'RE STAYING RIGHT HERE.
I'M SORRY.

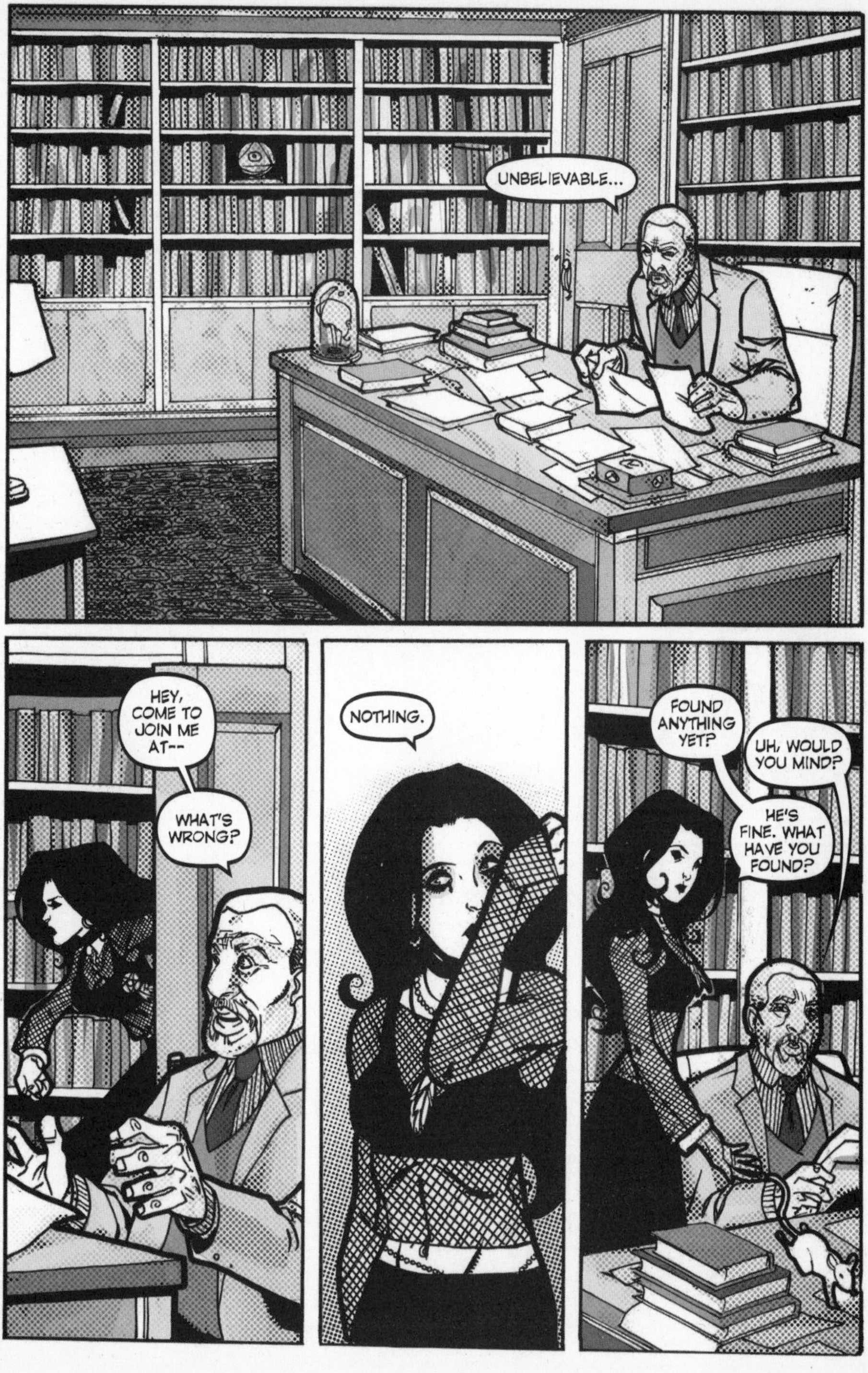
UNBELIEVABLE...
HEY, COME TO JOIN ME AT--
WHAT'S WRONG?
NOTHING.
FOUND ANYTHING YET?
UH, WOULD YOU MIND?
HE'S FINE. WHAT HAVE YOU FOUND?

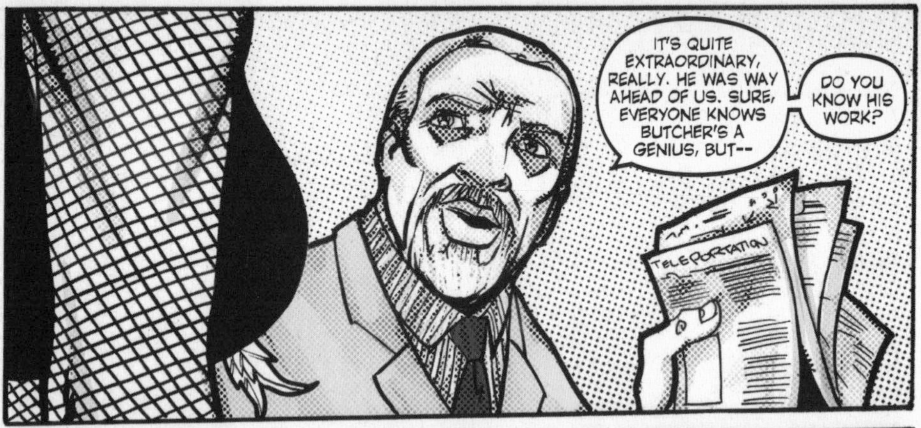
IT'S QUITE EXTRAORDINARY, REALLY. HE WAS WAY AHEAD OF US. SURE, EVERYONE KNOWS BUTCHER'S A GENIUS, BUT--
DO YOU KNOW HIS WORK?
TELEPORTATION

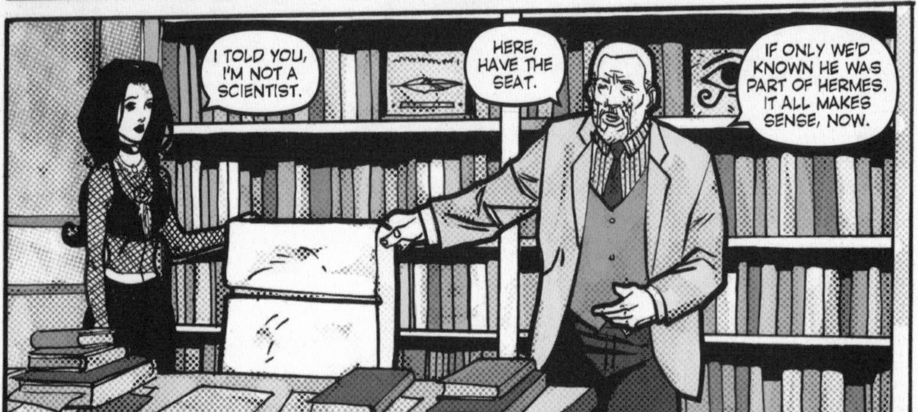
I TOLD YOU, I'M NOT A SCIENTIST.
HERE, HAVE THE SEAT.
IF ONLY WE'D KNOWN HE WAS PART OF HERMES. IT ALL MAKES SENSE, NOW.

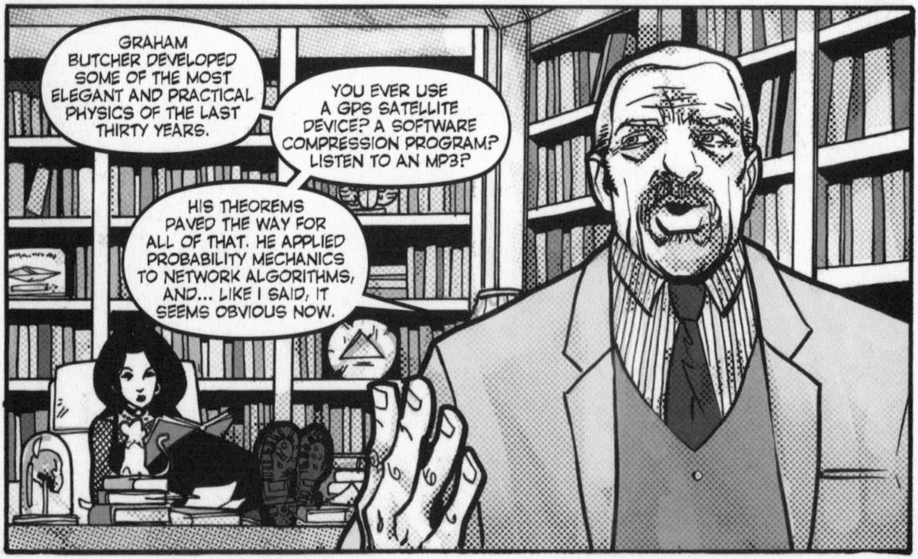
GRAHAM BUTCHER DEVELOPED SOME OF THE MOST ELEGANT AND PRACTICAL PHYSICS OF THE LAST THIRTY YEARS.
YOU EVER USE A GPS SATELLITE DEVICE? A SOFTWARE COMPRESSION PROGRAM? LISTEN TO AN MP3?
HIS THEOREMS PAVED THE WAY FOR ALL OF THAT. HE APPLIED PROBABILITY MECHANICS TO NETWORK ALGORITHMS, AND... LIKE I SAID, IT SEEMS OBVIOUS NOW.

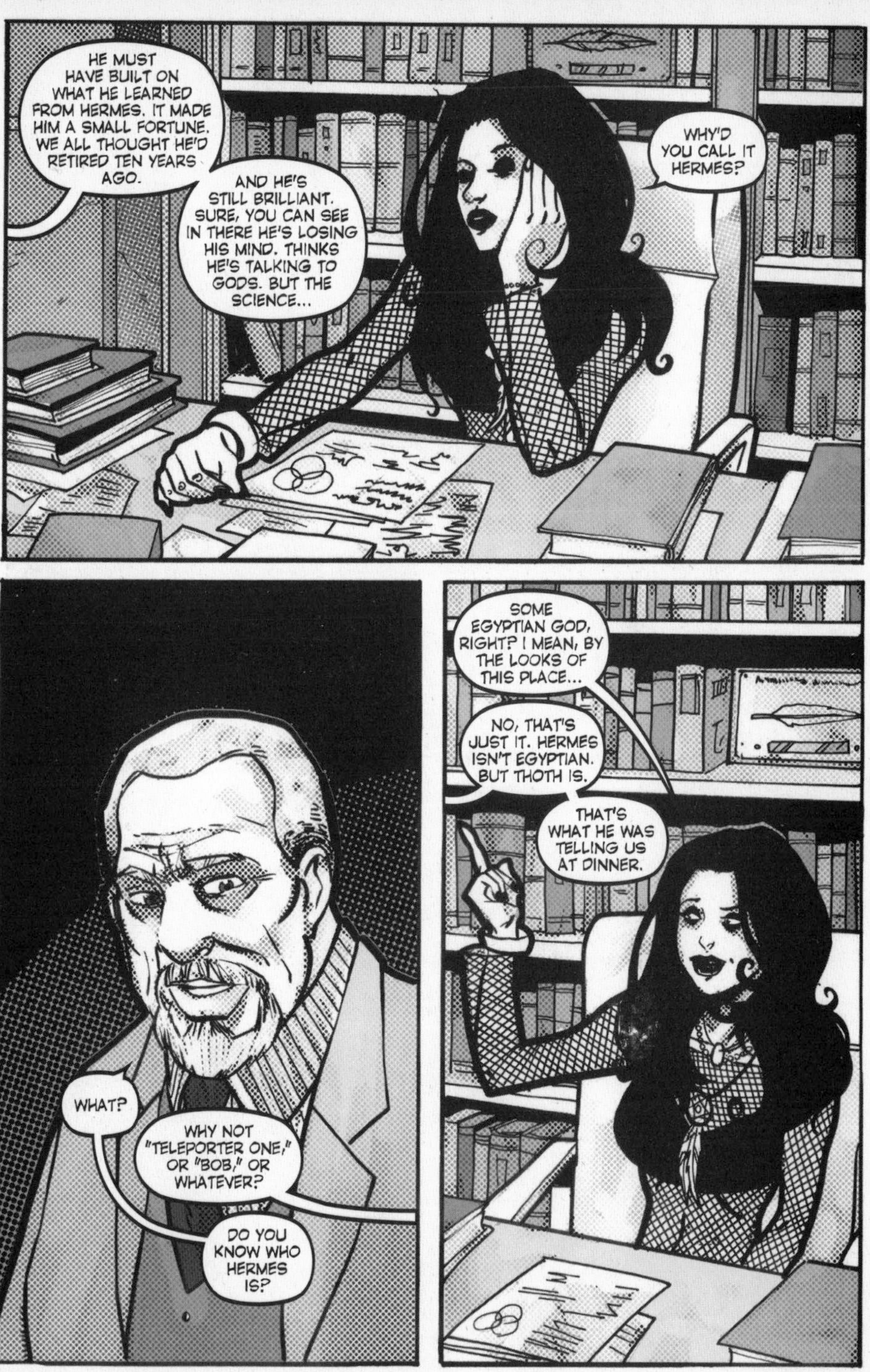
HE MUST HAVE BUILT ON WHAT HE LEARNED FROM HERMES. IT MADE HIM A SMALL FORTUNE. WE ALL THOUGHT HE'D RETIRED TEN YEARS AGO.
AND HE'S STILL BRILLIANT. SURE, YOU CAN SEE IN THERE HE'S LOSING HIS MIND. THINKS HE'S TALKING TO GODS. BUT THE SCIENCE...
WHY'D YOU CALL IT HERMES?
WHAT?
WHY NOT "TELEPORTER ONE," OR "BOB," OR WHATEVER?
DO YOU KNOW WHO HERMES IS?
SOME EGYPTIAN GOD, RIGHT? I MEAN, BY THE LOOKS OF THIS PLACE...
NO, THAT'S JUST IT. HERMES ISN'T EGYPTIAN. BUT THOTH IS.
THAT'S WHAT HE WAS TELLING US AT DINNER.

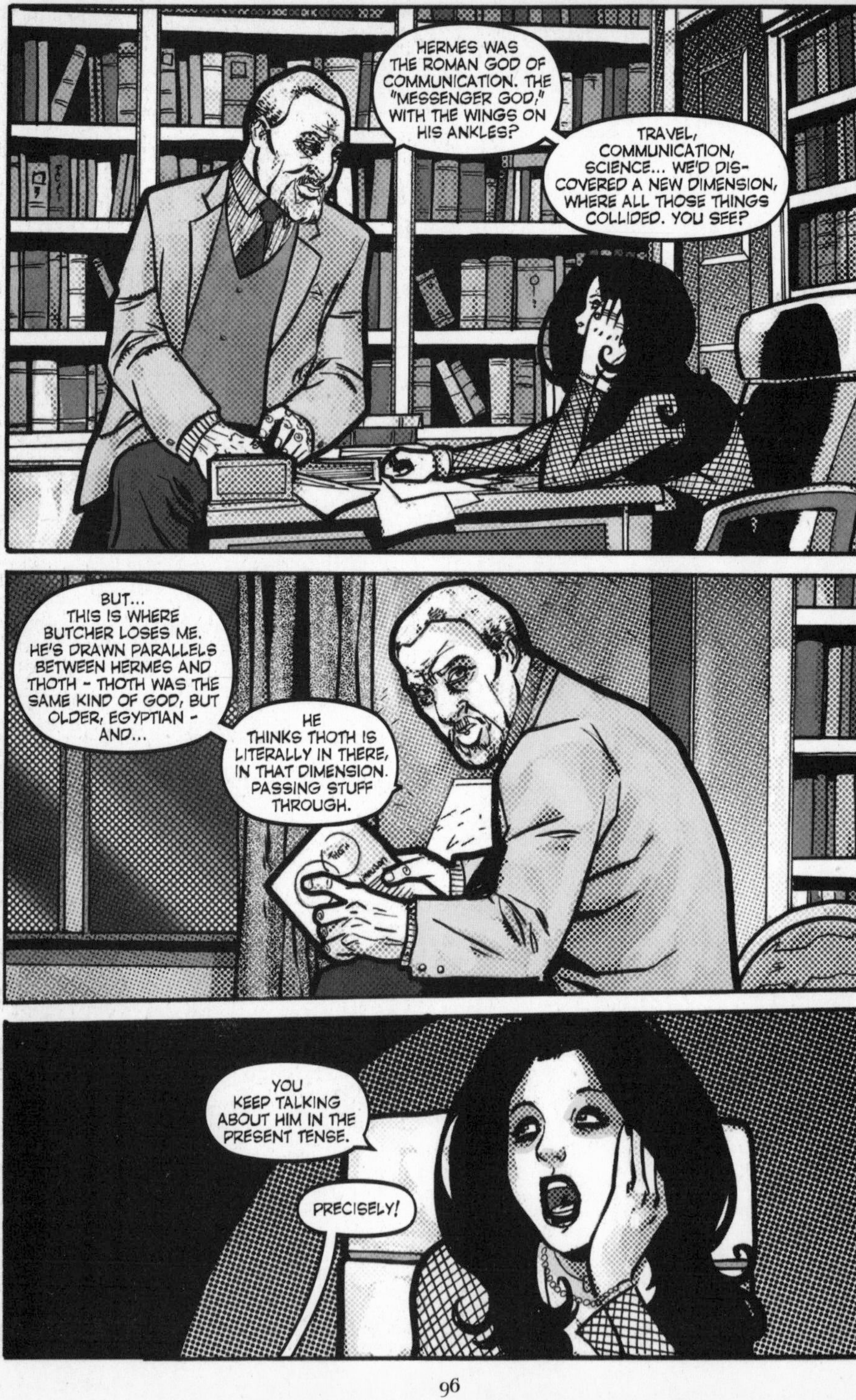
HERMES WAS THE ROMAN GOD OF COMMUNICATION. THE "MESSENGER GOD," WITH THE WINGS ON HIS ANKLES?
TRAVEL, COMMUNICATION, SCIENCE... WE'D DISCOVERED A NEW DIMENSION, WHERE ALL THOSE THINGS COLLIDED. YOU SEE?
BUT... THIS IS WHERE BUTCHER LOSES ME. HE'S DRAWN PARALLELS BETWEEN HERMES AND THOTH - THOTH WAS THE SAME KIND OF GOD, BUT OLDER, EGYPTIAN - AND...
HE THINKS THOTH IS LITERALLY IN THERE, IN THAT DIMENSION. PASSING STUFF THROUGH.
YOU KEEP TALKING ABOUT HIM IN THE PRESENT TENSE.
PRECISELY!

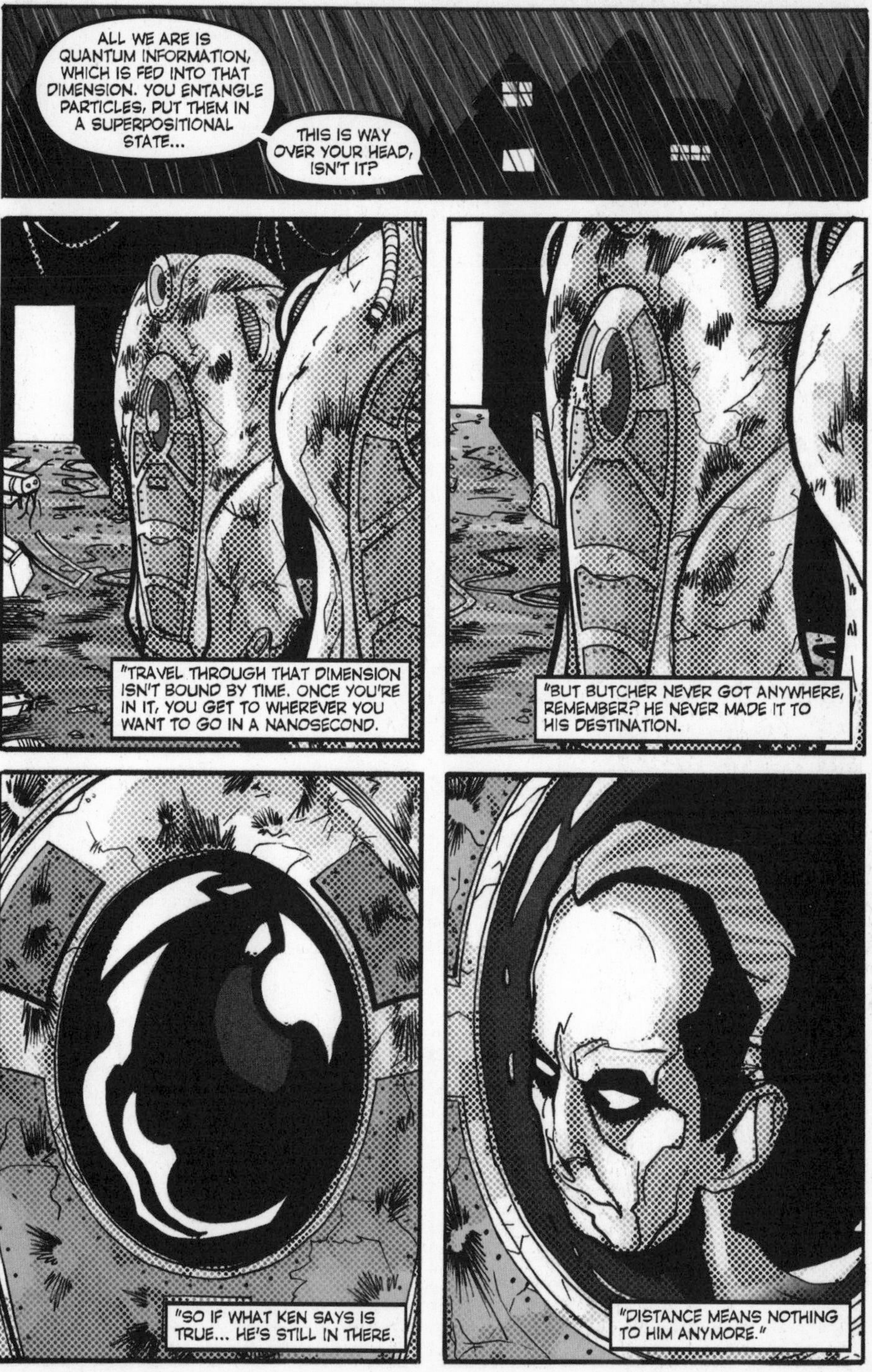

ALL WE ARE IS QUANTUM INFORMATION, WHICH IS FED INTO THAT DIMENSION. YOU ENTANGLE PARTICLES, PUT THEM IN A SUPERPOSITIONAL STATE...
THIS IS WAY OVER YOUR HEAD, ISN'T IT?
"TRAVEL THROUGH THAT DIMENSION ISN'T BOUND BY TIME. ONCE YOU'RE IN IT, YOU GET TO WHEREVER YOU WANT TO GO IN A NANOSECOND.
"BUT BUTCHER NEVER GOT ANYWHERE, REMEMBER? HE NEVER MADE IT TO HIS DESTINATION.
"SO IF WHAT KEN SAYS IS TRUE... HE'S STILL IN THERE.
"DISTANCE MEANS NOTHING TO HIM ANYMORE."

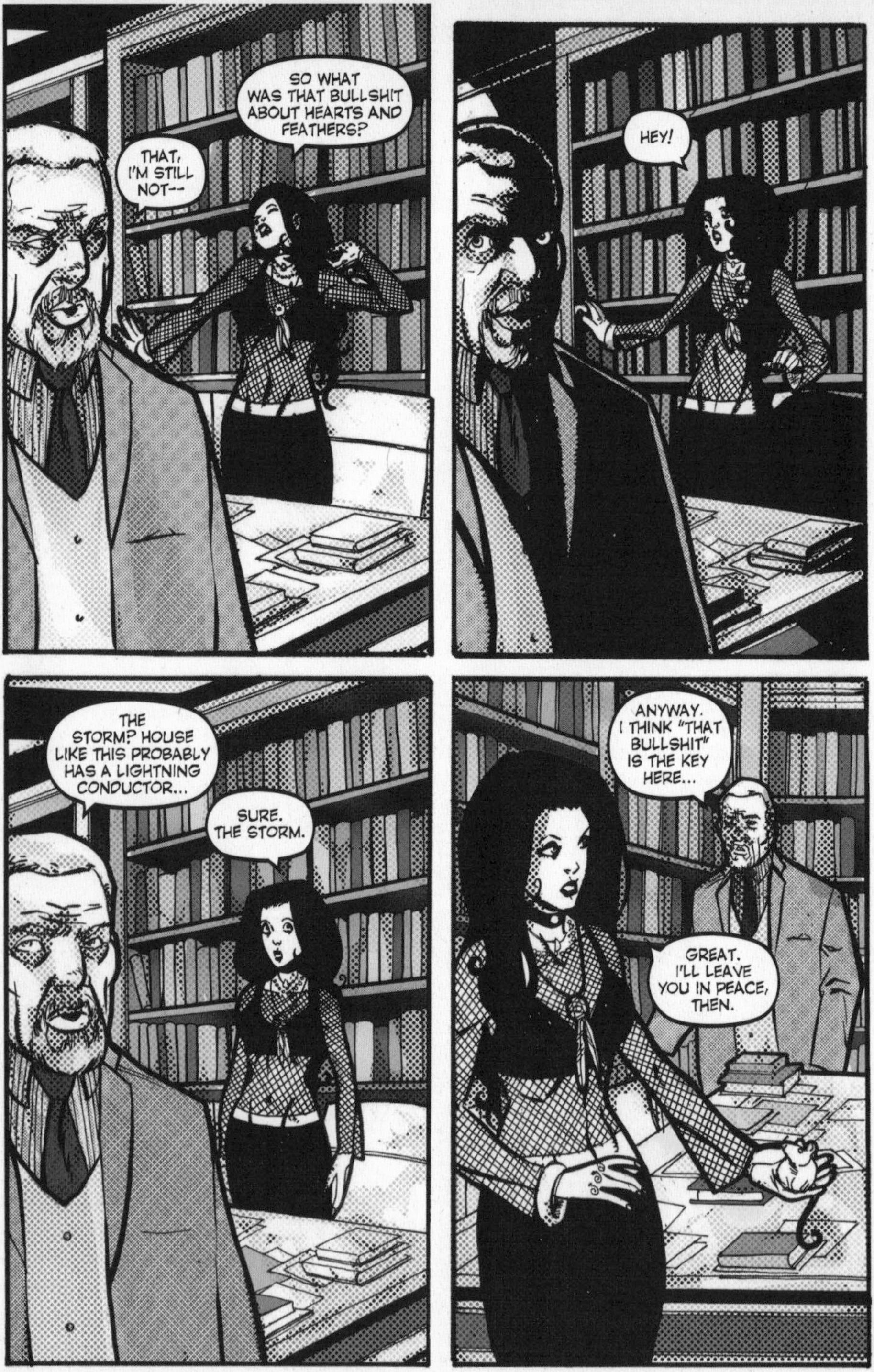
SO WHAT WAS THAT BULLSHIT ABOUT HEARTS AND FEATHERS?
THAT, I'M STILL NOT--
HEY!
THE STORM? HOUSE LIKE THIS PROBABLY HAS A LIGHTNING CONDUCTOR...
SURE. THE STORM.
ANYWAY. I THINK "THAT BULLSHIT" IS THE KEY HERE...
GREAT. I'LL LEAVE YOU IN PEACE, THEN.

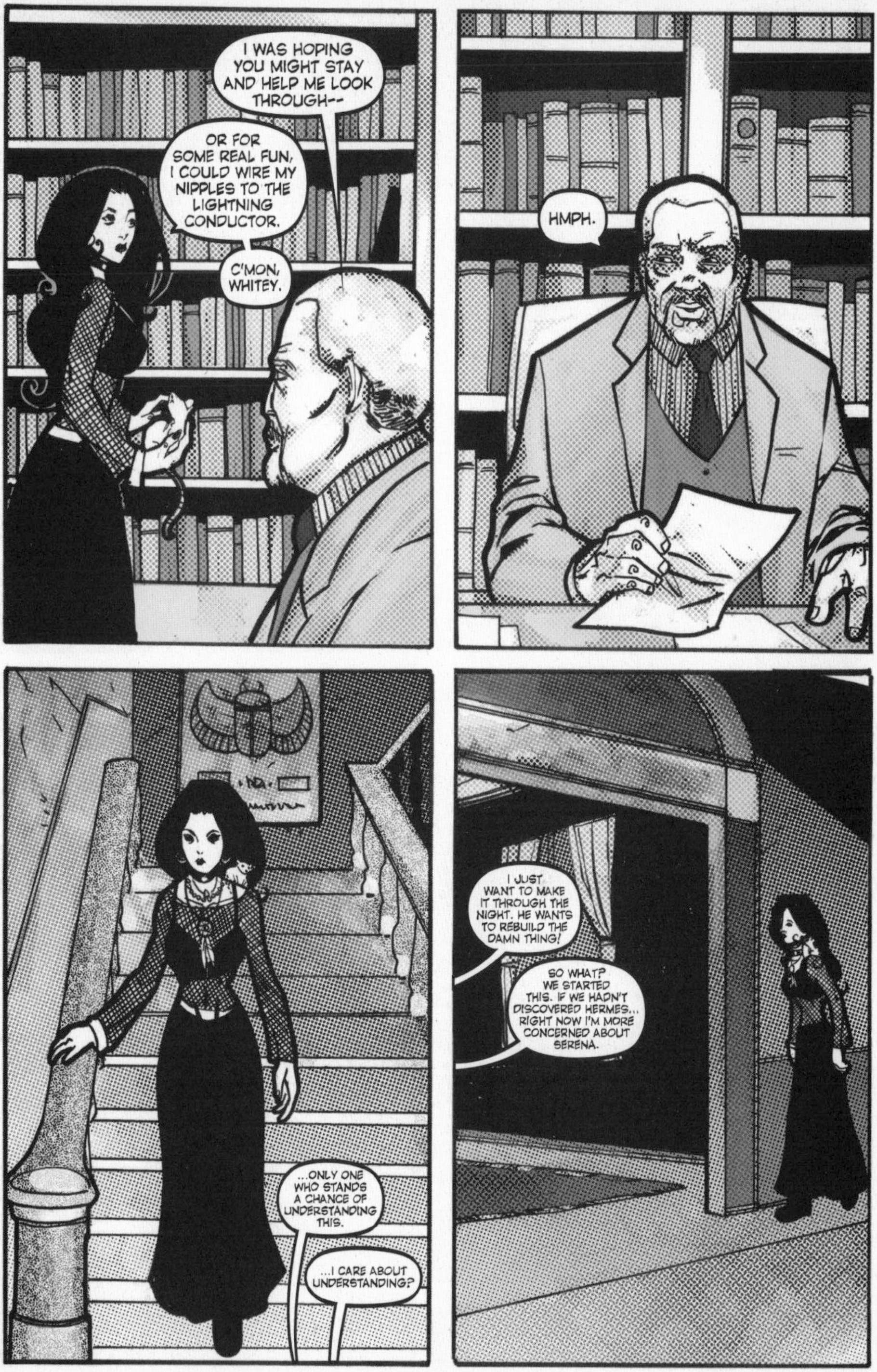
I WAS HOPING YOU MIGHT STAY AND HELP ME LOOK THROUGH--
OR FOR SOME REAL FUN, I COULD WIRE MY NIPPLES TO THE LIGHTNING CONDUCTOR.
C'MON, WHITEY.
HMPH.
...ONLY ONE WHO STANDS A CHANCE OF UNDERSTANDING THIS.
...I CARE ABOUT UNDERSTANDING?
I JUST WANT TO MAKE IT THROUGH THE NIGHT. HE WANTS TO REBUILD THE DAMN THING!
SO WHAT? WE STARTED THIS. IF WE HADN'T DISCOVERED HERMES... RIGHT NOW I'M MORE CONCERNED ABOUT SERENA.

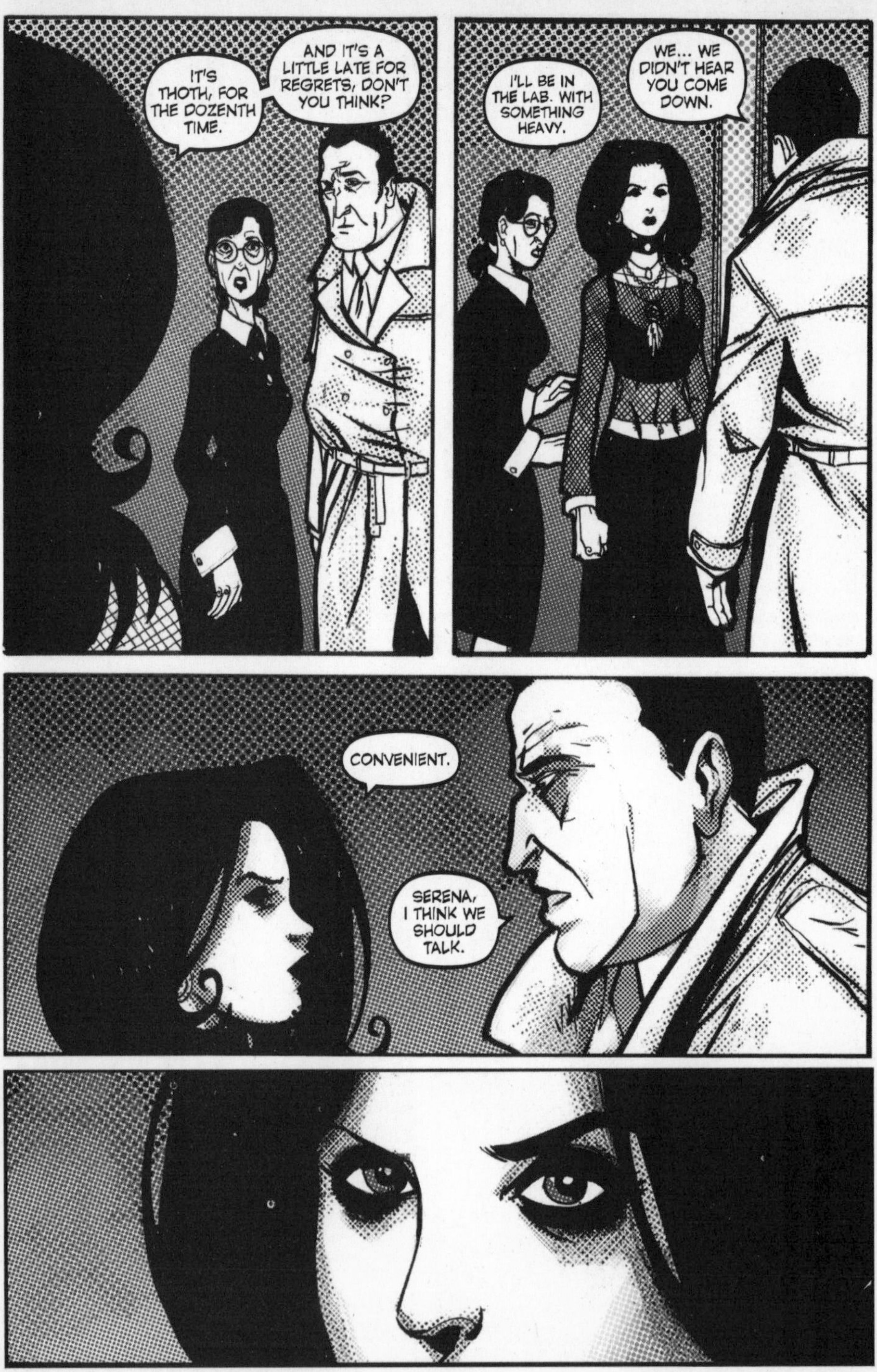
IT'S THOTH, FOR THE DOZENTH TIME.
AND IT'S A LITTLE LATE FOR REGRETS, DON'T YOU THINK?
WE... WE DIDN'T HEAR YOU COME DOWN.
I'LL BE IN THE LAB. WITH SOMETHING HEAVY.
CONVENIENT.
SERENA, I THINK WE SHOULD TALK.

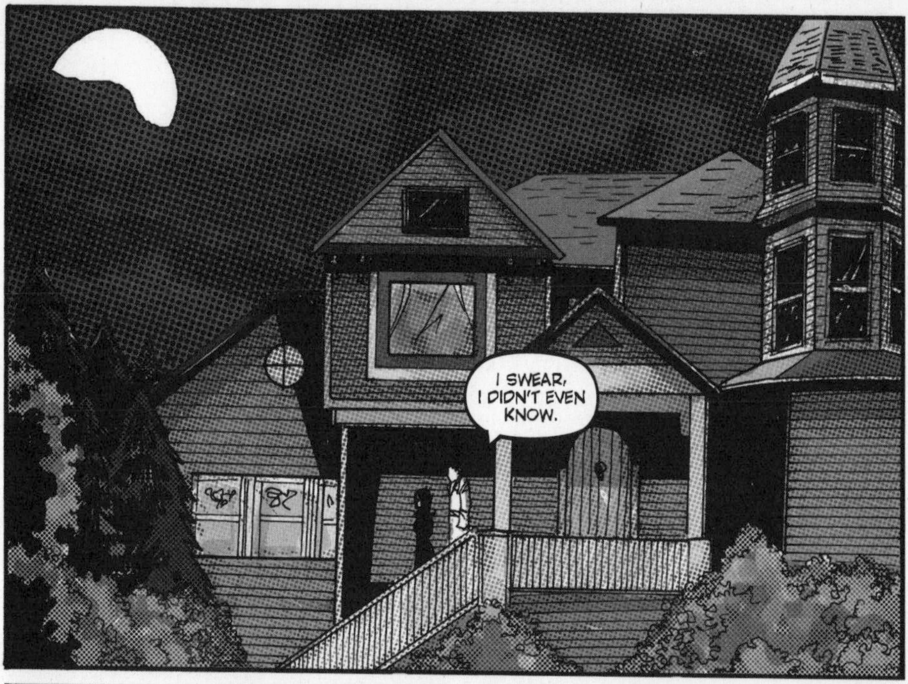
I SWEAR, I DIDN'T EVEN KNOW.
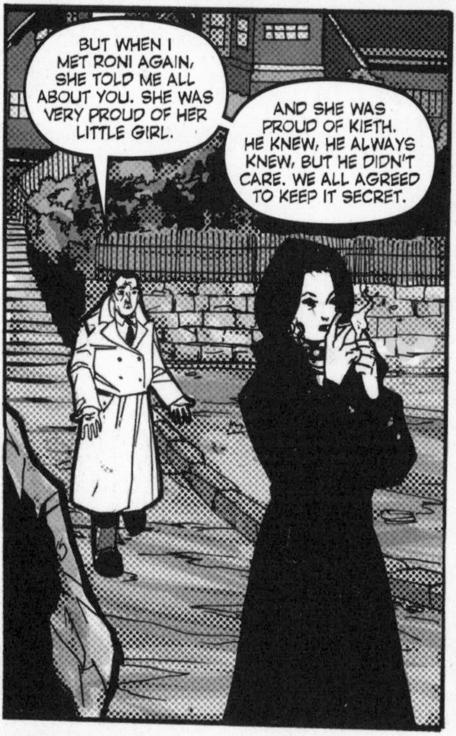
BUT WHEN I MET RONI AGAIN, SHE TOLD ME ALL ABOUT YOU. SHE WAS VERY PROUD OF HER LITTLE GIRL.
AND SHE WAS PROUD OF KIETH. HE KNEW, HE ALWAYS KNEW, BUT HE DIDN'T CARE. WE ALL AGREED TO KEEP IT SECRET.
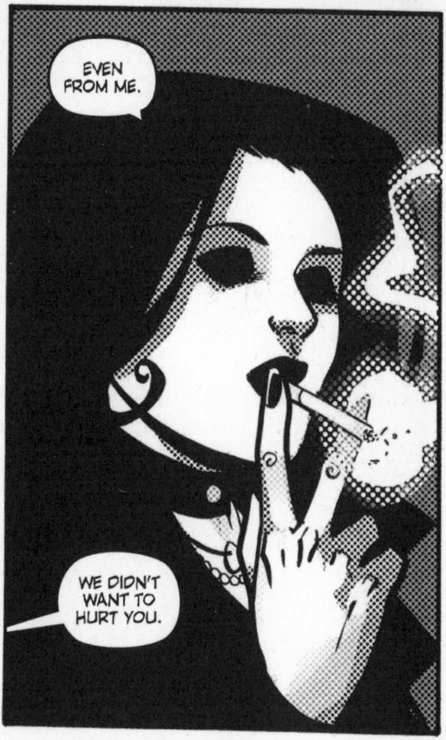
EVEN FROM ME.
WE DIDN'T WANT TO HURT YOU.

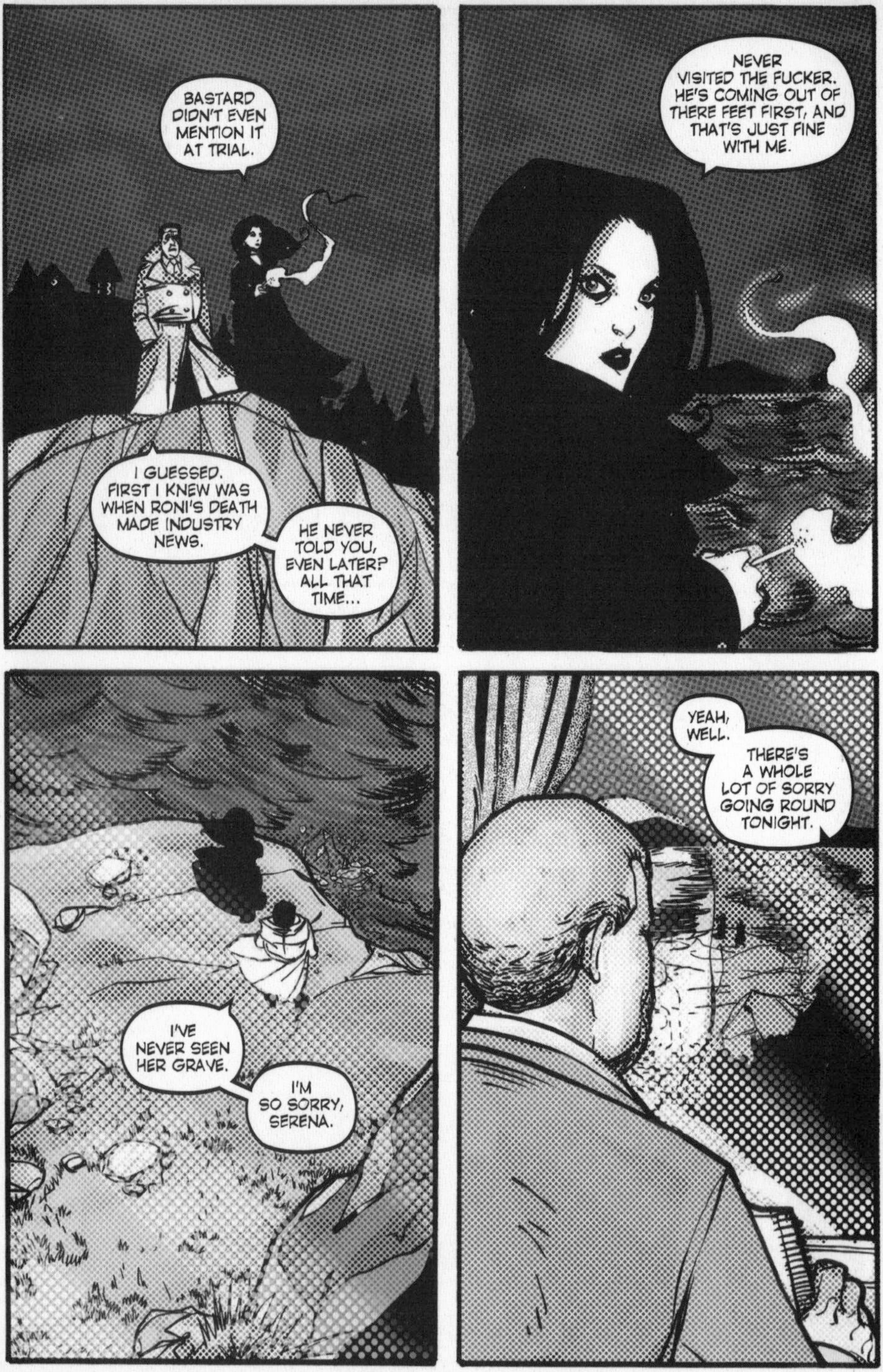
BASTARD DIDN'T EVEN MENTION IT AT TRIAL.
I GUESSED. FIRST I KNEW WAS WHEN RONI'S DEATH MADE INDUSTRY NEWS.
HE NEVER TOLD YOU, EVEN LATER? ALL THAT TIME...
NEVER VISITED THE FUCKER. HE'S COMING OUT OF THERE FEET FIRST, AND THAT'S JUST FINE WITH ME.
I'VE NEVER SEEN HER GRAVE.
I'M SO SORRY, SERENA.
YEAH, WELL.
THERE'S A WHOLE LOT OF SORRY GOING ROUND TONIGHT.

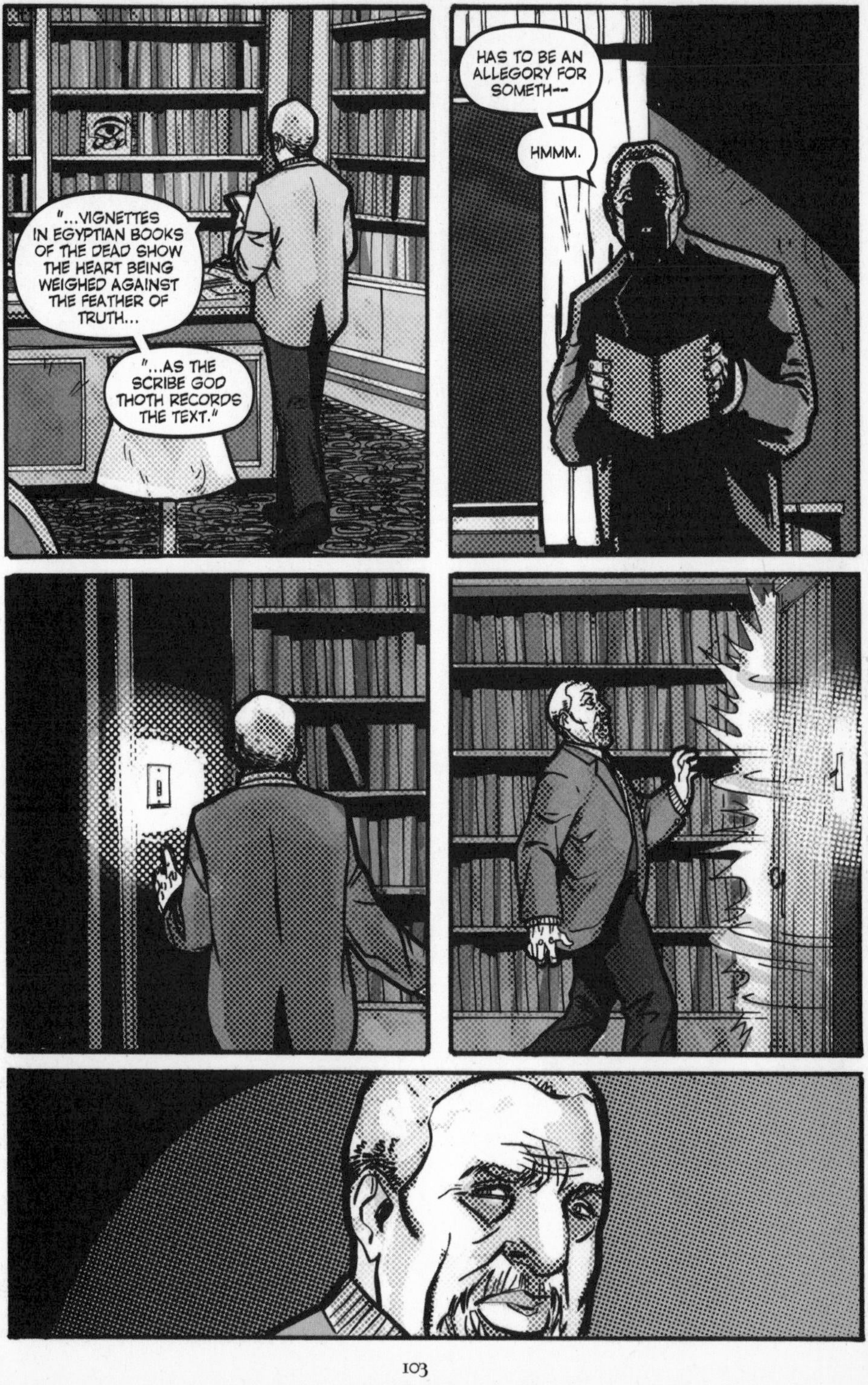
"...VIGNETTES IN EGYPTIAN BOOKS OF THE DEAD SHOW THE HEART BEING WEIGHED AGAINST THE FEATHER OF TRUTH...
"...AS THE SCRIBE GOD THOTH RECORDS THE TEXT."
HAS TO BE AN ALLEGORY FOR SOMETH--
HMMM.

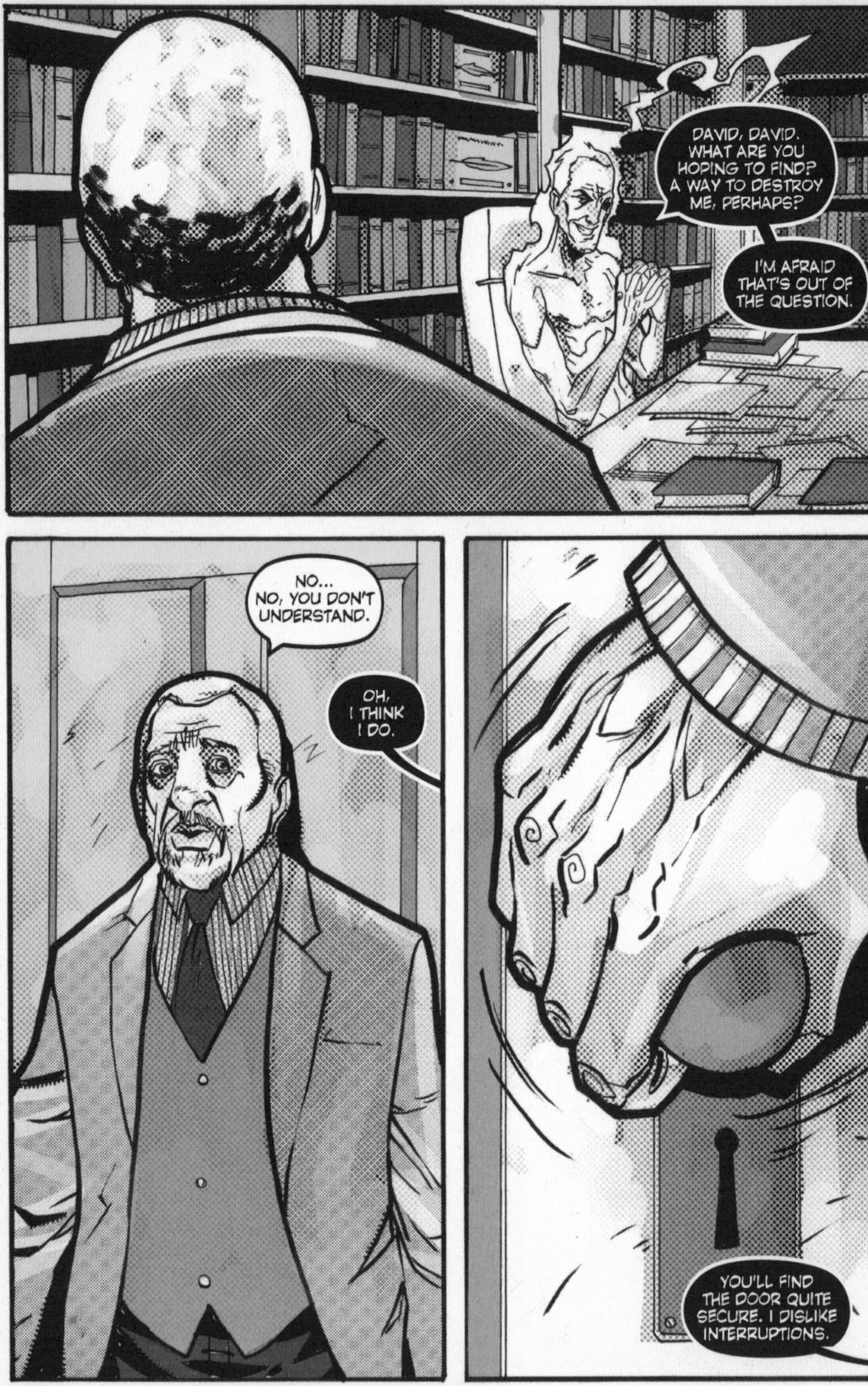
DAVID, DAVID. WHAT ARE YOU HOPING TO FIND? A WAY TO DESTROY ME, PERHAPS?
I'M AFRAID THAT'S OUT OF THE QUESTION.
NO... NO, YOU DON'T UNDERSTAND.
OH, I THINK I DO.
YOU'LL FIND THE DOOR QUITE SECURE. I DISLIKE INTERRUPTIONS.

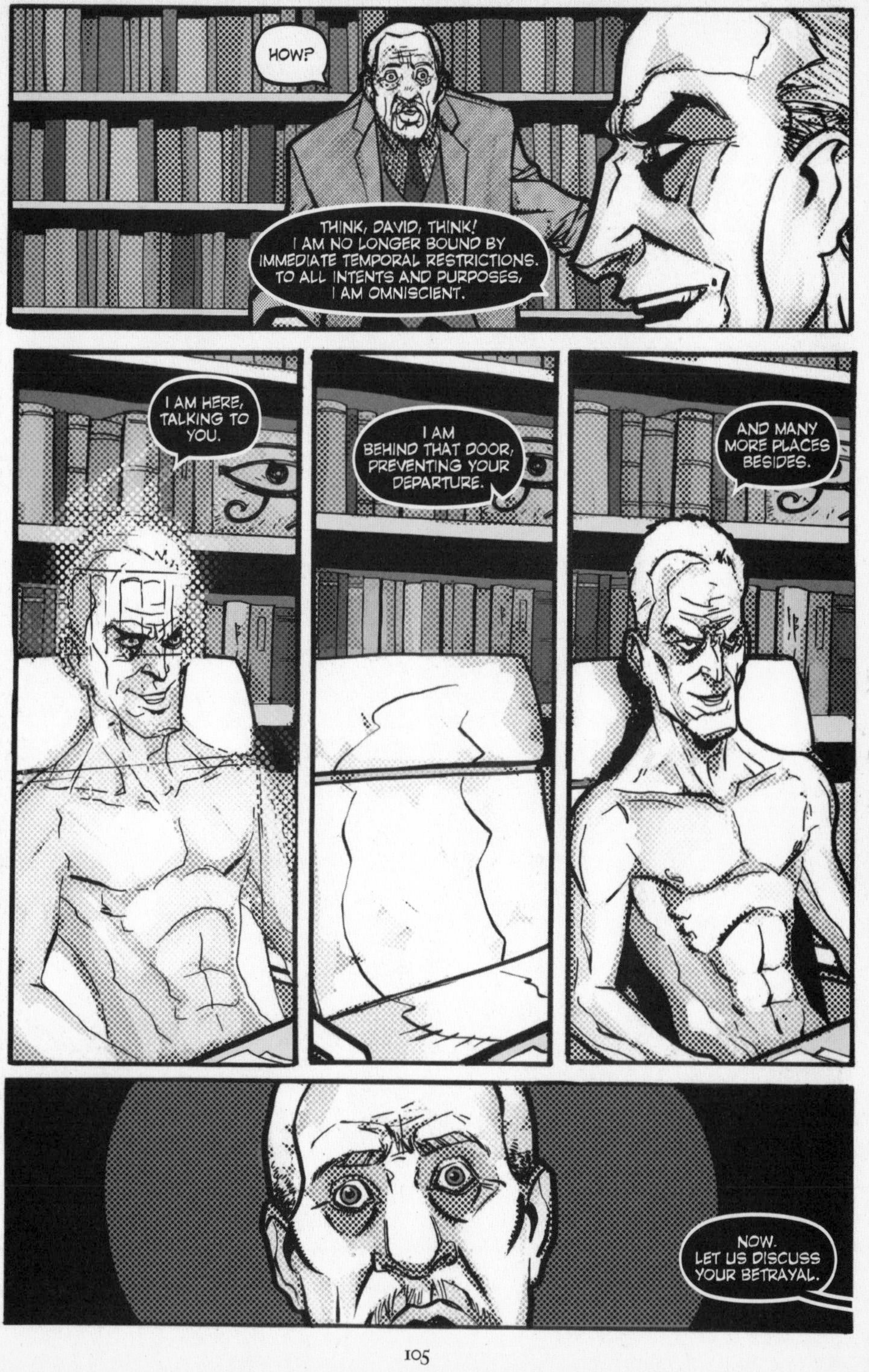
HOW?
THINK, DAVID, THINK! I AM NO LONGER BOUND BY IMMEDIATE TEMPORAL RESTRICTIONS. TO ALL INTENTS AND PURPOSES, I AM OMNISCIENT.
I AM HERE, TALKING TO YOU.
I AM BEHIND THAT DOOR, PREVENTING YOUR DEPARTURE.
AND MANY MORE PLACES BESIDES.
NOW. LET US DISCUSS YOUR BETRAYAL.

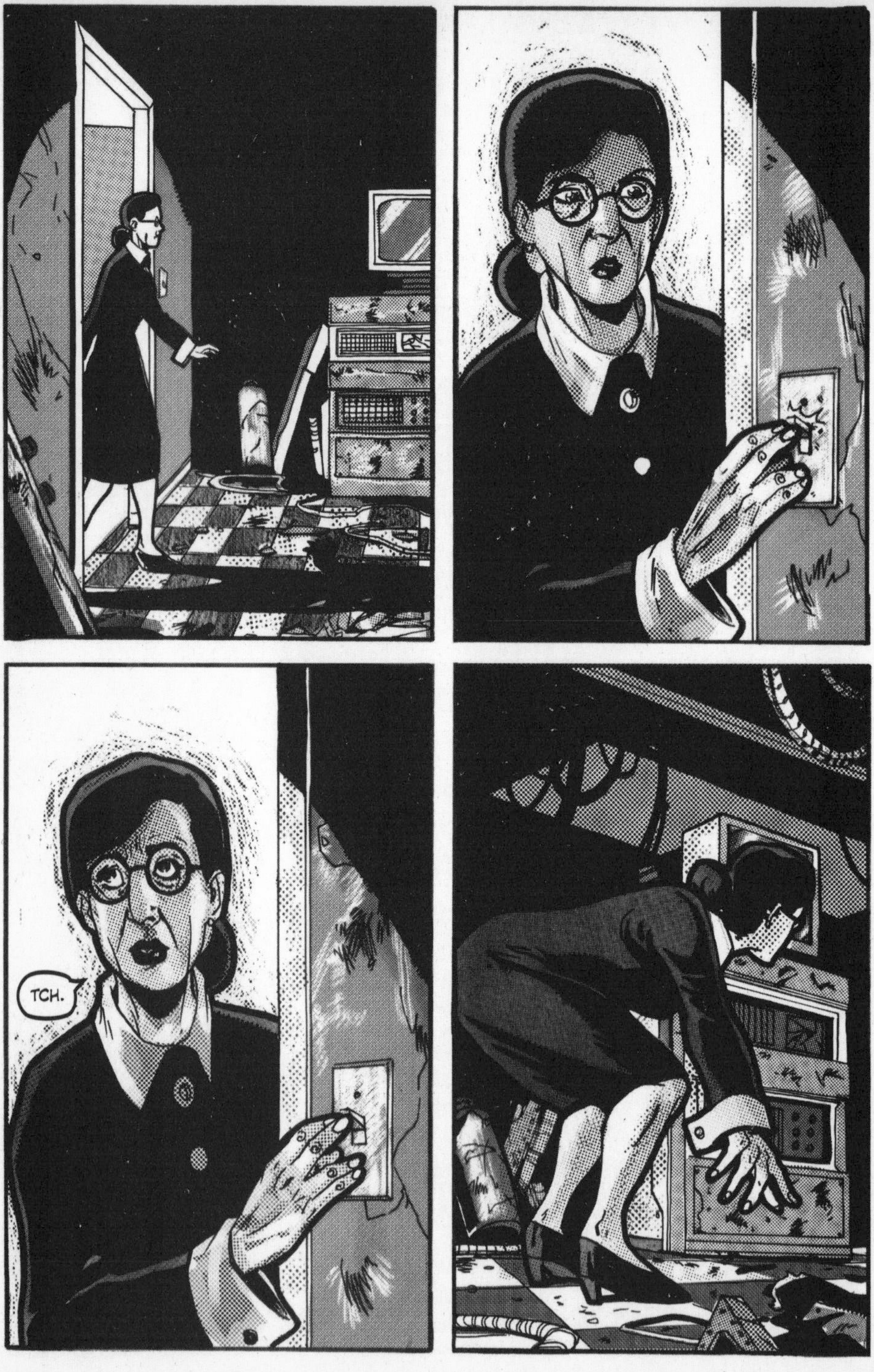
TCH.

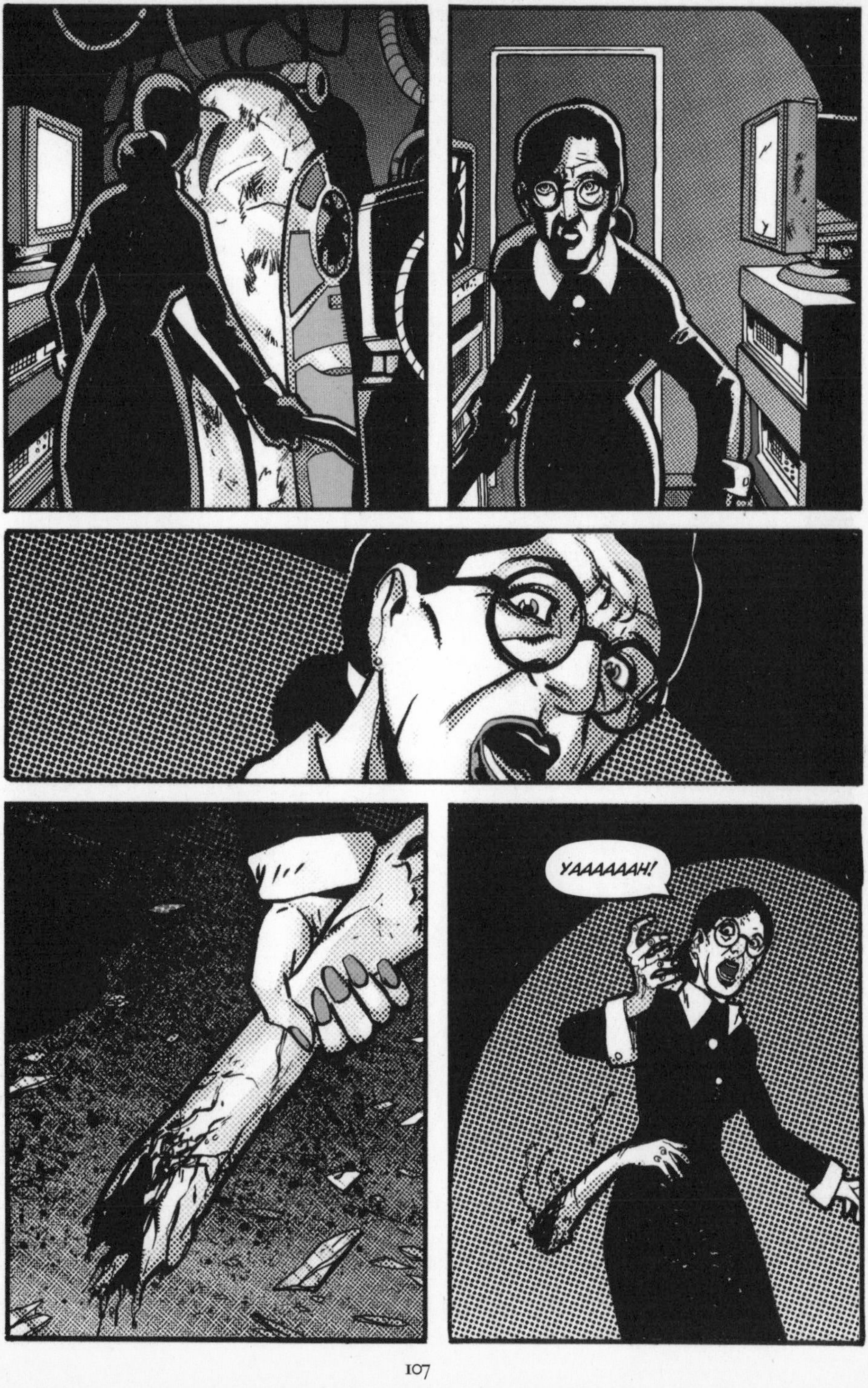
YAAAAAAH!

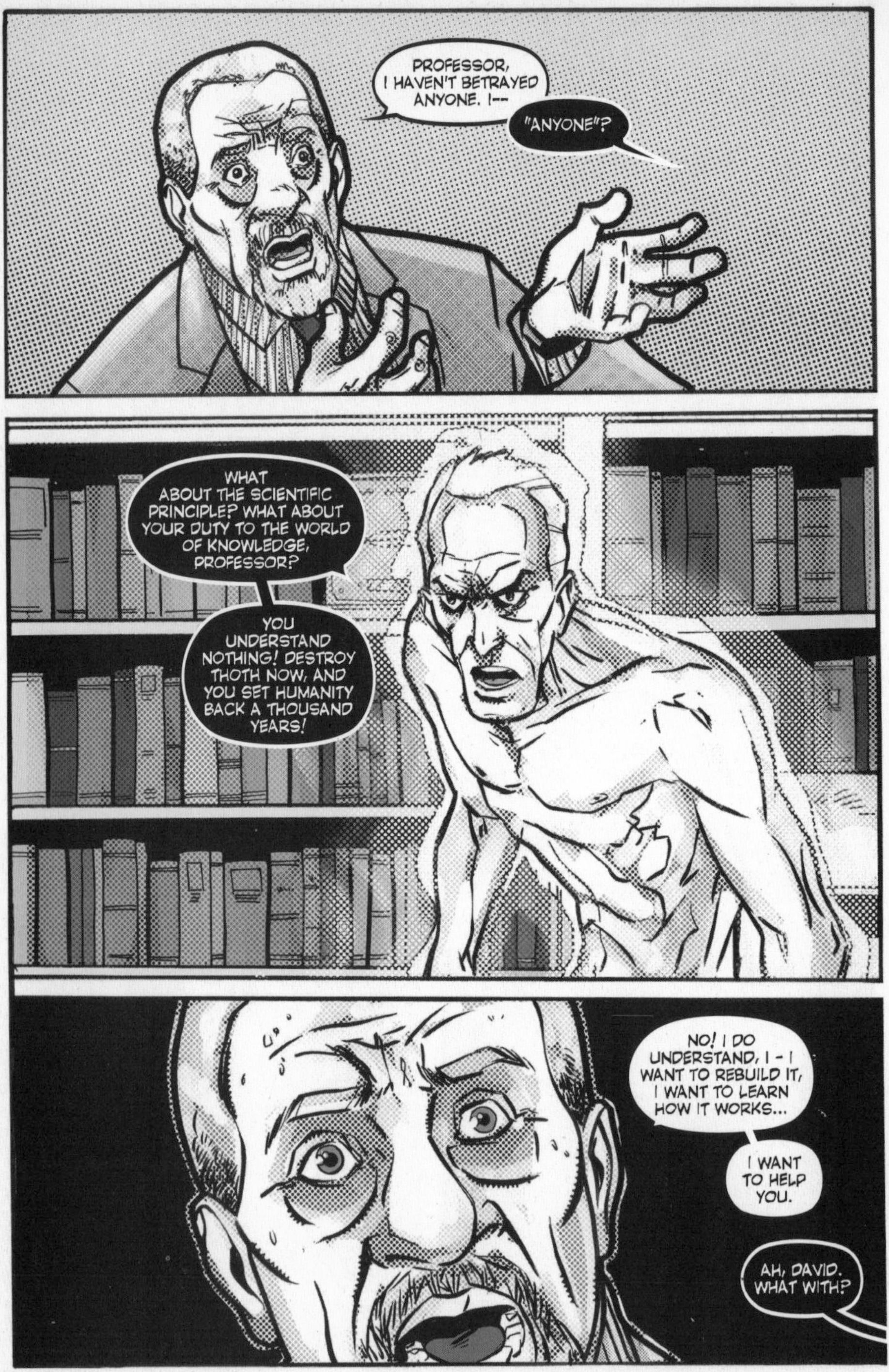
PROFESSOR, I HAVEN'T BETRAYED ANYONE. I--
"ANYONE"?
WHAT ABOUT THE SCIENTIFIC PRINCIPLE? WHAT ABOUT YOUR DUTY TO THE WORLD OF KNOWLEDGE, PROFESSOR?
YOU UNDERSTAND NOTHING! DESTROY THOTH NOW, AND YOU SET HUMANITY BACK A THOUSAND YEARS!
NO! I DO UNDERSTAND, I - I WANT TO REBUILD IT, I WANT TO LEARN HOW IT WORKS...
I WANT TO HELP YOU.
AH, DAVID. WHAT WITH?

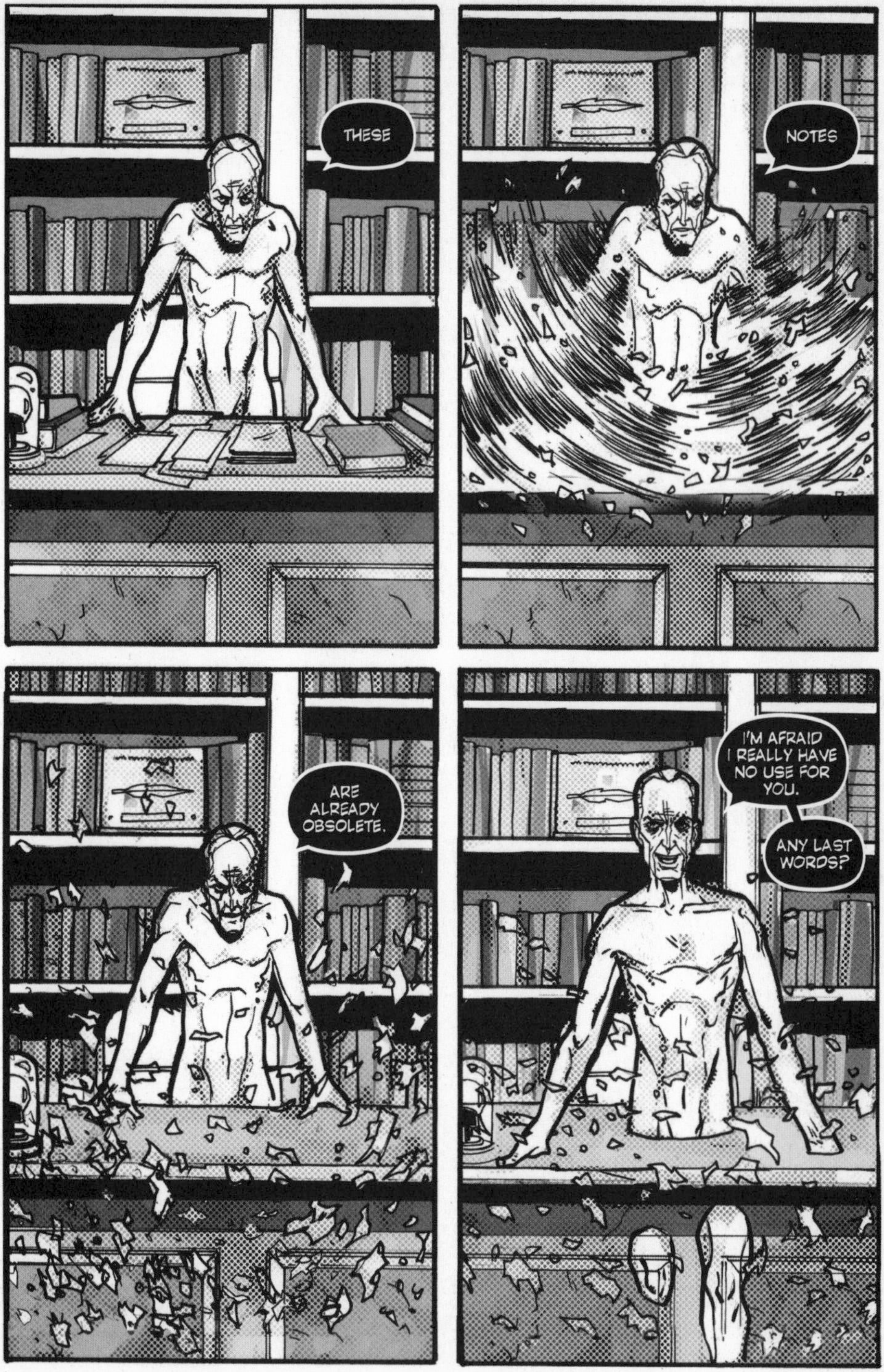
THESE
NOTES
ARE ALREADY OBSOLETE.
I'M AFRAID I REALLY HAVE NO USE FOR YOU.
ANY LAST WORDS?

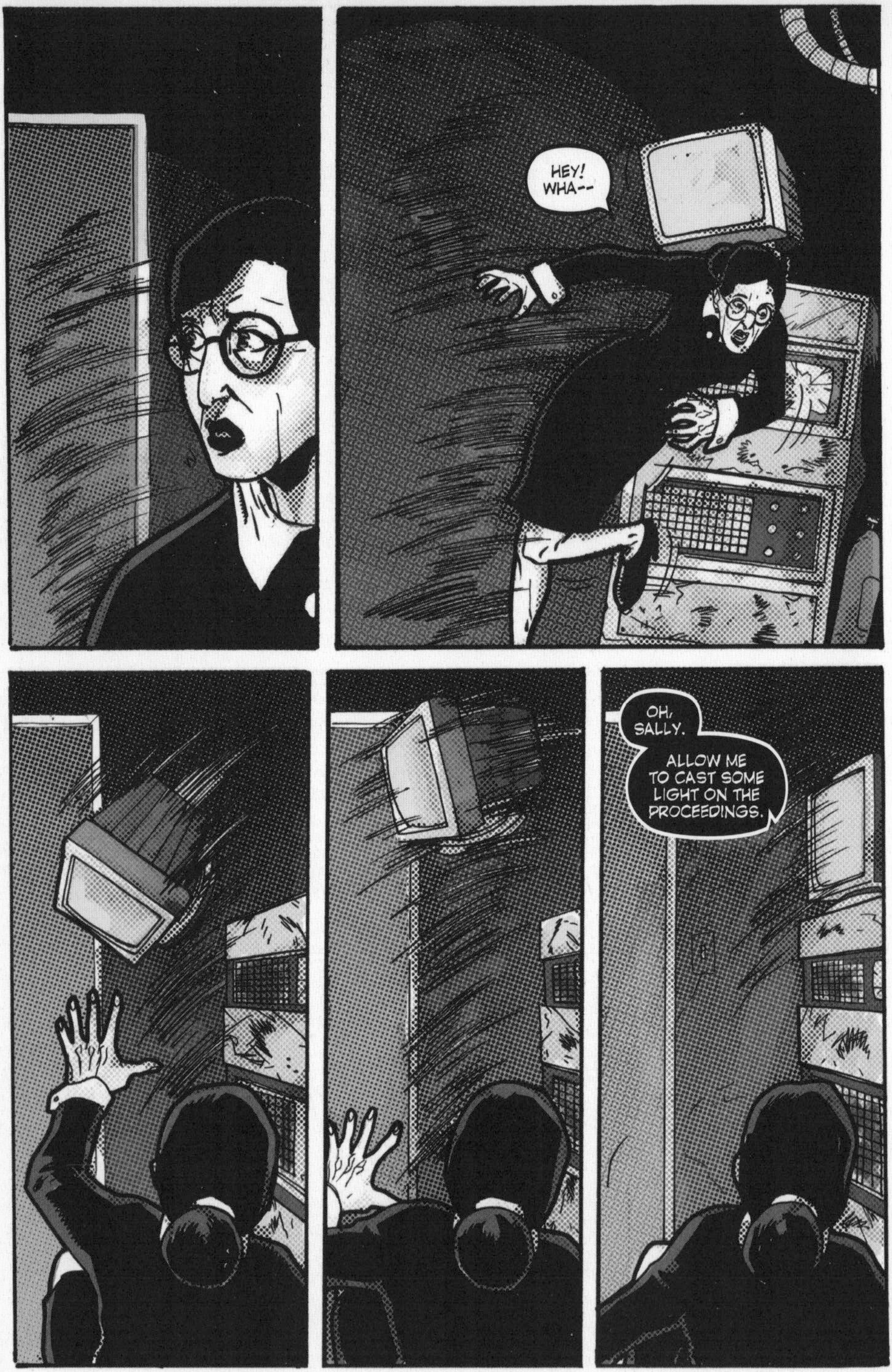
HEY! WHA--
OH, SALLY.
ALLOW ME TO CAST SOME LIGHT ON THE PROCEEDINGS.

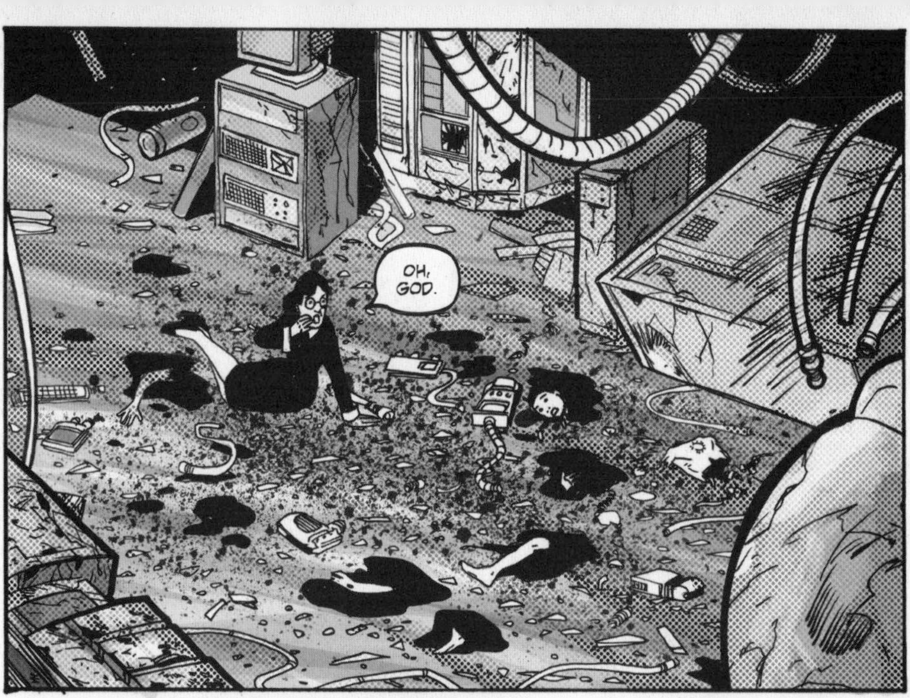
OH, GOD.

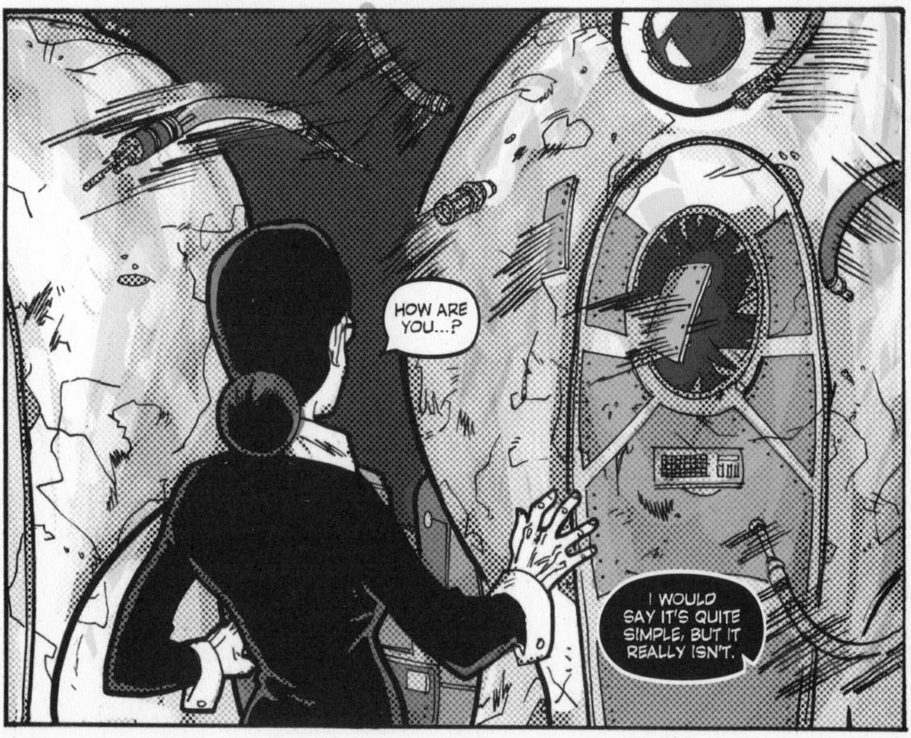
HOW ARE YOU...?
I WOULD SAY IT'S QUITE SIMPLE, BUT IT REALLY ISN'T.

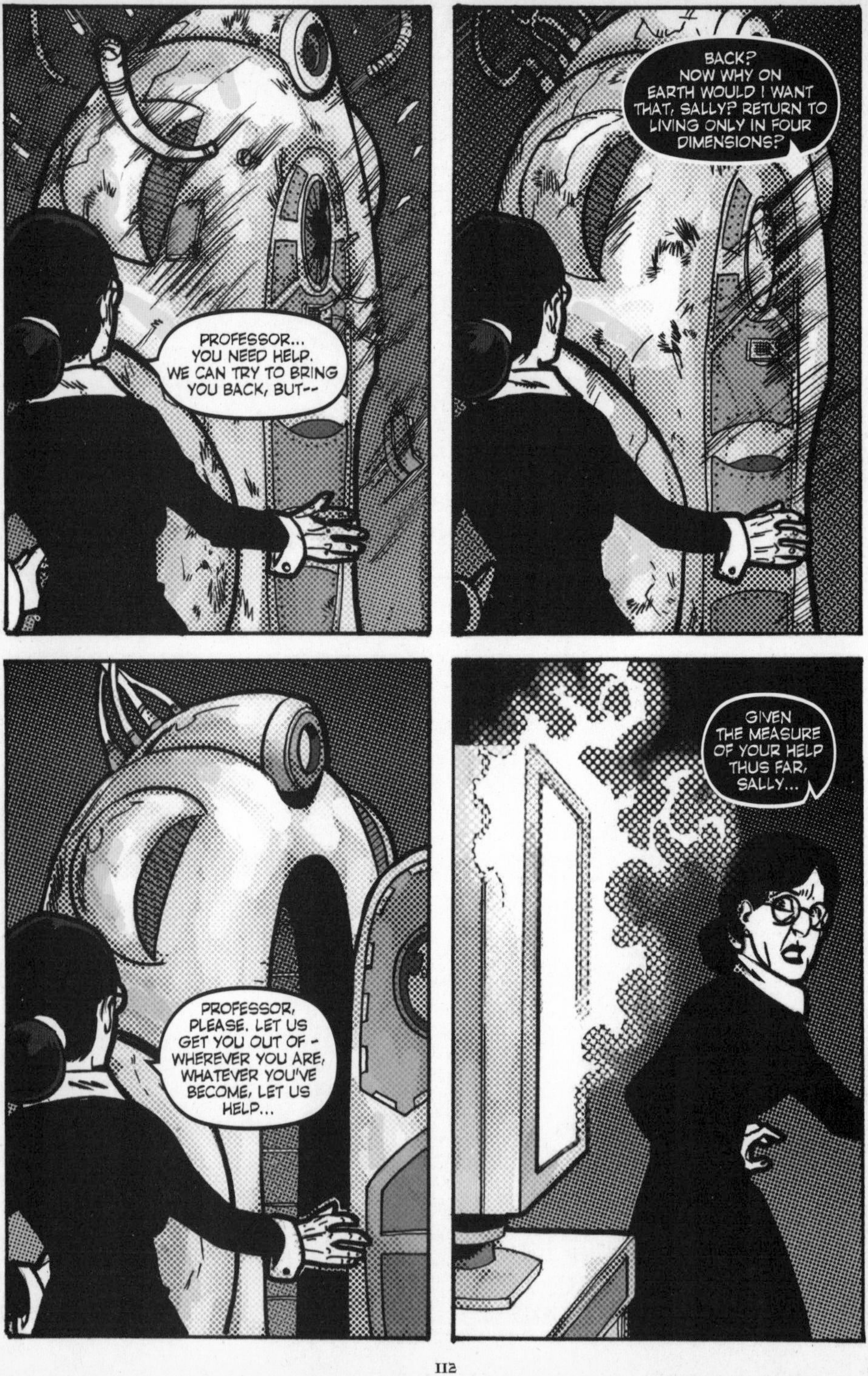
PROFESSOR... YOU NEED HELP. WE CAN TRY TO BRING YOU BACK, BUT--
BACK? NOW WHY ON EARTH WOULD I WANT THAT, SALLY? RETURN TO LIVING ONLY IN FOUR DIMENSIONS?
PROFESSOR, PLEASE. LET US GET YOU OUT OF - WHEREVER YOU ARE, WHATEVER YOU'VE BECOME, LET US HELP...
GIVEN THE MEASURE OF YOUR HELP THUS FAR, SALLY...

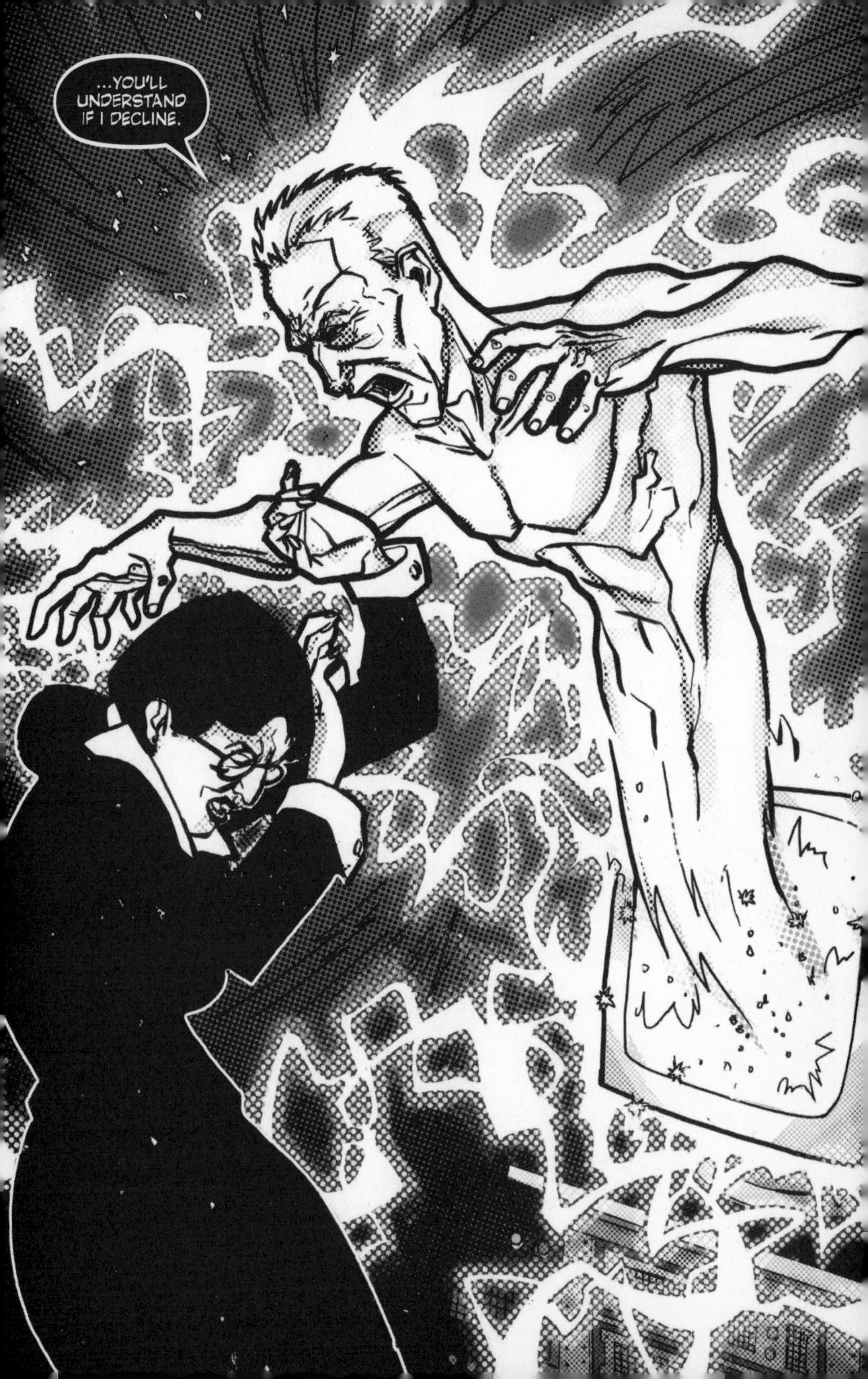
...YOU'LL UNDERSTAND IF I DECLINE.

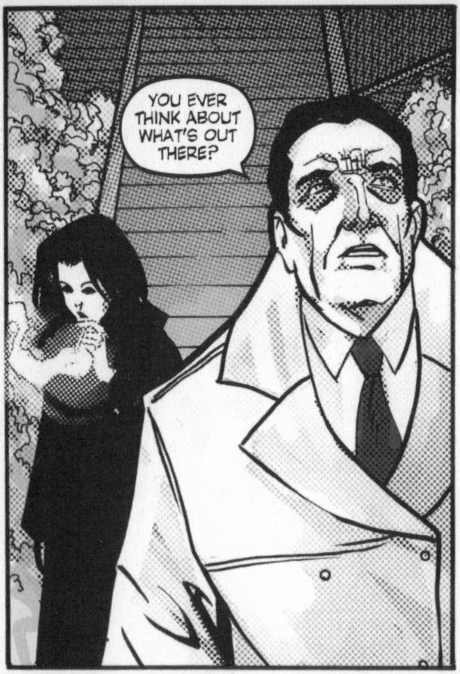
YOU EVER THINK ABOUT WHAT'S OUT THERE?

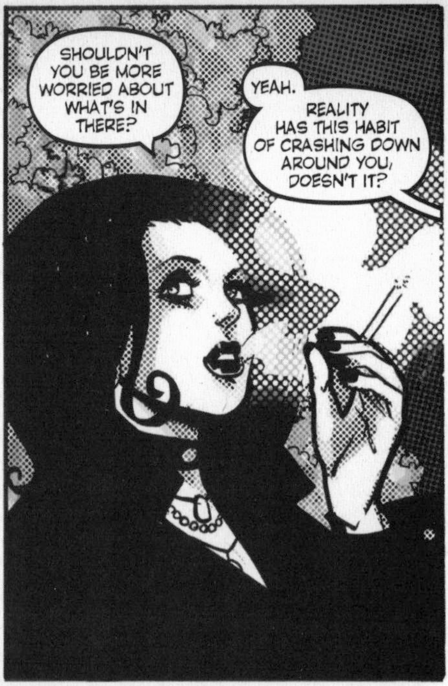
SHOULDN'T YOU BE MORE WORRIED ABOUT WHAT'S IN THERE?
YEAH.
REALITY HAS THIS HABIT OF CRASHING DOWN AROUND YOU, DOESN'T IT?

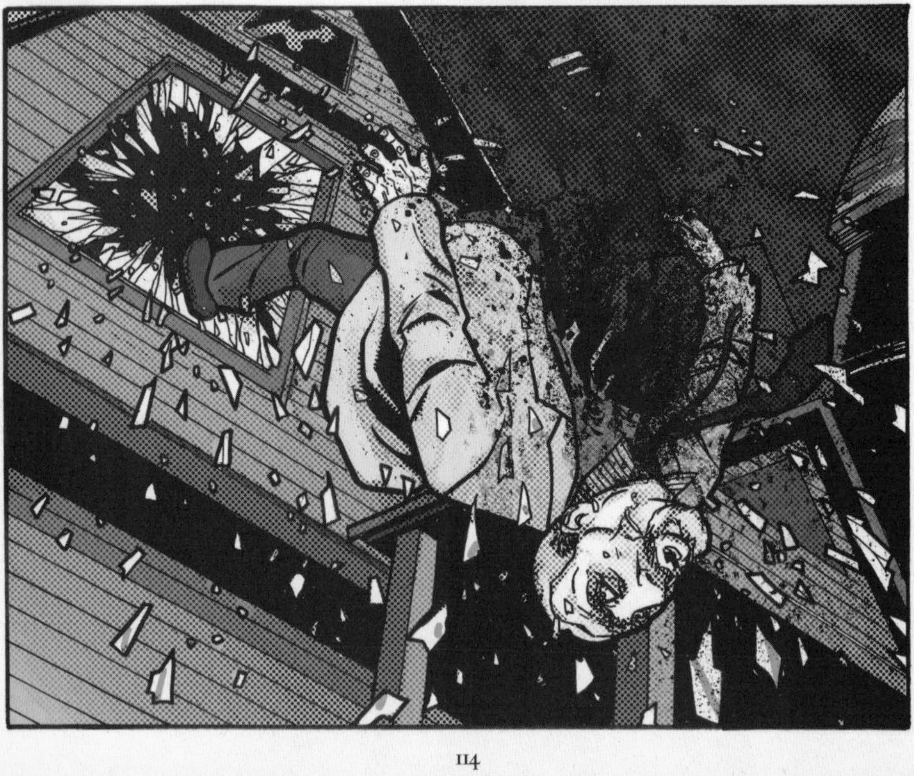

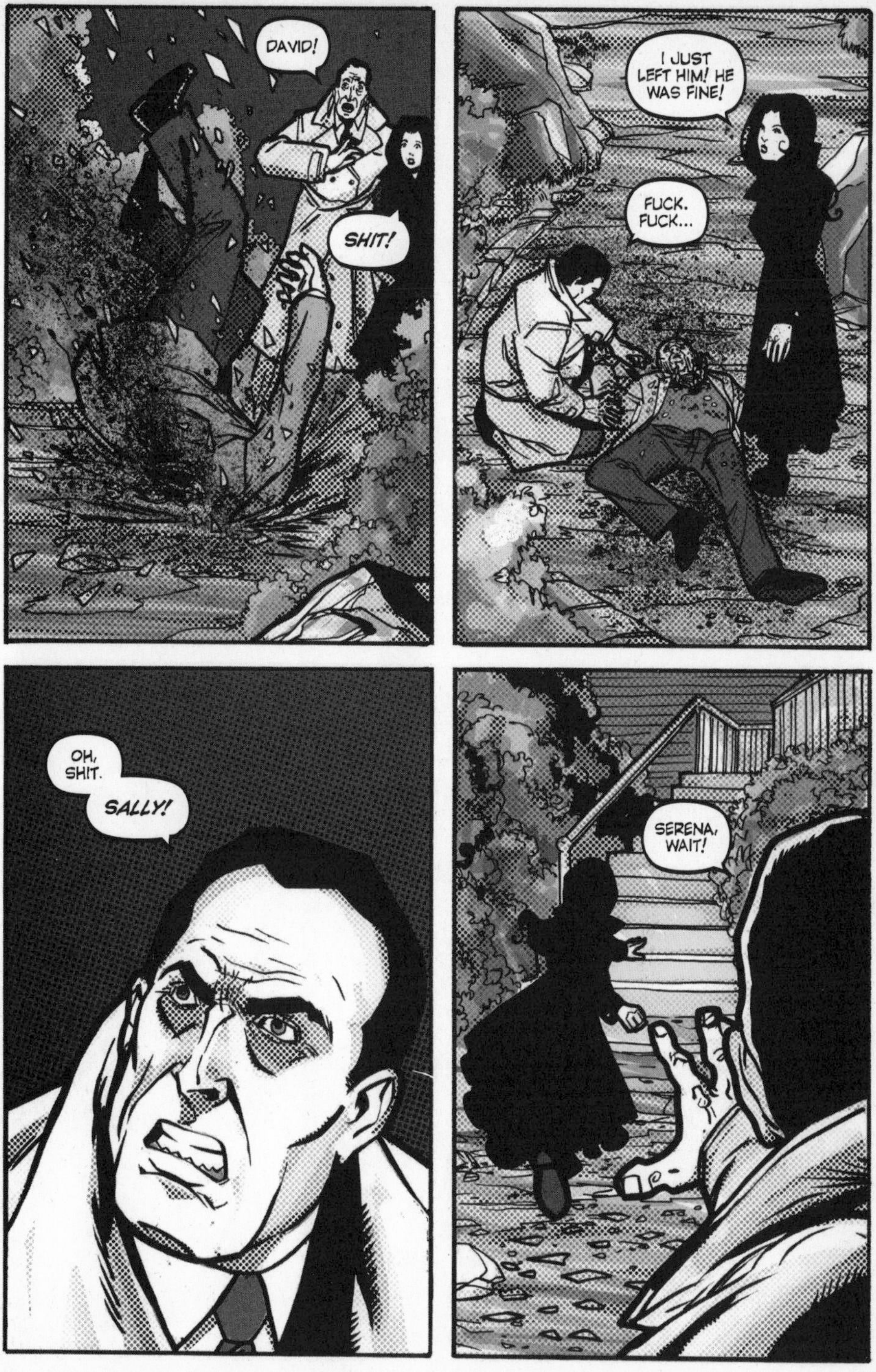
DAVID!
SHIT!
I JUST LEFT HIM! HE WAS FINE!
FUCK. FUCK...
OH, SHIT.
SALLY!
SERENA, WAIT!

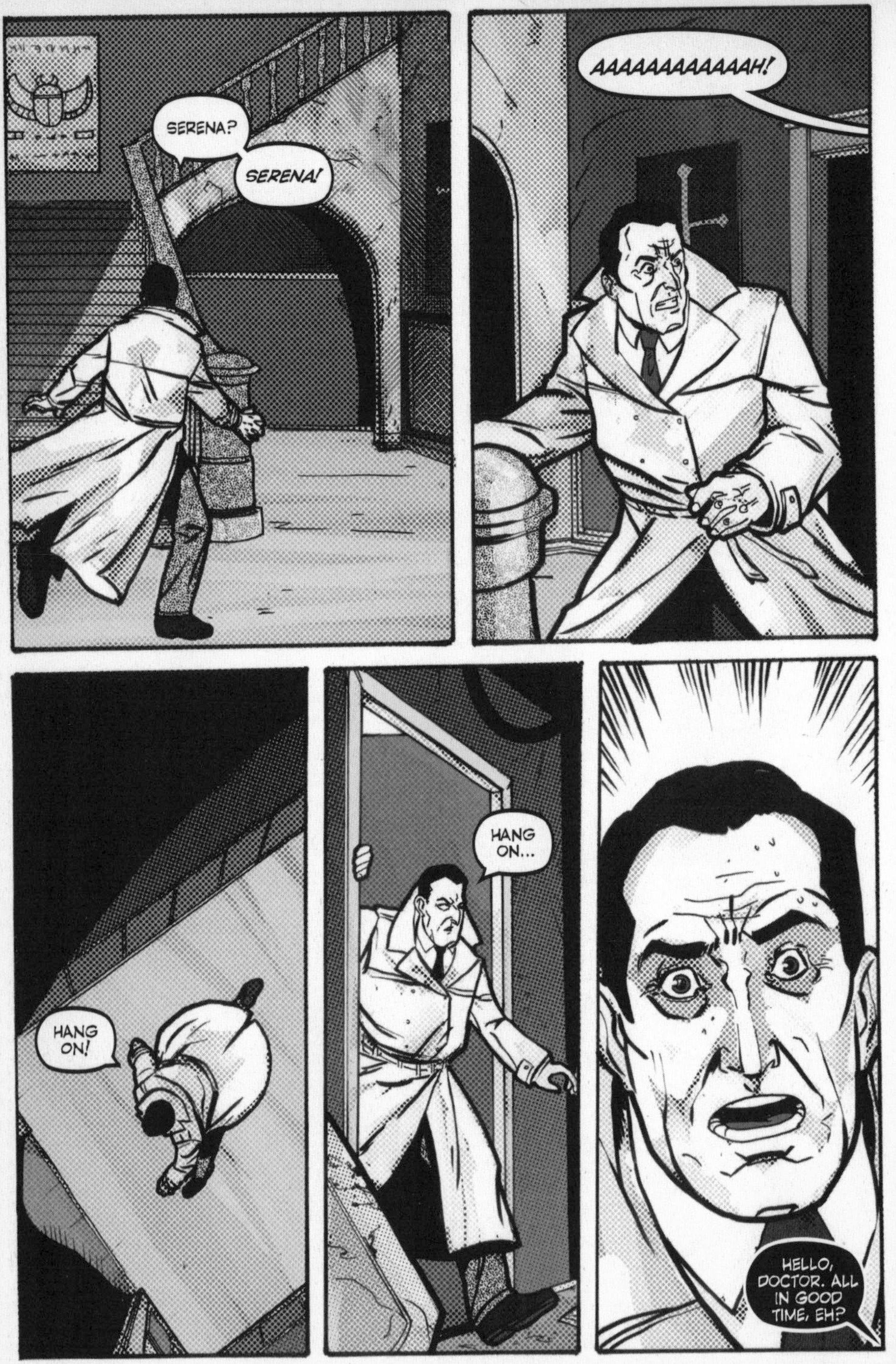
SERENA?
SERENA!
AAAAAAAAAAAAH!
HANG ON!
HANG ON...
HELLO, DOCTOR. ALL IN GOOD TIME, EH?

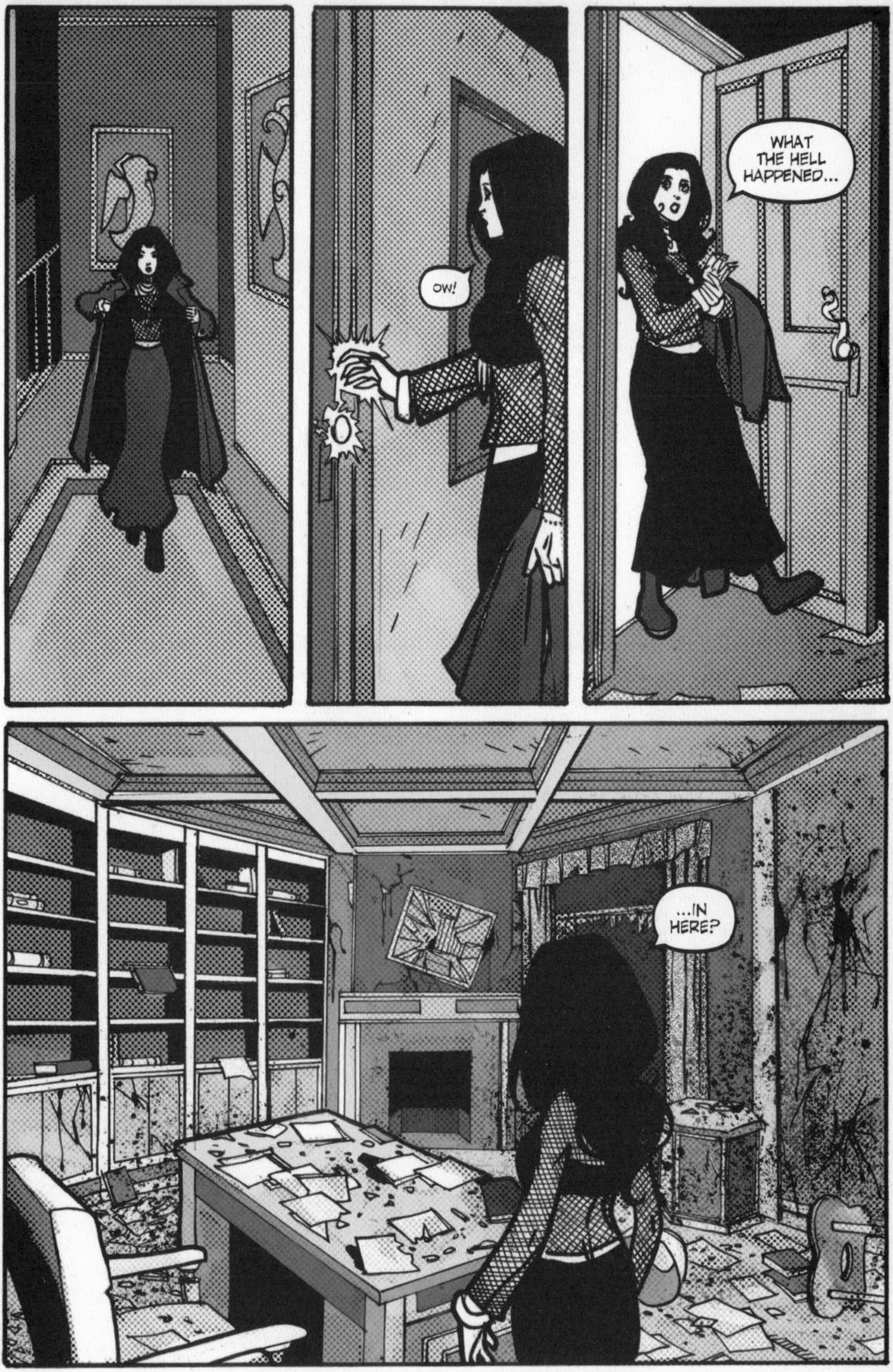
OW!
WHAT THE HELL HAPPENED...
...IN HERE?

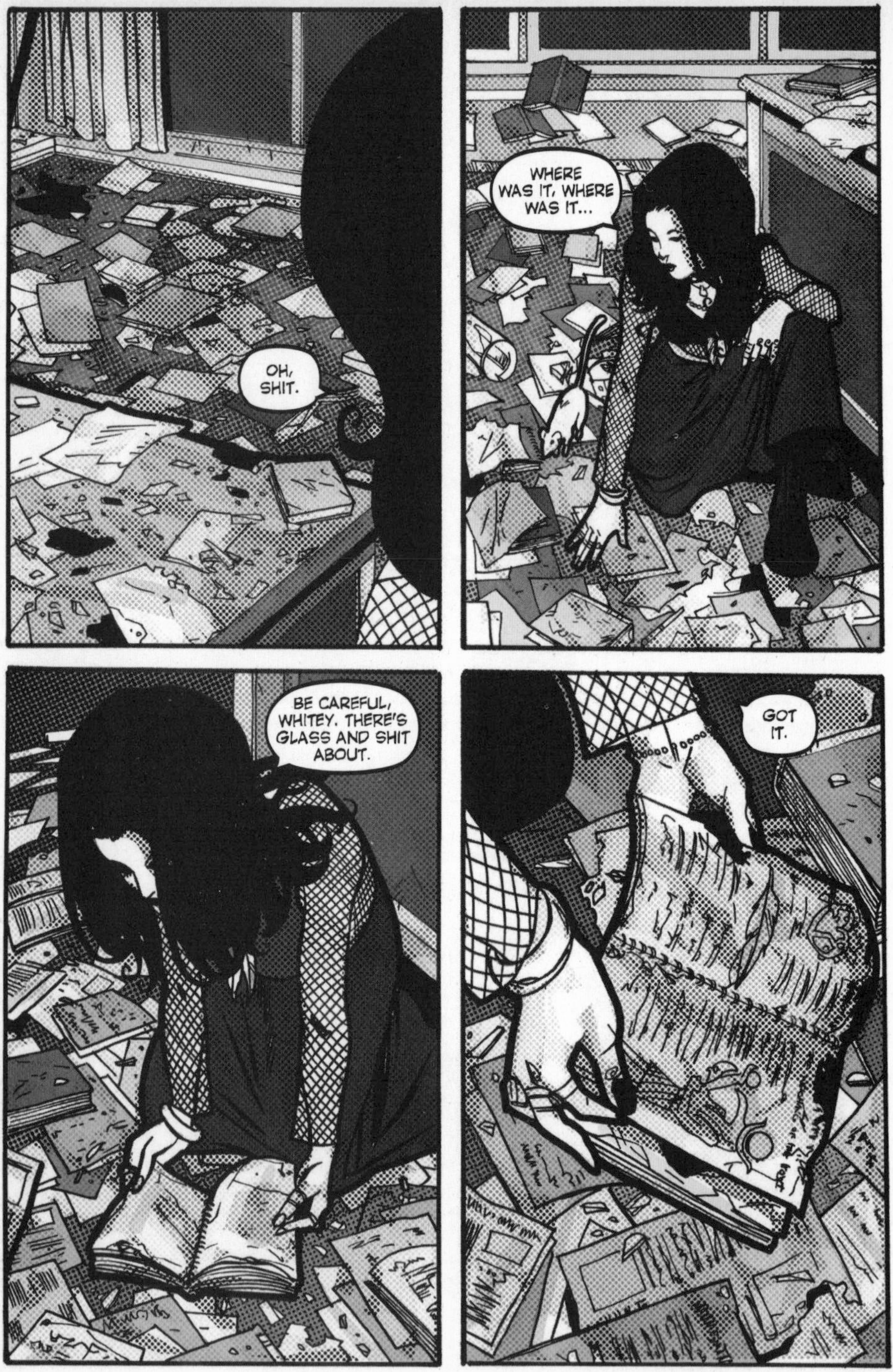
OH, SHIT.
WHERE WAS IT, WHERE WAS IT...
BE CAREFUL, WHITEY. THERE'S GLASS AND SHIT ABOUT.
GOT IT.

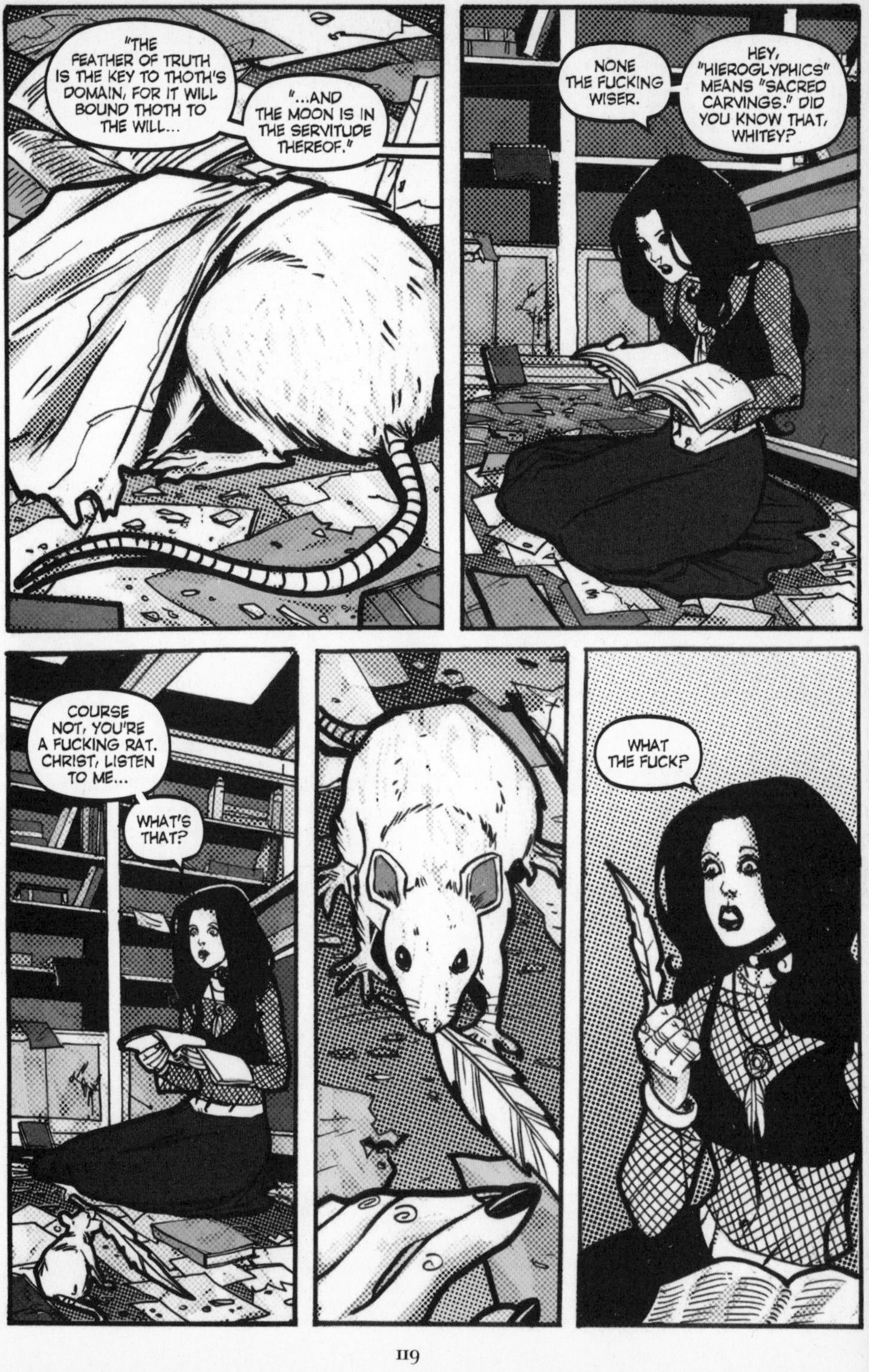
"THE FEATHER OF TRUTH IS THE KEY TO THOTH'S DOMAIN, FOR IT WILL BOUND THOTH TO THE WILL...
"...AND THE MOON IS IN THE SERVITUDE THEREOF."
NONE THE FUCKING WISER.
HEY, "HIEROGLYPHICS" MEANS "SACRED CARVINGS." DID YOU KNOW THAT, WHITEY?
COURSE NOT, YOU'RE A FUCKING RAT. CHRIST, LISTEN TO ME...
WHAT'S THAT?
WHAT THE FUCK?

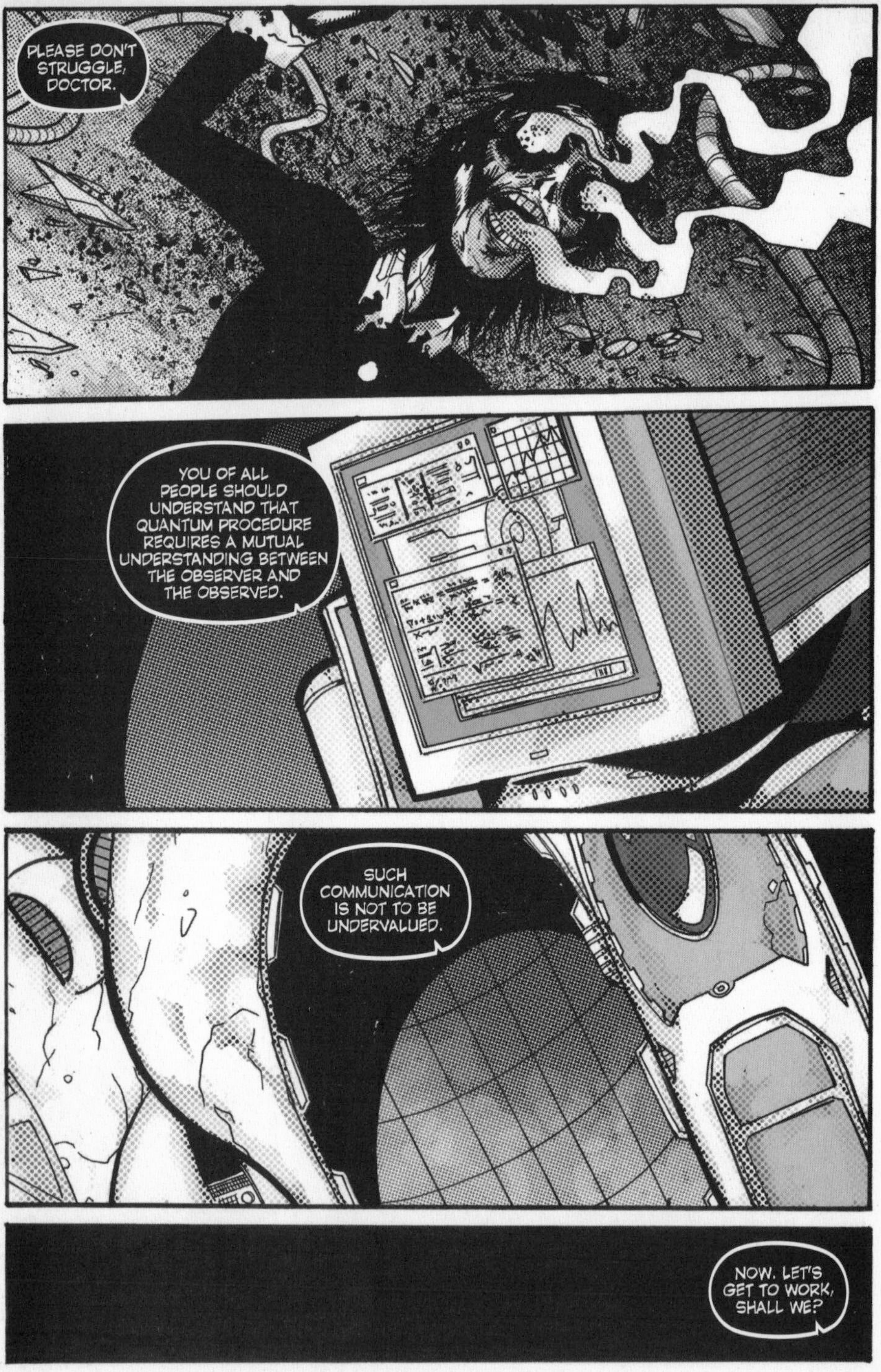
PLEASE DON'T STRUGGLE, DOCTOR.
YOU OF ALL PEOPLE SHOULD UNDERSTAND THAT QUANTUM PROCEDURE REQUIRES A MUTUAL UNDERSTANDING BETWEEN THE OBSERVER AND THE OBSERVED.
SUCH COMMUNICATION IS NOT TO BE UNDERVALUED.
NOW. LET'S GET TO WORK, SHALL WE?

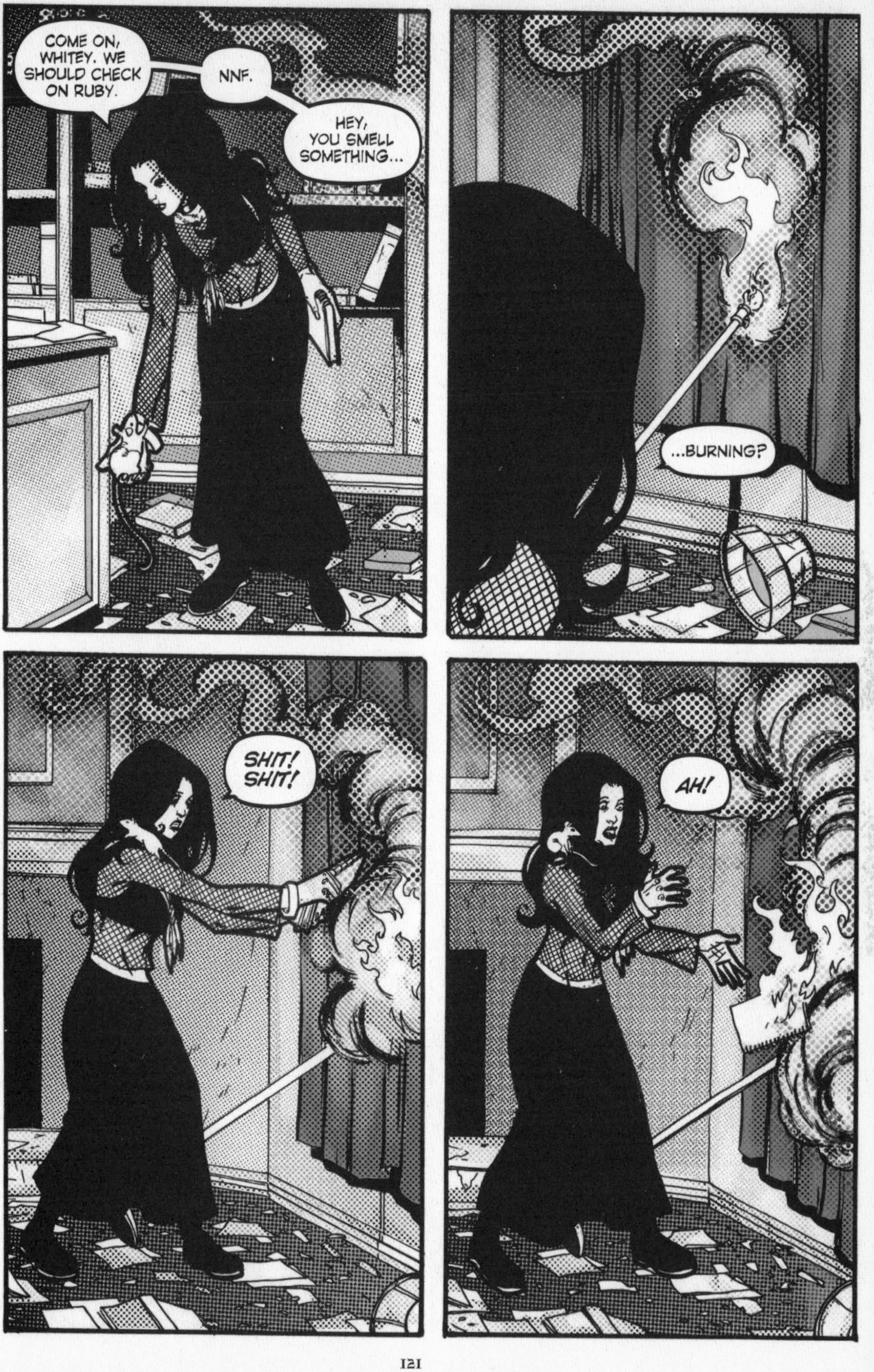
COME ON, WHITEY. WE SHOULD CHECK ON RUBY.
NNF.
HEY, YOU SMELL SOMETHING...
...BURNING?
SHIT! SHIT!
AH!

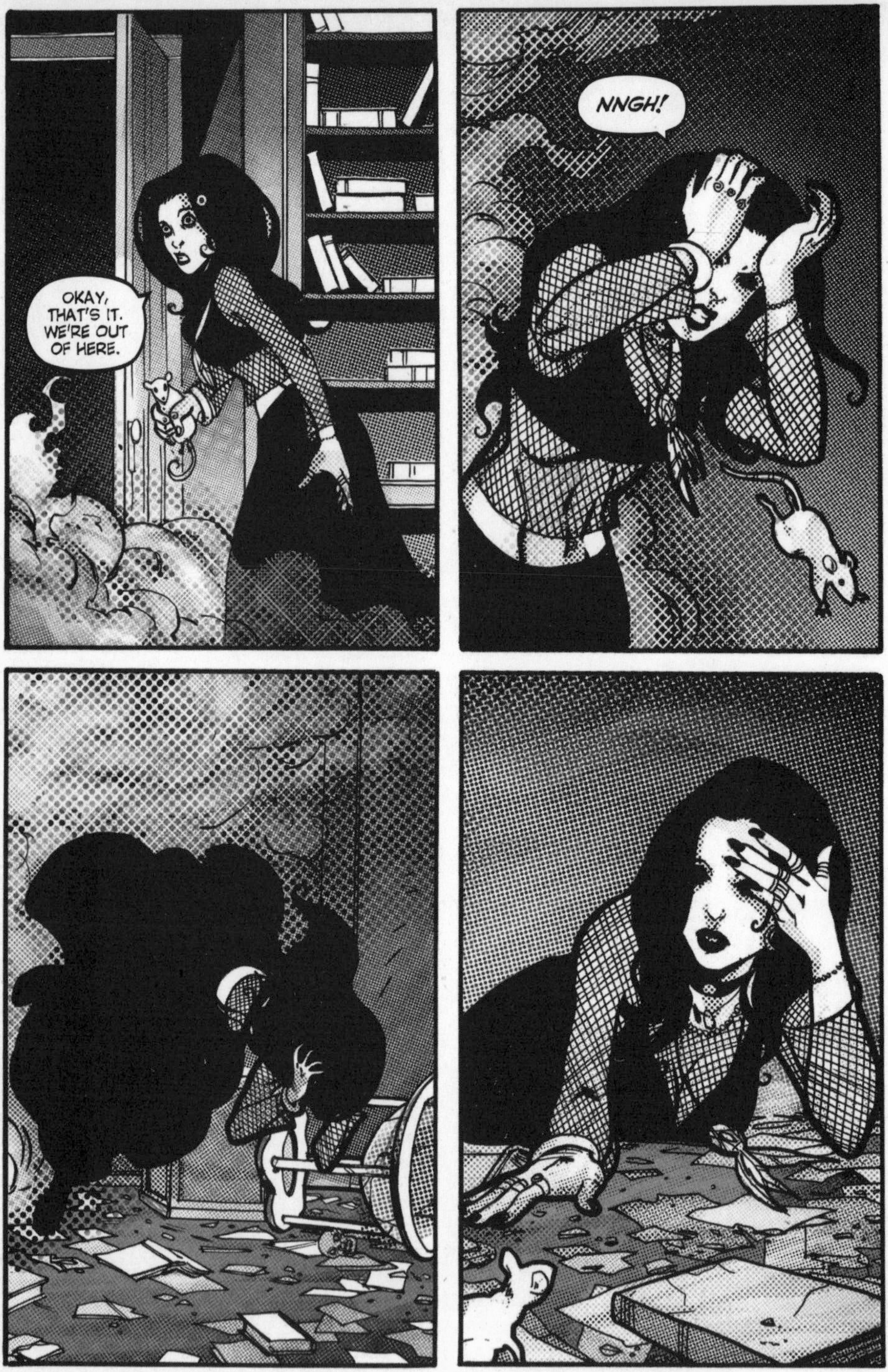
OKAY, THAT'S IT. WE'RE OUT OF HERE.
NNGH!

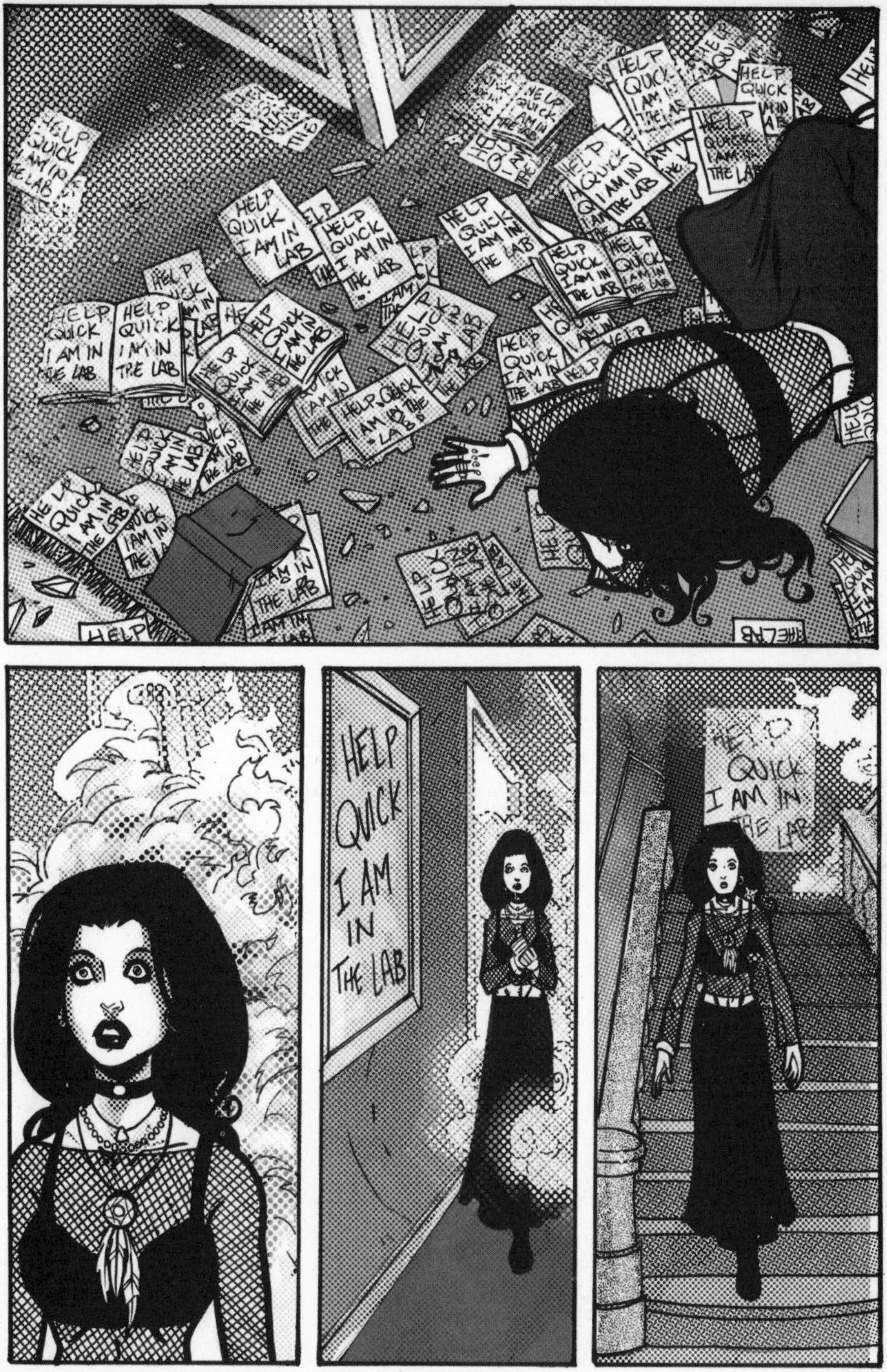
HELP QUICK I AM IN THE LAB
HELP QUICK I AM IN LAB
HELP QUICK I AM IN THE LAB
HELP QUICK I AM IN THE LAB

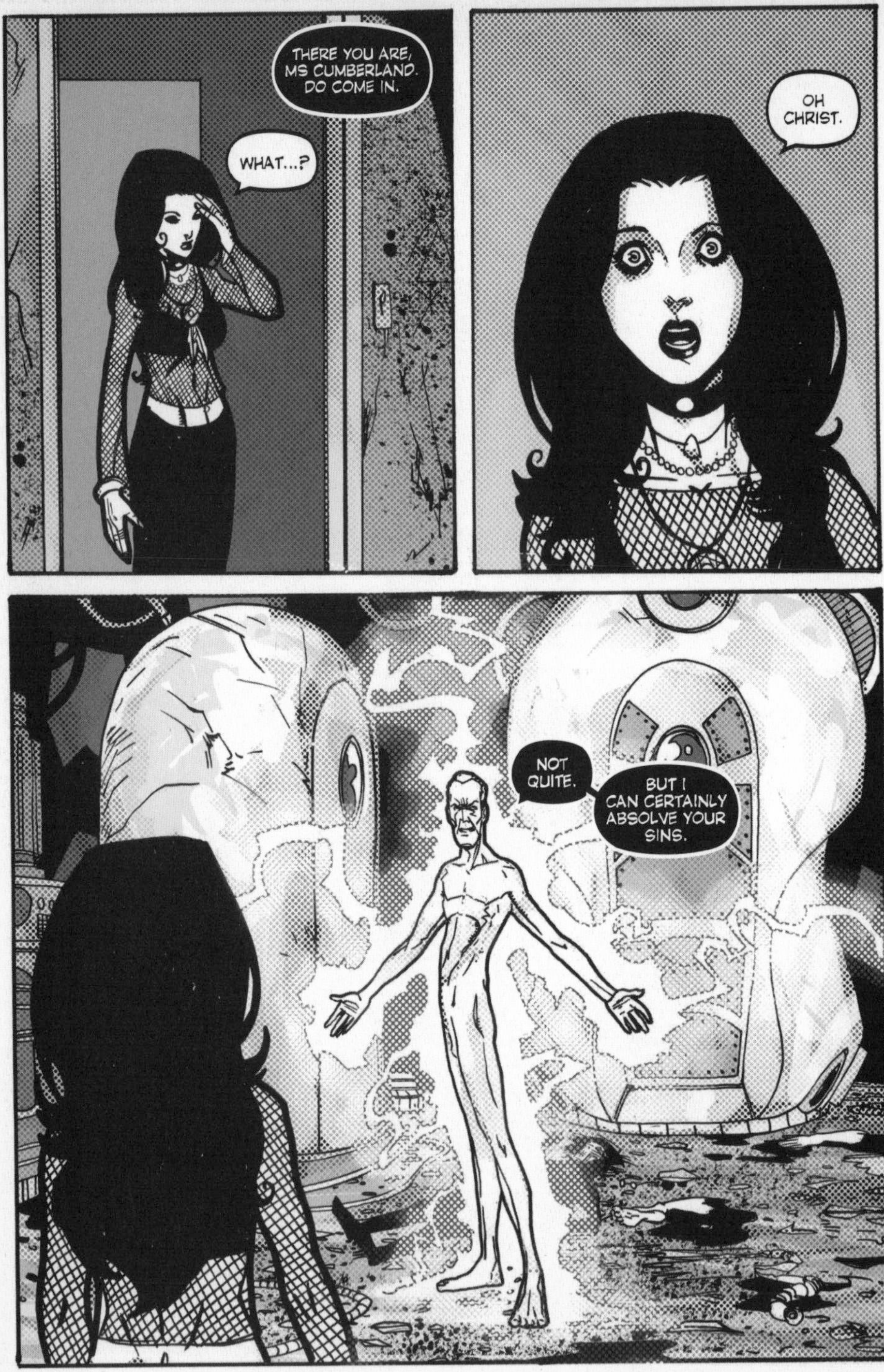
THERE YOU ARE, MS CUMBERLAND. DO COME IN.
WHAT...?
OH CHRIST.
NOT QUITE.
BUT I CAN CERTAINLY ABSOLVE YOUR SINS.

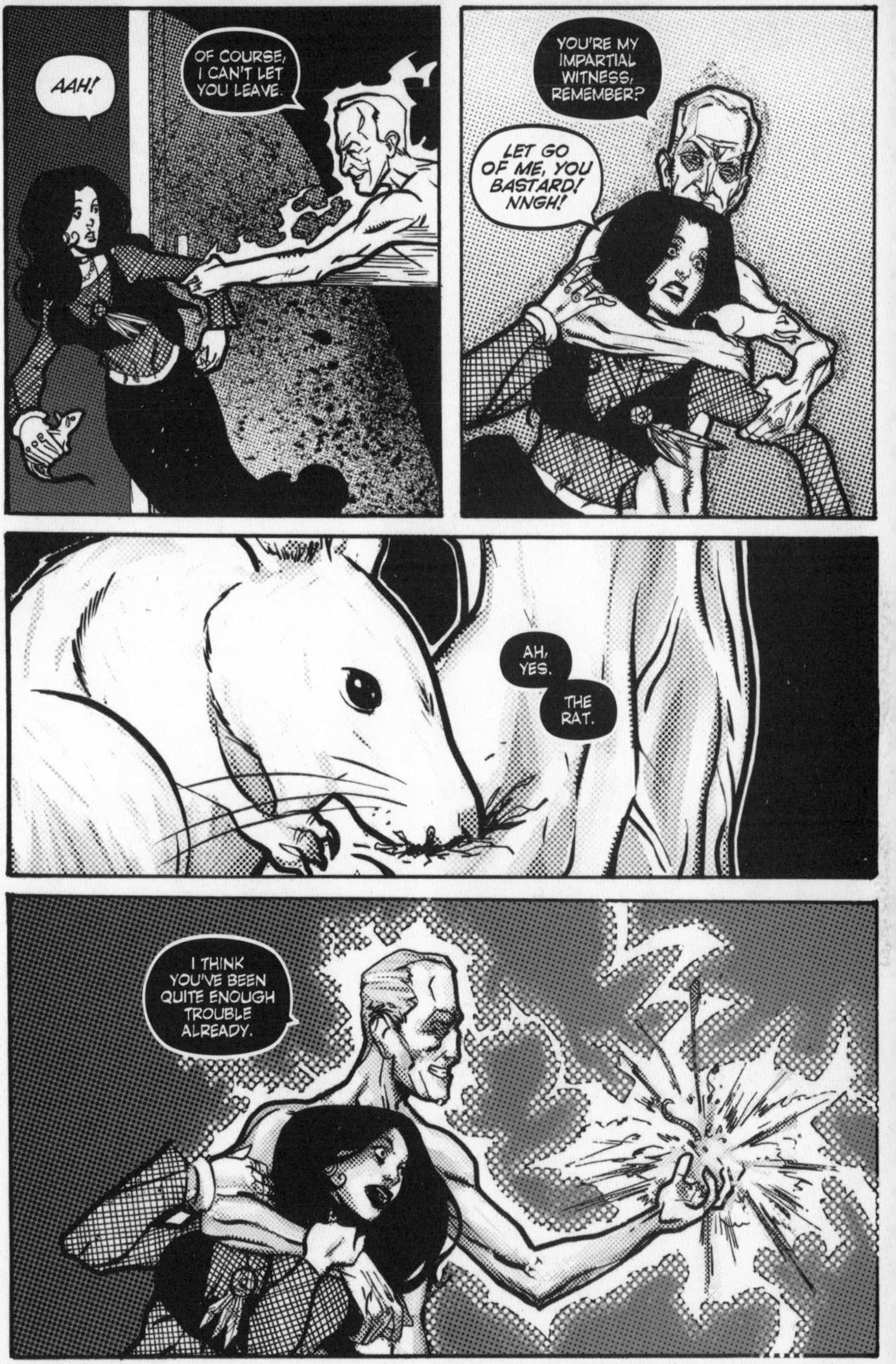
AAH!
OF COURSE, I CAN'T LET YOU LEAVE.
YOU'RE MY IMPARTIAL WITNESS, REMEMBER?
LET GO OF ME, YOU BASTARD! NNGH!
AH, YES.
THE RAT.
I THINK YOU'VE BEEN QUITE ENOUGH TROUBLE ALREADY.

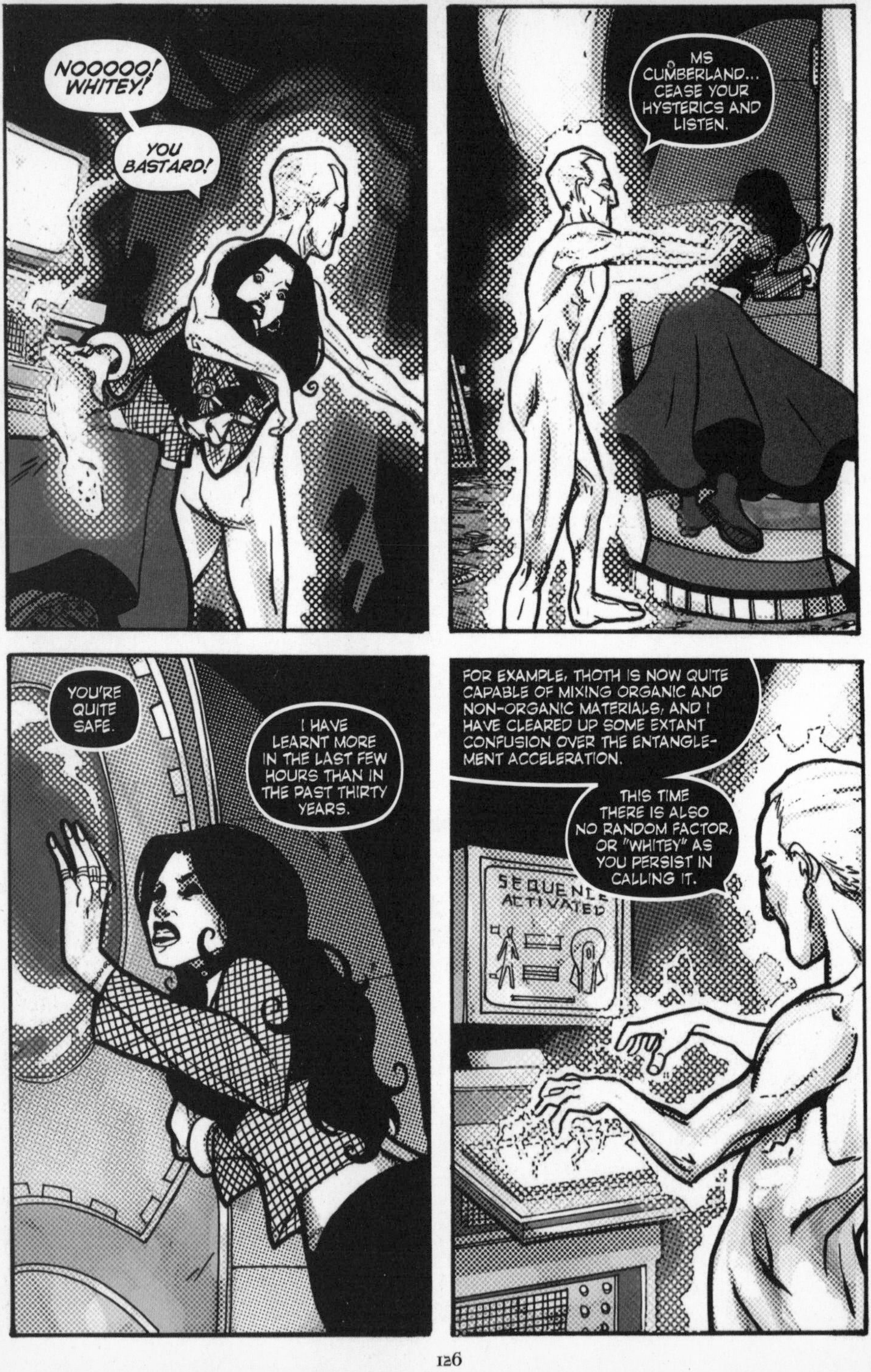
NOOOOO! WHITEY!
YOU BASTARD!
MS CUMBERLAND... CEASE YOUR HYSTERICS AND LISTEN.
YOU'RE QUITE SAFE.
I HAVE LEARNT MORE IN THE LAST FEW HOURS THAN IN THE PAST THIRTY YEARS.
FOR EXAMPLE, THOTH IS NOW QUITE CAPABLE OF MIXING ORGANIC AND NON-ORGANIC MATERIALS, AND I HAVE CLEARED UP SOME EXTANT CONFUSION OVER THE ENTANGLEMENT ACCELERATION.
THIS TIME THERE IS ALSO NO RANDOM FACTOR, OR "WHITEY" AS YOU PERSIST IN CALLING IT.
SEQUENCE ACTIVATED

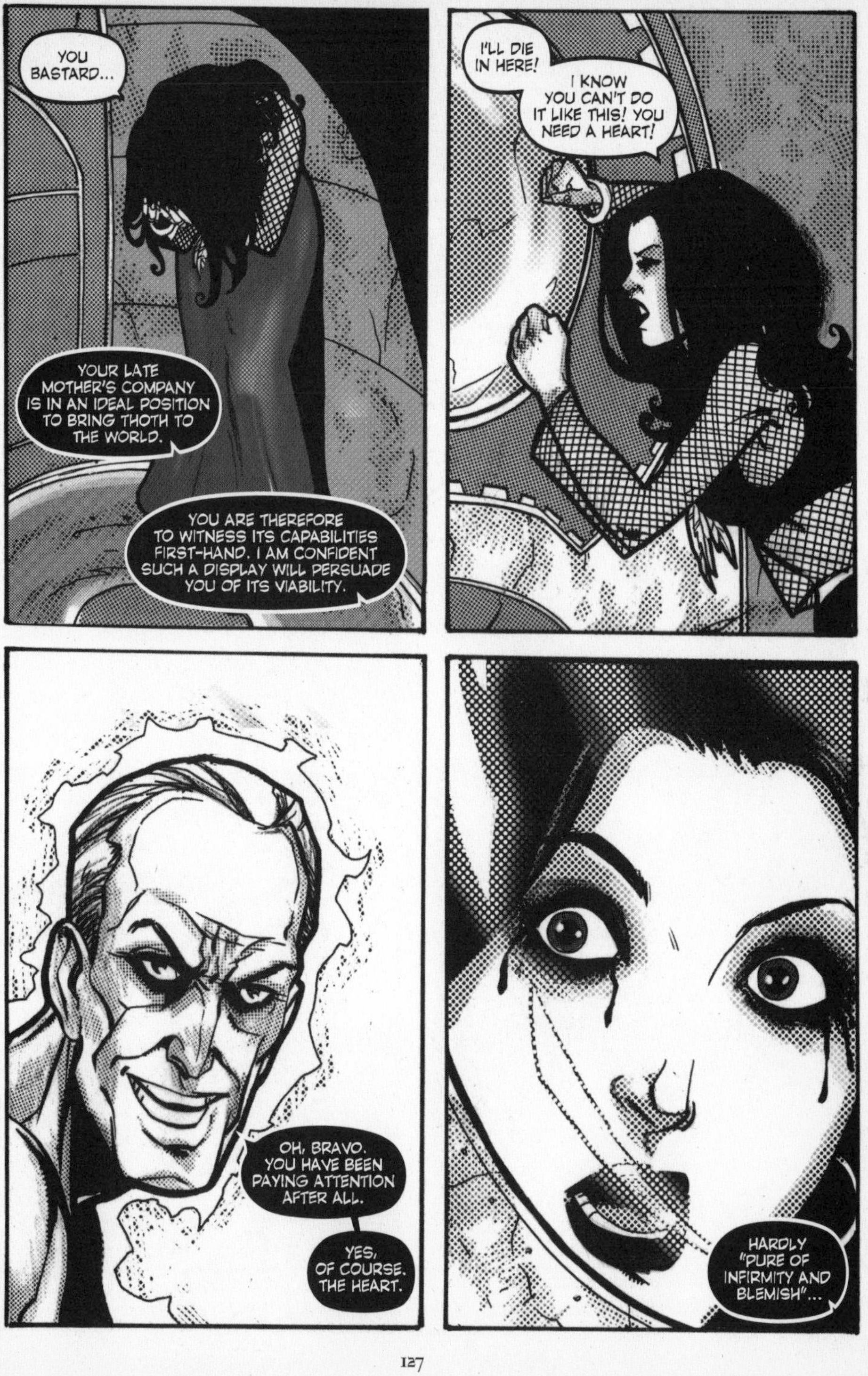
YOU BASTARD...
YOUR LATE MOTHER'S COMPANY IS IN AN IDEAL POSITION TO BRING THOTH TO THE WORLD.
YOU ARE THEREFORE TO WITNESS ITS CAPABILITIES FIRST-HAND. I AM CONFIDENT SUCH A DISPLAY WILL PERSUADE YOU OF ITS VIABILITY.
I'LL DIE IN HERE!
I KNOW YOU CAN'T DO IT LIKE THIS! YOU NEED A HEART!
OH, BRAVO. YOU HAVE BEEN PAYING ATTENTION AFTER ALL.
YES, OF COURSE. THE HEART.
HARDLY "PURE OF INFIRMITY AND BLEMISH"...

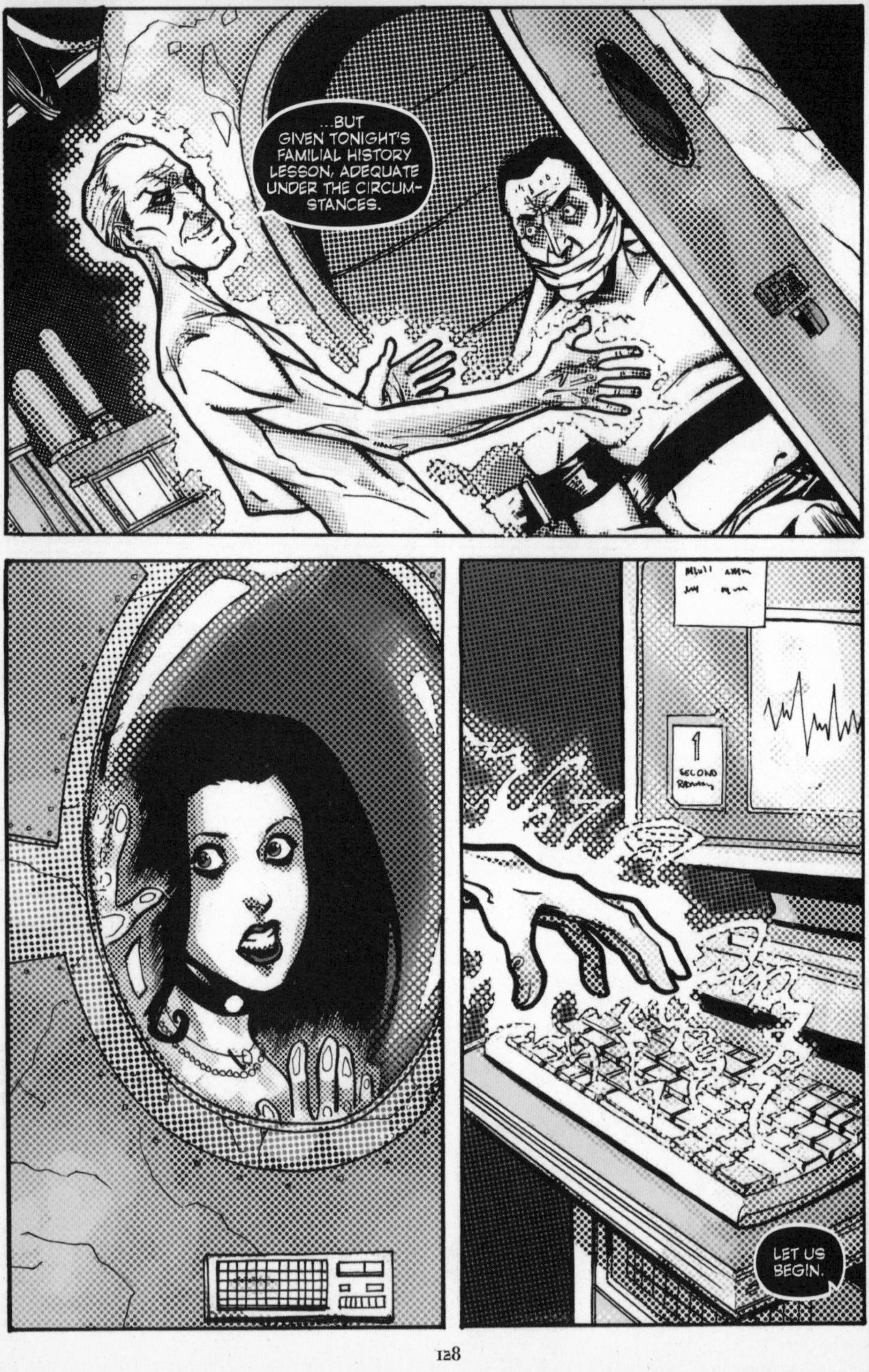
...BUT GIVEN TONIGHT'S FAMILIAL HISTORY LESSON, ADEQUATE UNDER THE CIRCUMSTANCES.
1 SECOND
LET US BEGIN.

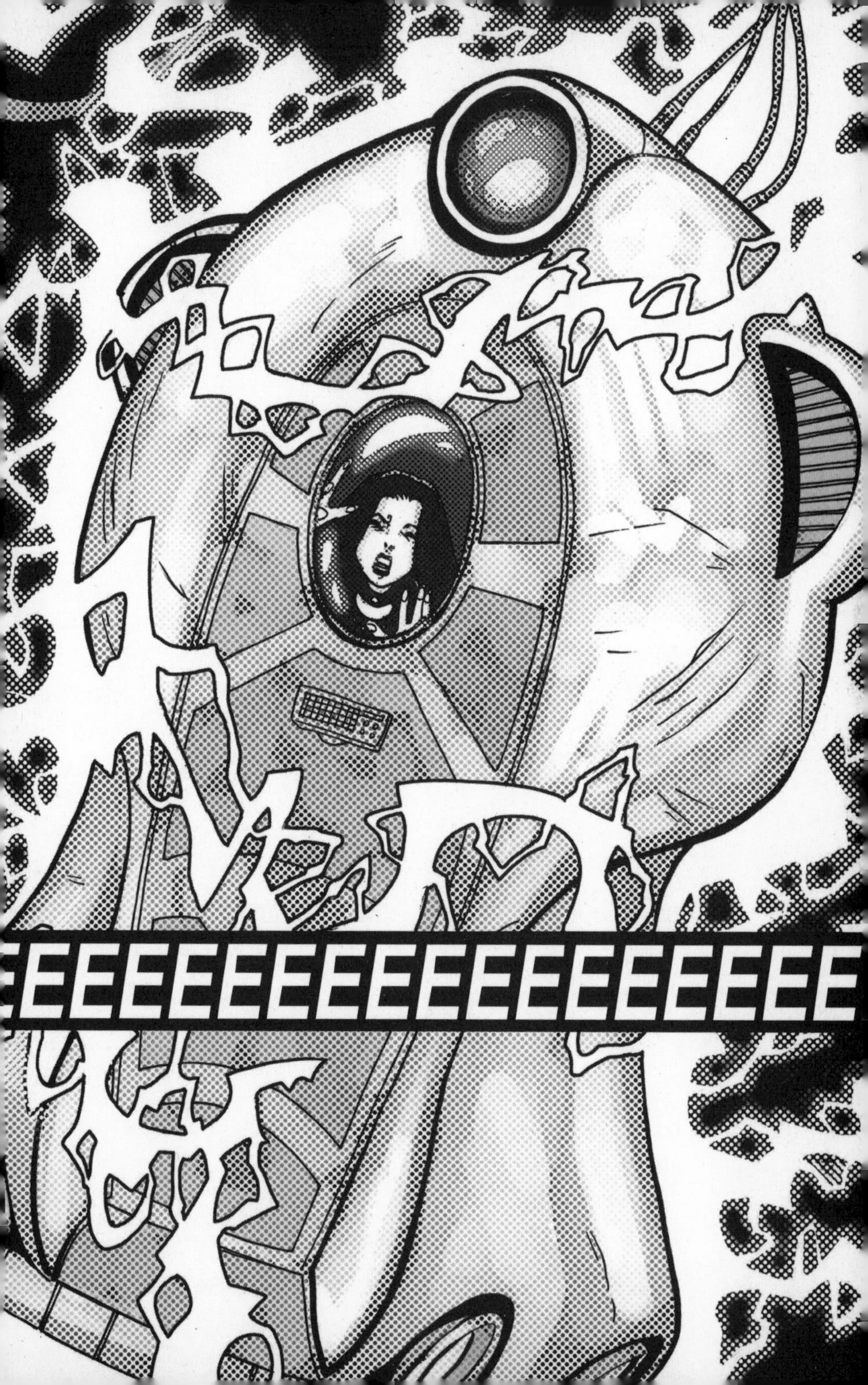
EEEEEEEEEEEEEEEEEEEEE

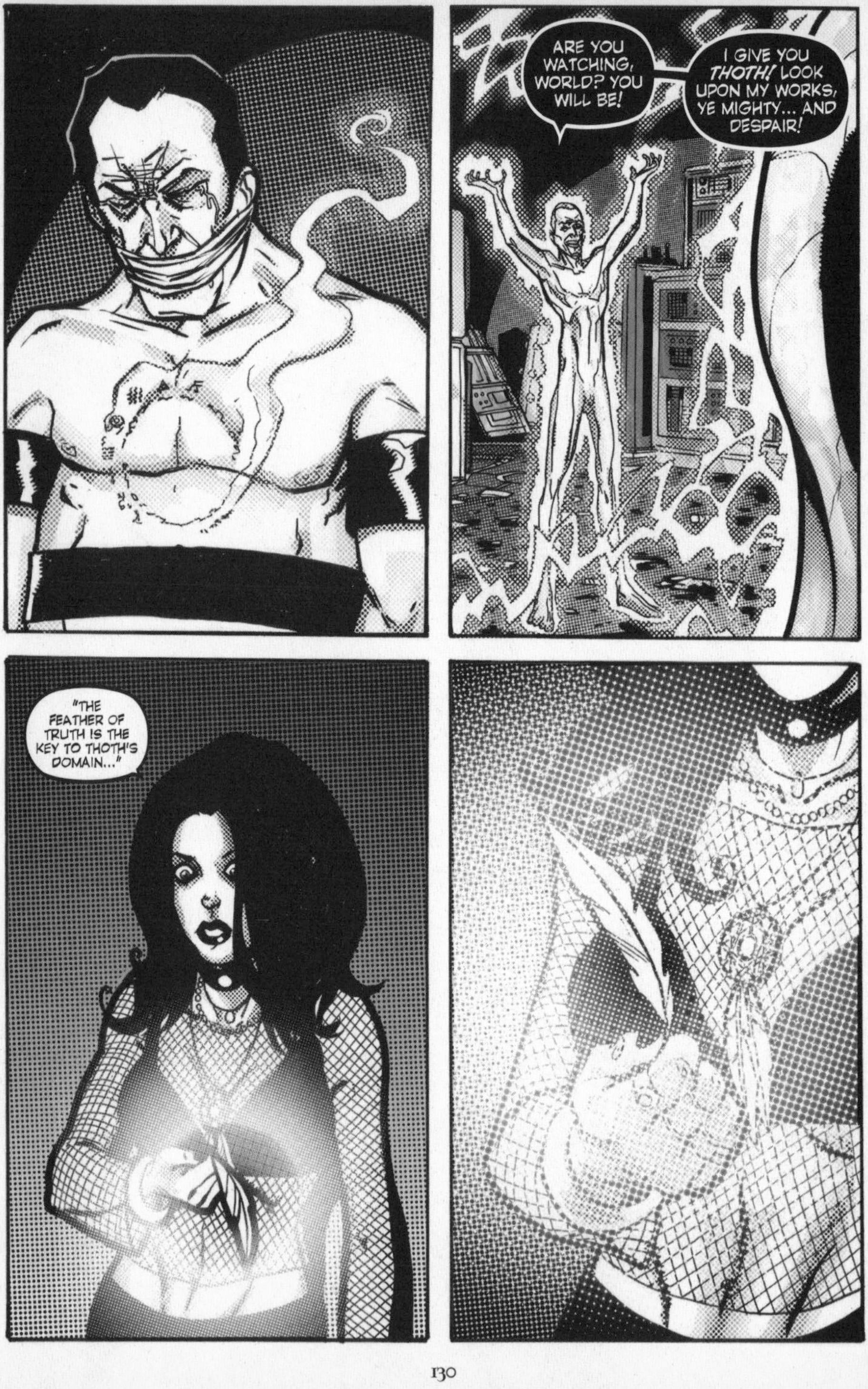
ARE YOU WATCHING, WORLD? YOU WILL BE!
I GIVE YOU *THOTH!* LOOK UPON MY WORKS, YE MIGHTY... AND DESPAIR!
"THE FEATHER OF TRUTH IS THE KEY TO THOTH'S DOMAIN..."

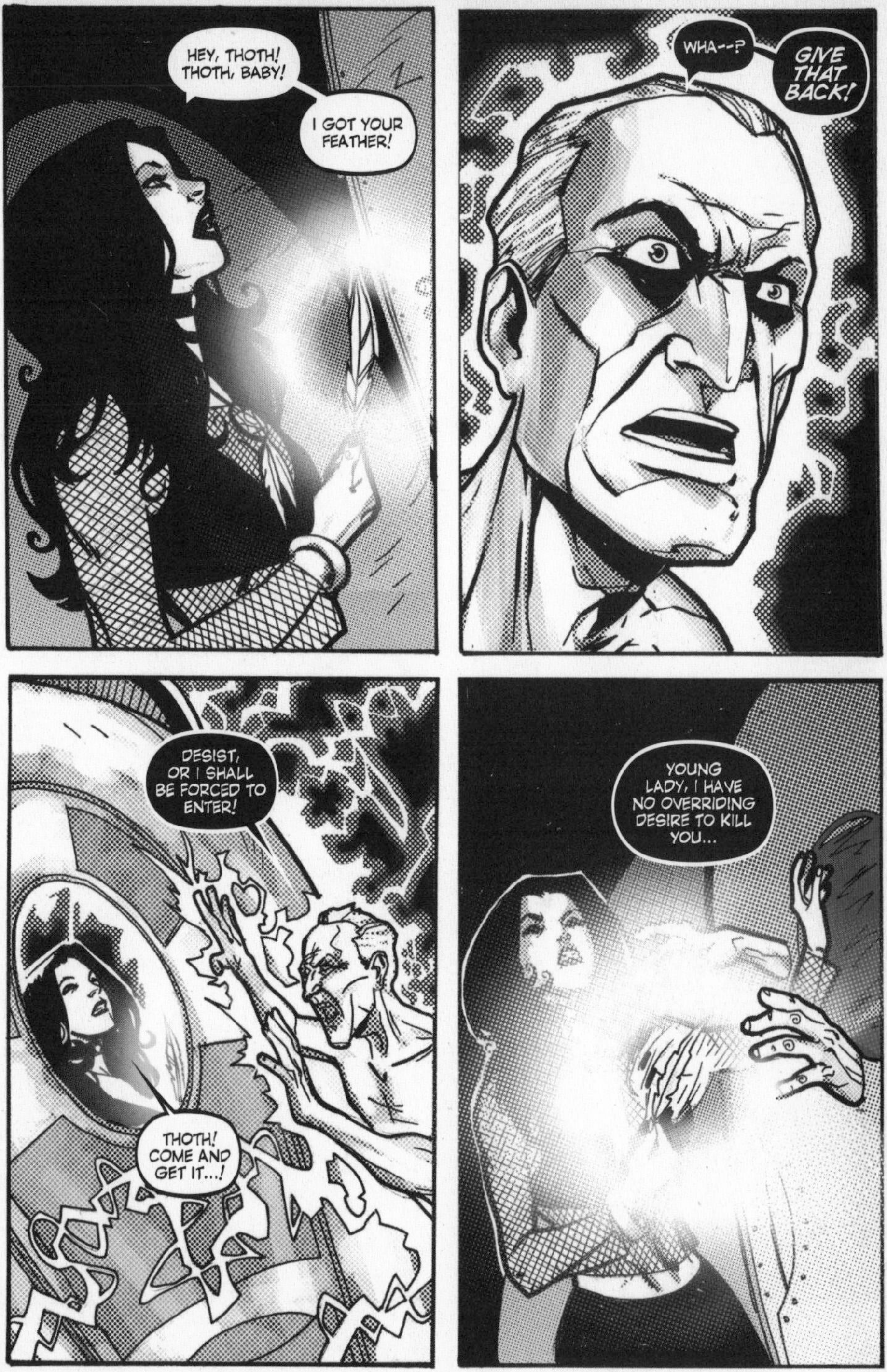
HEY, THOTH! THOTH, BABY!
I GOT YOUR FEATHER!
WHA--?
GIVE THAT BACK!
DESIST, OR I SHALL BE FORCED TO ENTER!
THOTH! COME AND GET IT...!
YOUNG LADY, I HAVE NO OVERRIDING DESIRE TO KILL YOU...

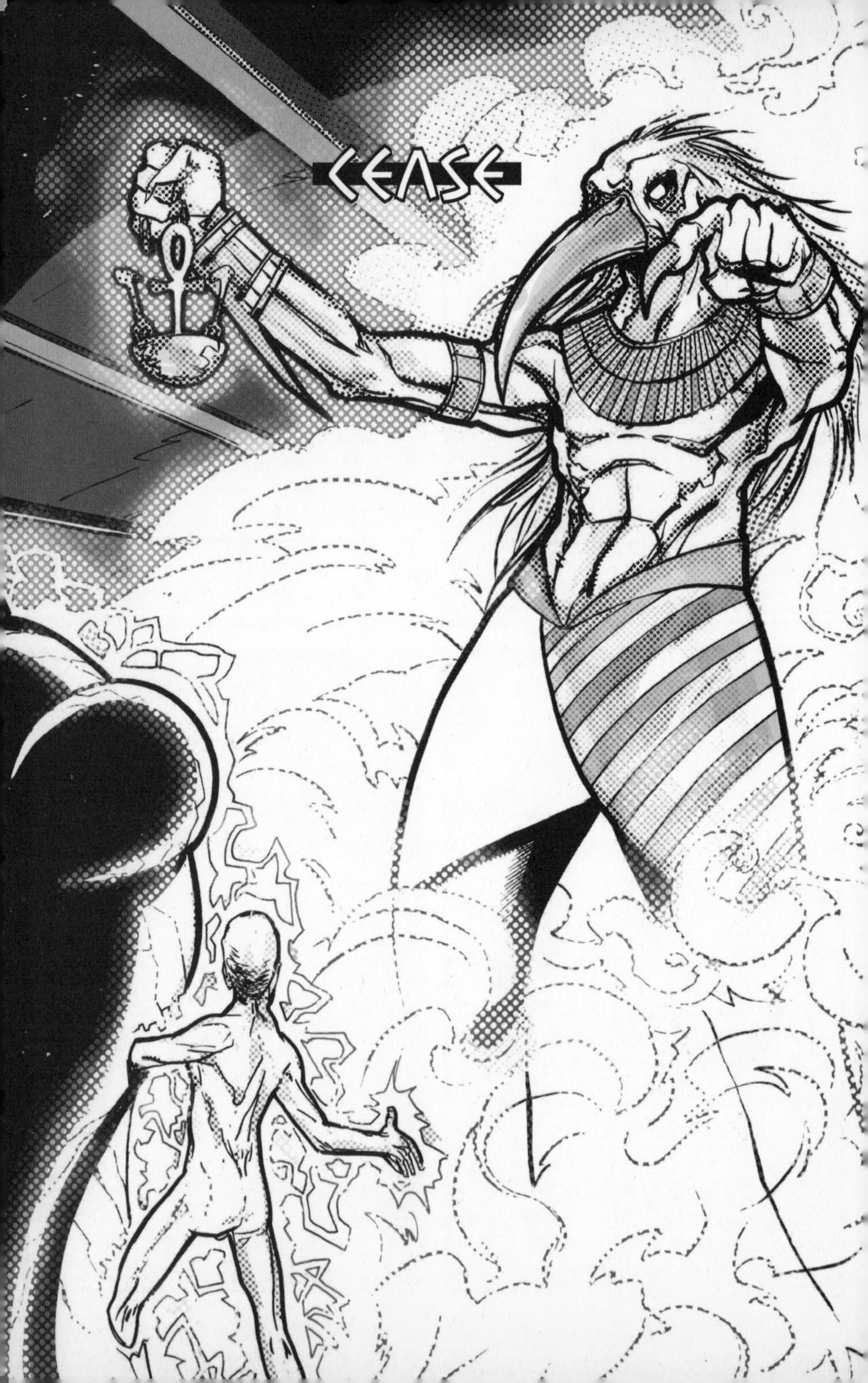
CEASE

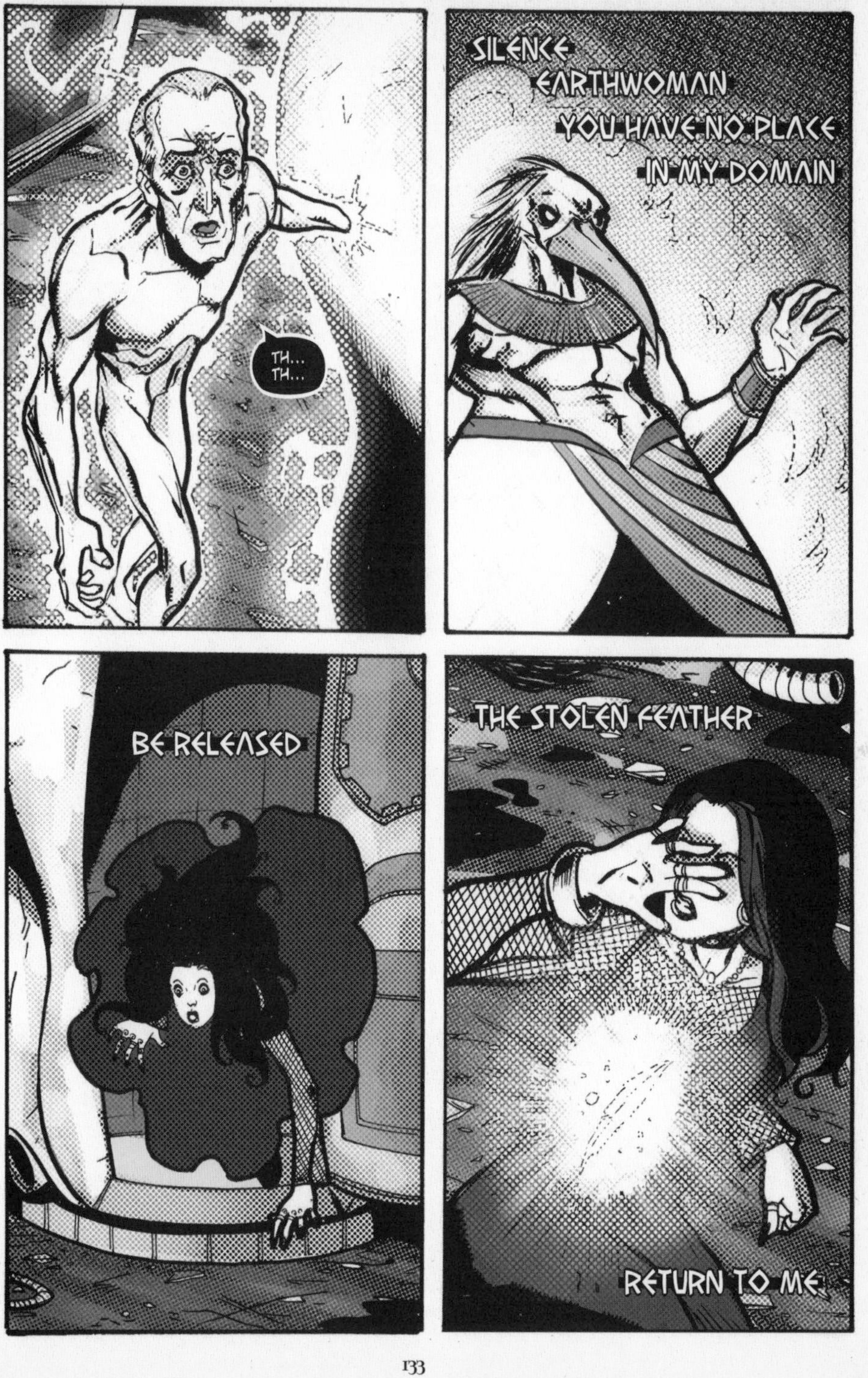
TH...
TH...
SILENCE
EARTHWOMAN
YOU HAVE NO PLACE
IN MY DOMAIN
BE RELEASED
THE STOLEN FEATHER
RETURN TO ME

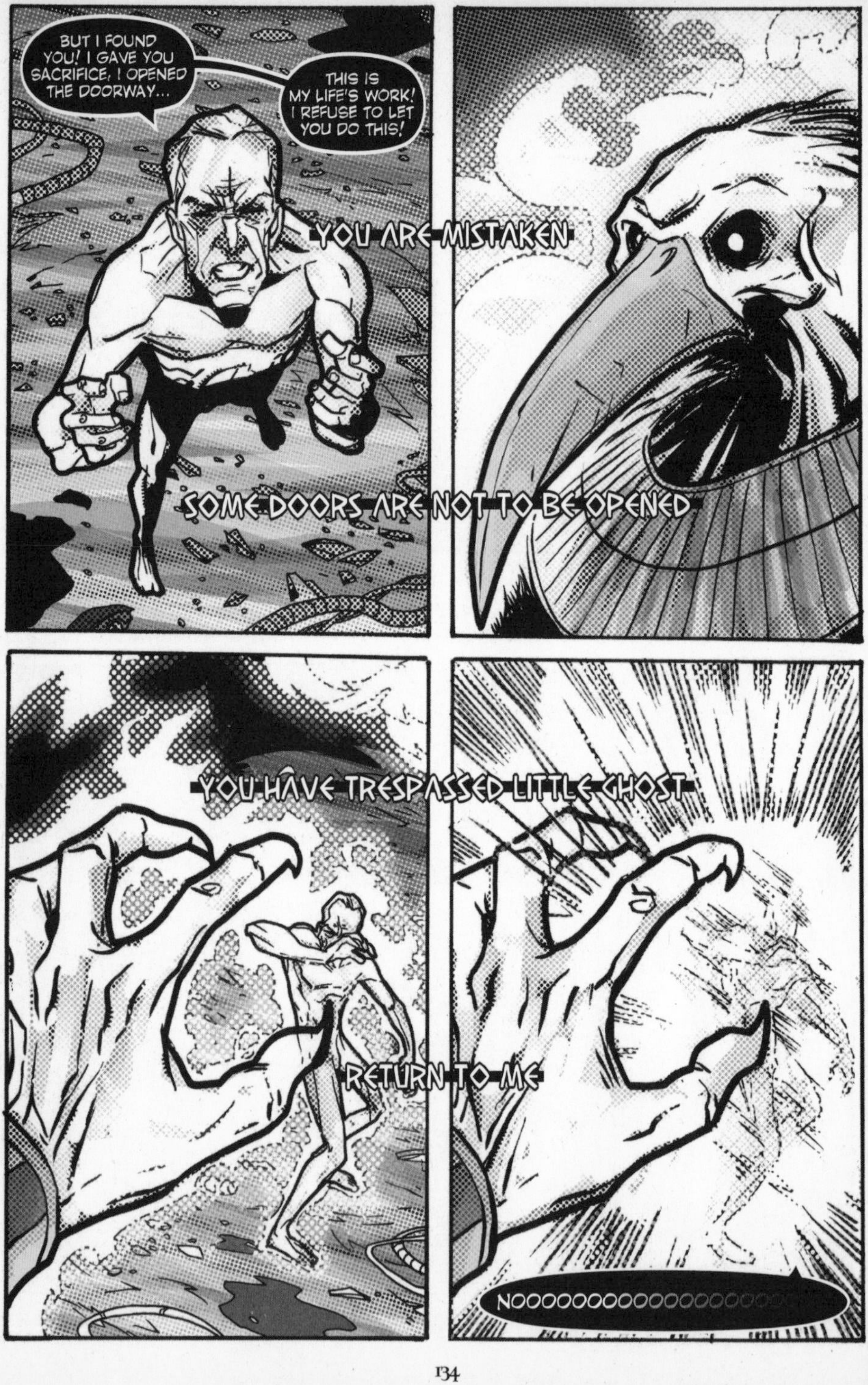
BUT I FOUND YOU! I GAVE YOU SACRIFICE, I OPENED THE DOORWAY...
THIS IS MY LIFE'S WORK! I REFUSE TO LET YOU DO THIS!
YOU ARE MISTAKEN
SOME DOORS ARE NOT TO BE OPENED
YOU HAVE TRESPASSED LITTLE GHOST
RETURN TO ME
NOOOOOOOOOOOOOOOOOOO

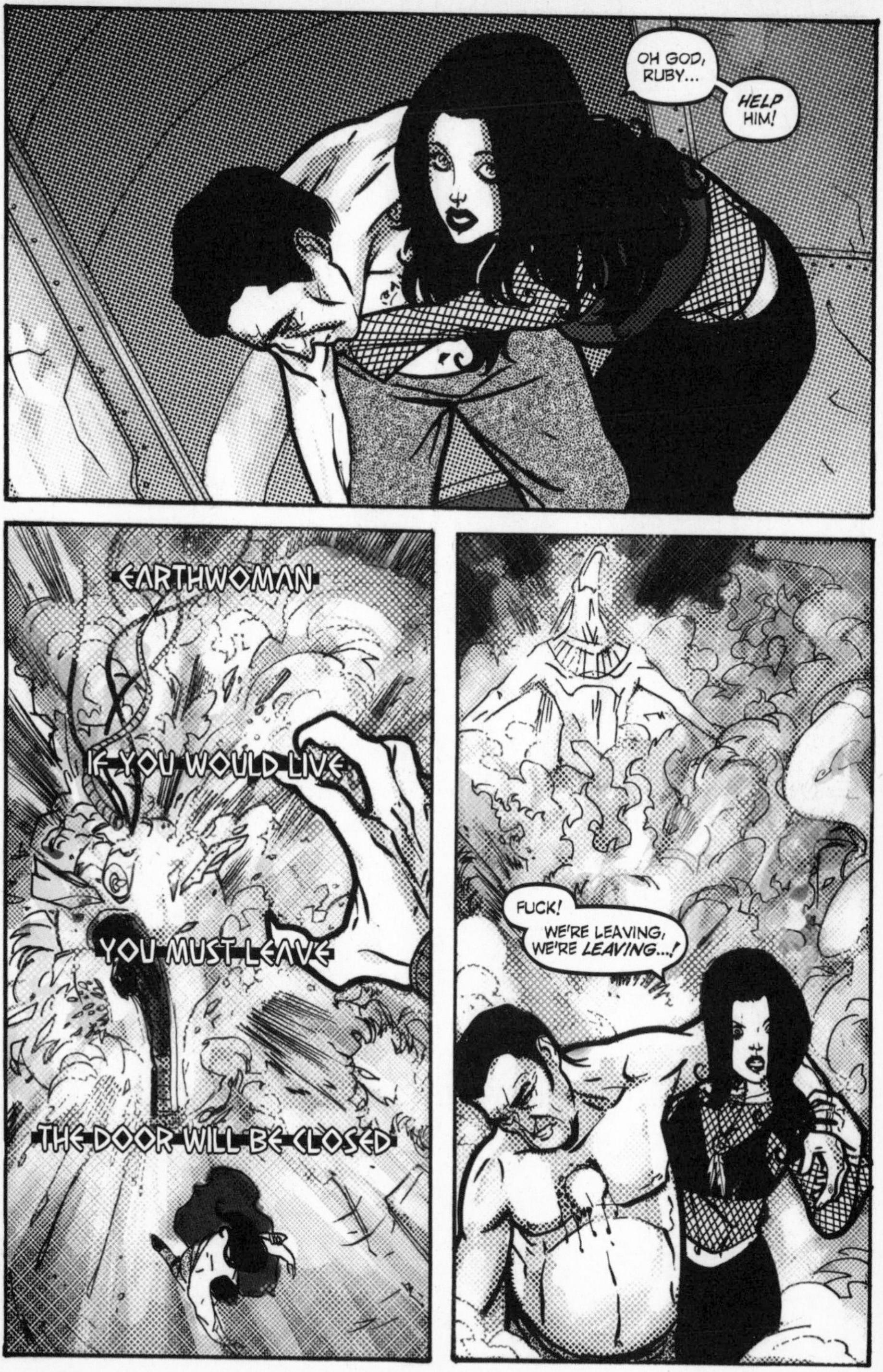
OH GOD, RUBY...
HELP HIM!
EARTHWOMAN
IF YOU WOULD LIVE
YOU MUST LEAVE
THE DOOR WILL BE CLOSED
FUCK!
WE'RE LEAVING, WE'RE LEAVING...!

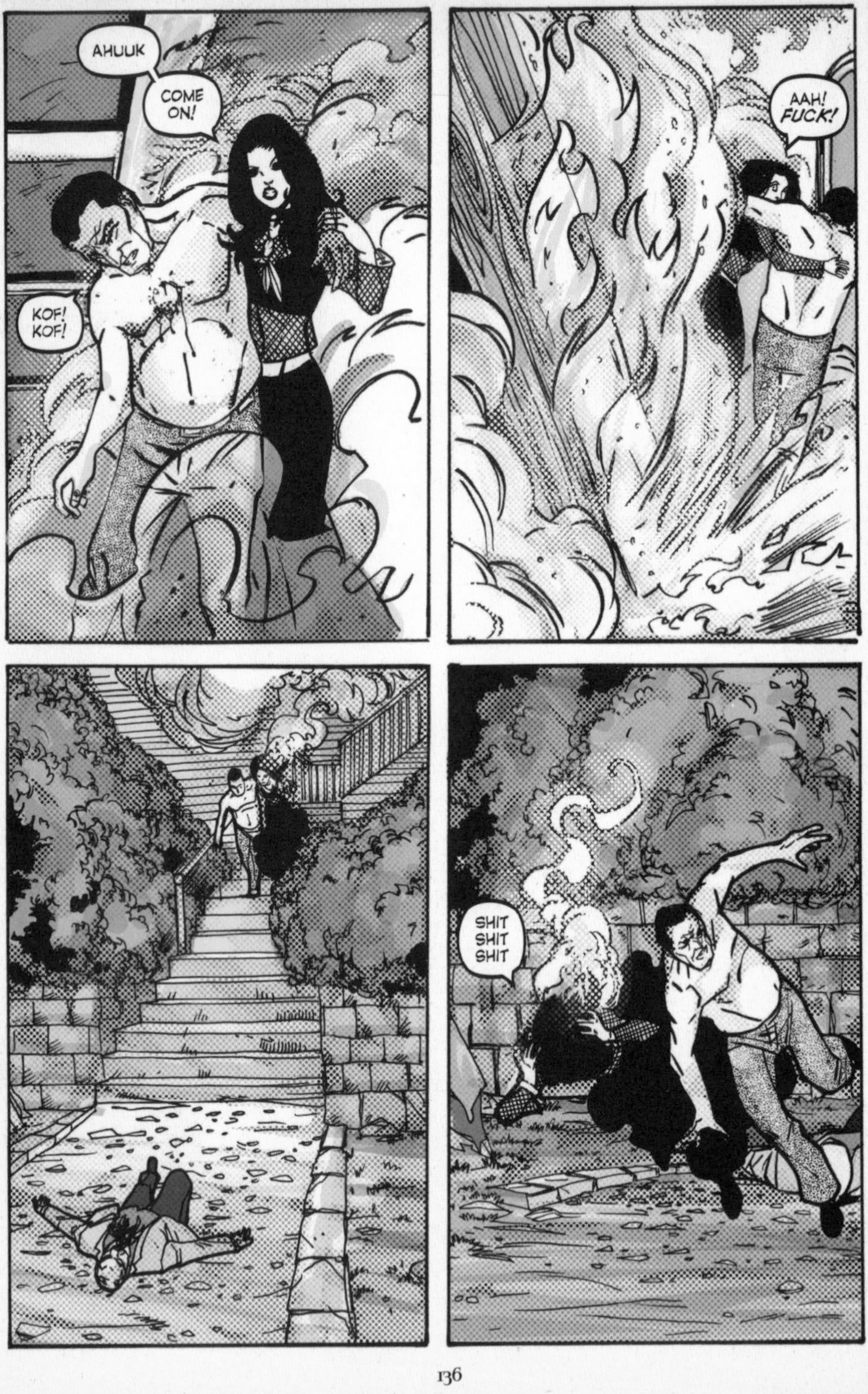
AHUUK
COME ON!
KOF! KOF!
AAH! FUCK!
SHIT SHIT SHIT

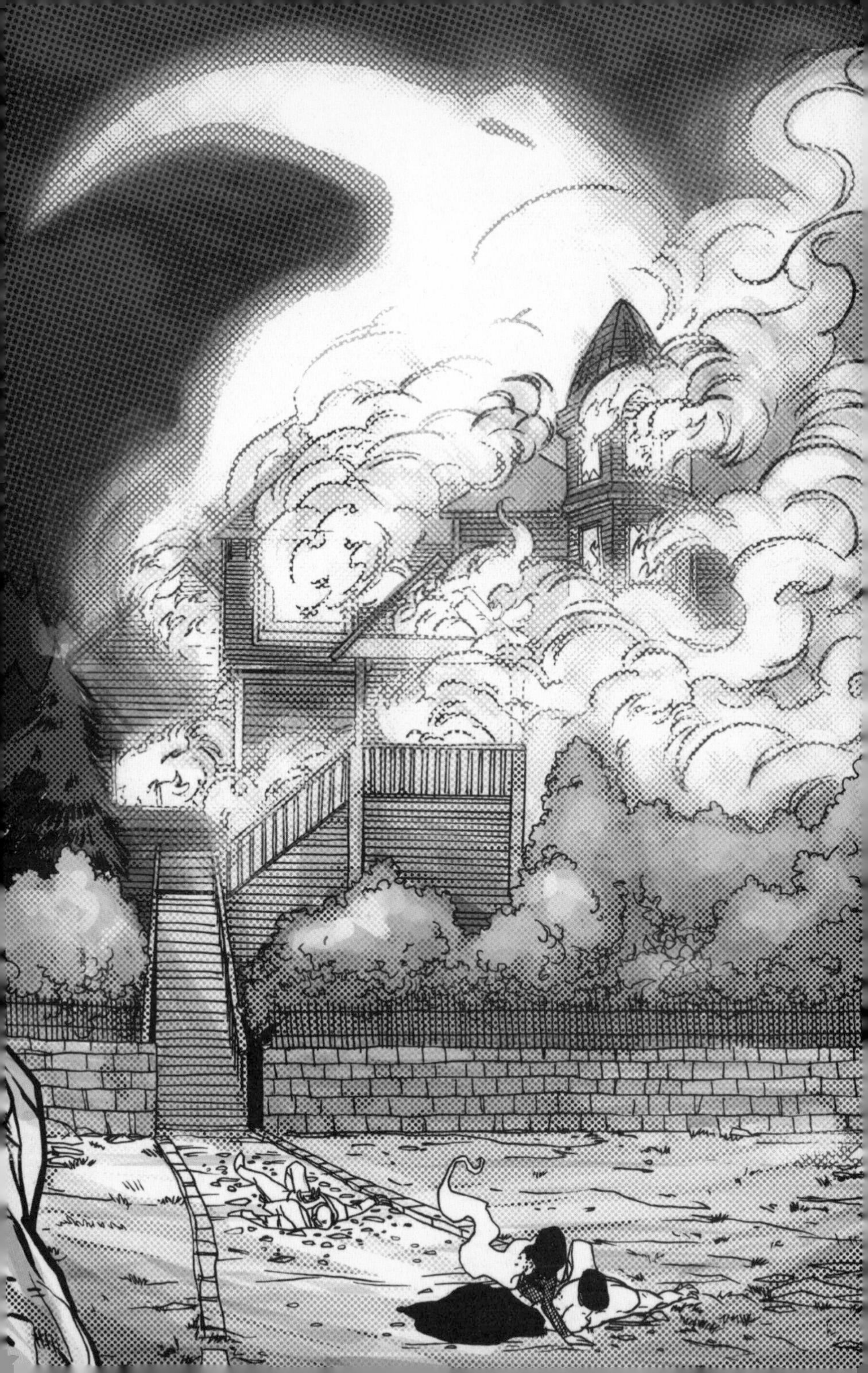

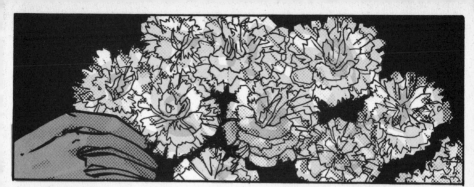

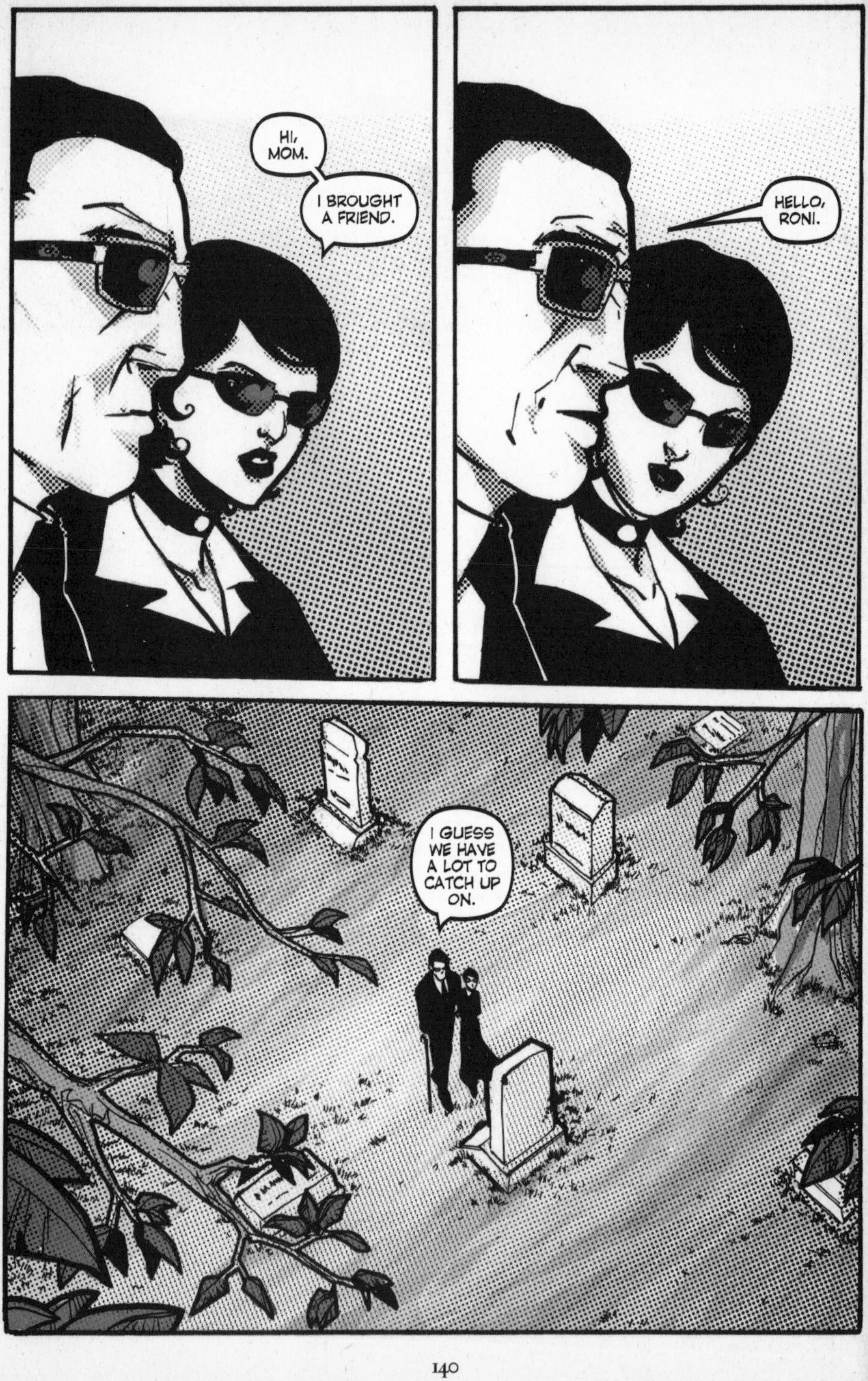
HI, MOM.
I BROUGHT A FRIEND.
HELLO, RONI.
I GUESS WE HAVE A LOT TO CATCH UP ON.